# LIBRARY OF NEW TESTAMENT STUDIES
# 319

*formerly the Journal for the Study of the New Testament Supplement series*

*Editor*
Mark Goodacre

*Editorial Board*
John M.G. Barclay, Craig Blomberg, Kathleen E. Corley,
R. Alan Culpepper, James D.G. Dunn, Craig A. Evans,
Stephen Fowl, Robert Fowler, Simon J. Gathercole, Michael Labahn,
John S. Kloppenborg, Robert Wall, Robert L. Webb, Catrin H. Williams

# PLAYING THE TEXTS
# 13

*Series Editor*
George Aichele, Adrian College, Michigan

# Transfigured

*A Derridean Rereading of the Markan Transfiguration*

Andrew P. Wilson

t&t clark

NEW YORK • LONDON

Copyright © 2007 by Andrew P. Wilson

All rights reserved. No part of this book may be reproduced, stored in a retrieval system, or transmitted in any form or by any means, electronic, mechanical, including photocopying, recording, or otherwise, without the written permission of the publisher, T & T Clark International.

T & T Clark International, 80 Maiden Lane, New York, NY 10038

T & T Clark International, The Tower Building, 11 York Road, London SE1 7NX

T & T Clark International is a Continuum imprint.

Printed in the United States of America

*Library of Congress Cataloging-in-Publication Data*

Wilson, Andrew P.
   Transfigured : a Derridean rereading of the Markan transfiguration / Andrew P. Wilson.
     p. cm. — (The library of New Testament studies ; #319)
   Includes bibliographical references and index.
   ISBN-13: 978-0-567-02601-9 (hardcover : alk. paper)
   ISBN-10: 0-567-02601-9 (hardcover : alk. paper)
   1. Jesus Christ—Transfiguration. 2. Bible. N.T. Mark IX, 2-8—Criticism, interpretation, etc. 3. Derrida, Jacques. I. Title. II. Series.

BT410.W56 2007
                        226.3'06—dc22

## Contents

| | |
|---|---|
| Acknowledgments | vii |
| Abbreviations | ix |
| Introduction | xi |

**Chapter 1**
**INTRODUCING DERRIDA AND DECONSTRUCTION** — 1
  Introduction — 1
  I. Structures, Signifiers, and Centers — 2
  II. *Différance* — 7
  III. Foundations of Sand — 9
  IV. Derrida and the Tower of Babel—"Des Tours de Babel" — 10
  V. A Question of Method — 14
  VI. Philosophy and de Man — 15
  Conclusion — 20

**Chapter 2**
**THE CRITICAL "OTHER": DERRIDEAN THEORY WITHIN BIBLICAL STUDIES** — 22
  Introduction — 22
  I. The Self and the Other — 22
  II. Reading Critically and Critiquing the Reader:
    The Evidence of Style — 24
  III. Beyond Deconstruction: Acknowledging Otherness — 38
  IV. Beauty and the Enigma — 47
  Conclusion — 49

**Chapter 3**
**THE MARKAN TRANSFIGURATION IN BIBLICAL STUDIES** — 52
  Introduction — 52
  Part 1. Mark's Glorious Process — 53
  Part 2. Reading Mark 9:2–8 — 60
  I. Defining the Transfiguration — 60
  II. Mark's Loss of Face — 64

| | |
|---|---|
| III. Mark Stutters | 66 |
| IV. Elijah Then Moses | 67 |
| V. Peter Misses the Point | 73 |
| VI. Terror of Incrimination | 77 |
| VII. Cloudy Commands | 79 |
| VIII. Ending Alone | 82 |
| Conclusion | 83 |

**Chapter 4**
**REREADING THE MARKAN TRANSFIGURATION**    86

| | |
|---|---|
| Introduction | 86 |
| Part 1. The Spluttering Sun and the Palimpsest | 88 |
| I. Aristotle's Sun | 88 |
| II. The Fuller Glory of the Robes | 93 |
| III. Reflections on/of Glory | 99 |
| IV. Erased Face | 103 |
| V. Cloud of Absence and Presence | 105 |
| Part 2. Peter's Terrifying Insight | 108 |
| I. Keeping the *Mysterium Tremendum* | 108 |
| II. Peter's "Error" | 112 |
| III. End of Fear | 115 |
| IV. Tomb without End | 118 |
| Conclusion | 124 |

**Chapter 5**
**NEW FIGURATIONS: IMPLICATIONS AND FUTURE DIRECTIONS**    126

| | |
|---|---|
| Introduction | 126 |
| Part 1. Transfiguring Transfiguration | 128 |
| Part 2. Poetic Comment | 133 |
| I. *Transfiguration*—The One-Legged *Pas de Deux* | 133 |
| II. Vision of Bees | 140 |
| Part 3. Reading the Sacred Text | 142 |
| Part 4. Sacred Literature, Sacred Scripture | 145 |
| I. Unbinding the Text? | 149 |
| Conclusion | 155 |

| | |
|---|---|
| Conclusion | 158 |
| Bibliography | 163 |
| Index of Biblical Passages | 179 |
| Index of Names | 183 |

ACKNOWLEDGMENTS

This book began in Australia as a vague idea for a doctoral project. Since that time it has accompanied me across three continents and from one side of the world to the other. Needless to say, it takes a long time to travel that far and requires a lot of resources to complete a project of this type. I wouldn't have lasted the distance were I not also accompanied by a number of people and institutions at various times and in various places along the way.

In Australia, I am indebted to my family, who enabled me to begin this journey and who sustained me throughout. Tom, Corrie, Damian, Simon, Marita, and a trailing list of extended family, too long to name but no less appreciated. I am also grateful to a number of friends and mentors, especially Sophia, Leo, Wendy, and David.

From my time in the United Kingdom and the years spent in the Department of Biblical Studies at the University of Sheffield, I value the creative and encouraging ethos and the openness to a broad range of approaches to the study of biblical literature. In particular, I am grateful to my Ph.D. supervisors, R. Barry Matlock and Stephen D. Moore, for setting me on my course and accompanying me on that most intense part of the journey. Friends and colleagues—Jamie, Mandy, Claire, James, Peter, Patrick—provided much needed encouragement and diversion along the way. I was fortunate to have received generous support from the University of Sheffield. The award was a crucial step in enabling the project that was to become this book.

In Canada, I am indebted to the University of Alberta for its most generous support of my research. Special thanks to Francis, Bennett and Joseph and to Ted Blodgett, whose poetry inspired a reading that was to become my fourth chapter. This book was eventually completed with the assistance and support of Mt. Allison University, and I have particular appreciation for the members of the Department of Religious Studies who help contribute to an astonishingly creative and collegial work environment. Thanks to Barb, Colin, John, and Marilyn.

Thanks are due to George Aichele for his insightful, incisive, and speedy reading of the manuscript and his willingness to include this book in his "Playing the Texts" series. I am also appreciative of Henry Carrigan, whose guidance of this project throughout the publication process was always gracious, even in the face of the inevitable delays.

This book wouldn't be complete if I did not thank my wife, Fiona, someone who has lived and breathed this project almost as much as I have. Thank you for being my most constant companion, for your encouragement and your love. I look forward to our journey continuing.

# ABBREVIATIONS

| | |
|---|---|
| AB | Anchor Bible |
| BCC | The Bible and Culture Collective |
| *Bib* | *Biblica* |
| *BibInt* | *Biblical Interpretation: A Journal of Contemporary Approaches* |
| *CBQ* | *Catholic Biblical Quarterly* |
| *DRev* | *Downside Review* |
| *ExpTim* | *Expository Times* |
| *EvQ* | *Evangelical Quarterly* |
| FB | Forschung zu Bibel |
| GCT | Gender, Culture, Theory |
| *HAR* | *Hebrew Annual Review* |
| *Int* | *Interpretation* |
| *IDB* | *The Interpreter's Dictionary of the Bible* |
| *ISBE* | *International Standard Bible Encyclopedia* |
| *JBL* | *Journal of Biblical Literature* |
| JSNTSup | Journal for the Study of the New Testament, Supplementary Series |
| JSOTSup | Journal for the Study of the Old Testament, Supplementary Series |
| *Neot* | *Neotestamentica* |
| NIBC | New International Biblical Commentary |
| *NovT* | *Novum Testamentum* |
| NTS | New Testament Studies |
| RB | Revue biblique |
| RBL | Review of Biblical Literature |
| *RSR* | *Recherches de science religieuse* |
| *SJOT* | *Scandanavian Journal of the Old Testament* |
| *WTJ* | *Westminster Theological Journal* |

## Introduction

The Markan transfiguration (Mark 9:2–8) is all about light, sound, and spectacle. On the mountaintop, Jesus is transformed; his robes shine with a divine whiteness. Two of the most eminent figures of the Hebrew Bible miraculously appear. The disciples looking on are dumbstruck, terrified by the awesome spectacle. And if that is not enough, the cloud of God's presence descends on the scene as a booming voice proclaims Jesus' divine identity and mission. This is a scene that brims with vivid images of glorious presences and unequivocal theological revelations. Or so it seems.

Commentators make much of Mark's theology in this scene. The general trend of their interpretations is to identify the transfiguration as a high point in Mark's presentation of God's glory, a scene that is second only to, or that facilitates, the culmination of that glory in the parousia. Light, sound, and all that sparkles are therefore of prime importance in such readings. But have commentators been blinded by their dazzling evaluations of Mark's theology? For, despite all the splendor and sparkle, the Markan transfiguration remains a difficult scene to interpret. On closer inspection, there is much that commentators find enigmatic and troublesome in this scene. There are many gaps, absences, and awkward moments that potentially interrupt and undermine the apparent clarity of this vision.

In this book, I investigate the imagery of the Markan transfiguration, with a particular focus on its ambiguity and otherness. My motivating question is to ask what we could see if we were to squint past the sunlike glory (Markan and interpretive) that dominates this vision. As such, I am not interested in pinning down the pericope's meaning, in finally ironing out its troublesome spots, or blotting out its difficulties. Rather, I focus precisely on these problematic elements, which I reevaluate so that the transfiguration may be reread from an altered perspective. Reading from this altered perspective will involve a response to scholarship on the transfiguration that questions certain connections and patterns that commentators take for granted. Of particular interest will be the way glory is evaluated, be it in the intimate associations with light and spectacle, or alternatively through the types of connections that are made between this scene and other parts of the Gospel. My rereading will seek to look anew at the complex combinations of images that are assembled on the mountaintop and ask how meaning might be alternatively generated in this scene. What factors shape the way the transfiguration is understood? What is revealed in this scene once the perspective is shifted? In the end, the rereading takes me less toward *what* the scene means than toward *how* it means.

The work of Jacques Derrida will be central to the orientation of this rereading of the transfiguration. Derridean theory (deconstruction and his later work) identifies monolithic or totalizing approaches to textual meaning and is particularly interested in the continuing legacy of metaphysics on Western thought. In his later work, Derrida further calls into question the very method and style of scholarship and in doing so implicates the critic in the criticism. In this way, Derrida deals with the way the critic is mirrored by the text and explores the image that is reflected back as much as he attends to the traditional approaches to reading. Moreover, Derrida's later works read texts as textuality first. In other words, rather than bringing a set of metaphysical ideas to a text, ideas that would associate light with glory, for instance, Derrida concentrates on what he considers the preconditions for meaning—iterability, difference, intertextuality—and uses these qualities of inscription to inform his reading. In this way, he engages with a sense of "otherness" that draws together and realigns the reader (subject), the reading (method), and the read (text).

I have chosen to call this process a "rereading," rather than a "deconstruction," because I am not concerned only with exposing the metaphysical presuppositions that inform and perpetuate readings of this passage. I am proposing an alternative reassembly of this text, an alternative interpretation that is just as metaphysical and subject to deconstruction as is the traditional model. My interest is in re-creation and rereading. Such a process, when accompanied by Derridean theory, reveals that the terms are altered to the extent that the resulting interpretation is guided more by text than idea.

Although making use of Derridean theory, this book by no means functions as a thorough introduction to Derridean thought or to deconstruction. This enterprise has already been undertaken in capable ways, both for the larger field of literary criticism (Culler 1982; Leitch 1983; Taylor 1984; Bennington 1993; Rorty 1995; Caputo 1997) and increasingly within our own discipline of biblical studies (Moore 1989; Seeley 1994; BCC 1995; Counet 2000; Sherwood 2000). Naturally, I will also not be claiming to draw on the whole Derridean corpus. The works that I have selected are works that I consider useful in developing further the particular themes and images that emerge from a rereading of the transfiguration, a rereading that concentrates on those repressed and neglected elements, the gaps and fissures that have either been overlooked or de-emphasized in traditional scholarly approaches.

My approach to the Markan transfiguration and to its imagery is a literary approach. Because of this focus, it is also worth noting that there are certain elements that I will not be dealing with in this book. In the first instance, it is unnecessary to speculate on the historical reality behind the text. While an interesting project in and of itself, a question such as this is not centrally relevant in my literary-theoretical approach to the biblical text. Furthermore, speculations on the

*Introduction* xiii

literary and historical origins of this particular text and the use made of it by the evangelist in his specific social and religious context will also be of little use here. Therefore, although at times I will refer to the "evangelist" or to "Mark," I am not seeking to evoke a historical author. I merely use these names for convenience. A final disclaimer is that, of course, Mark's version of the transfiguration is not the only one available in the biblical corpus. Matthew's and Luke's might also benefit from an inquiry such as mine, but to include them would be beyond the scope of this present project. Therefore, aside from occasional comparisons, I will not be investigating the use made of this story by the other Gospels, nor, for that matter, will I be seeking to discover the origins of this story as shared by the Synoptic writers nor attempting to establish an original preexisting form for this story. It should therefore be clear that what follows will not be a traditional (and broad) commentary on the Markan transfiguration or the transfiguration story in general. The outline of the book is as follows.

In the first part of chap. 1, I introduce some key Derridean ideas. Following on from this, as an illustration of his approach and also as a depiction of some of his key textual interests, I take a well-known deconstructive reading of a biblical text undertaken by Derrida himself, "Des Tours de Babel" (2002b). Next, I clarify that Derrida's work goes beyond, and is different from, the deconstructivist movement, and I end this part of the chapter with a brief look at Derrida's reception within the field of philosophy, investigating a particular criticism of Derrida's work from analytic philosophy and one attempt to come to terms with this. Exploration of other (later) Derridean works will be undertaken at the same time as my rereading in chap. 4 so that text and theory may be read side-by-side.

Mindful that Derrida's influence in biblical studies is primarily in the form of deconstructive readings, in chap. 2, I undertake a brief sampling of these deconstructive readings. This sampling will prove useful to illustrate Derrida's reception in biblical studies and to give an indication of the type of work that has been done so far. Because I will not be undertaking a deconstructive reading myself, it will not be necessary to provide an exhaustive account of this type of reading within biblical studies. It will be enough to present a selection of readings that prove useful in setting up my own rereading, which follows in chap. 4. As such, while looking at these examples, I will investigate two major themes that impact on my own rereading. These themes involve the interaction between critic and text and the implications for using Derridean theory beyond the scope of the deconstructive approach. I end by looking at the relationship between text and critic and the need to reformulate the sense of the critic from one that is coherent and distant to one that is thoroughly implicated and in some ways indistinguishable from the text. I also look to the impact of this style of critique, finding an evocative example in the poetic work of Francis Landy.

In chap. 3, I survey recent scholarship on the Markan transfiguration narrative. The focus of this chapter is twofold. First, I ask how scholars interpret the images of the transfiguration story and, second, where the gaps and glosses are, the repressed and problematic elements that either elude or vex traditional approaches to this story. I conclude this chapter with the insight that a certain theological conception underlies readings of the Markan transfiguration. A very particular notion of glory is shared by the majority of commentators, and it is a notion that appears to influence the way this text is interpreted.

Chapter 4 constitutes my rereading of the Markan transfiguration. Here, I draw on the insights gained from the previous chapters, as well as making further use of Derrida's work, to propose a rereading that presents very different emphases and conclusions than those given in traditional readings. This chapter has three parts. The first will be influenced by Derrida's essay "White Mythology" (1974b), which deals with the place of metaphor within philosophy. Here I look to the images of light that so fill this vision and, along with Derrida, question their clarity and reliability. The second part draws from *The Gift of Death* (1995), which charts the reemergence of the daemonic and indeterminate within religious discourse along with associated ethical implications. In so doing, I reinterpret Peter's error and the significance of the disciples' fear. Finally, the Markan transfiguration will be linked with the scene at the empty tomb, and the implications of the promise made in the transfiguration will be reinterpreted in light of this ending and alongside *The Post Card* (1987). The latter investigates the fruitfulness of textual indeterminacy through Derrida's development of the postal metaphor.

The implications of my rereading will be investigated in chap. 5. Here, the literary reinterpretation of the Markan transfiguration story will be extended beyond the Bible and beyond the writings of Derrida. Blanchot's notion of a poetic transfiguration, a notion he develops from a reading of the work of Rainer Maria Rilke, will be elucidated. From here, a more recent poetic work will be explored as an intertext of the transfiguration narrative: Blodgett and Brault's *Transfiguration*. It will emerge from this reading that a literary approach to biblical texts not only implicates the reader/critic but also challenges those theological/ideological conceptions at work in traditional interpretation. Finally, I turn to the work of three writers, all of whom demonstrate a literary approach to the work of biblical studies and theology, but in markedly different ways: Kevin Hart, Richard Kearney, and George Aichele. Hart investigates the sense of *écriture* as scripture and explores the possibility of a theology compatible with Derridean theory. In *The God Who May Be* (2001), Kearney undertakes a hermeneutical reading of the transfiguration tradition to support his conception of a "God without being." While dialoguing with Hart, Aichele questions the enduring presence of an increasingly destabilized Christian canon and argues that postcanonical possibilities ought to be possible. In light of the traditional theological perspectives that inform interpretations of the transfiguration story and in light of Derrida's challenge to scholarly approaches and to subjectivity, I conclude that, while the way forward is far from clear, the approach to this text, and also the theology one brings to it, ought to be recast.

Chapter 1

INTRODUCING DERRIDA AND DECONSTRUCTION

*Introduction*

The story of the tower of Babel (Gen 11:1–9) tells of a world unified under the power of a single language. To the Babelians, the potential of this sense of perfect linguistic communion appears to be limitless. But God expresses some concern at the powerful consequences of a world united in this way: "And the Lord said: 'Look, they are one people and they have all one language; and this is only the beginning of what they will do; nothing that they propose to do will now be impossible for them'" (Gen 11:6).[1] And so this univocity is short lived, and the Babelians' worst fears are realized when the incomprehensibility that results from God's intervention leads to confusion, disorganization, and the rapid and far-flung dissemination of their world.

In a sense, Jacques Derrida's major theoretical challenge, leveled squarely at the history of metaphysics, has consequences that appear to parallel the worst fears of the Babelians. Derrida, too, challenges myths of completeness, of unity, and the apparently seamless homogeneity that have formed the immensely broad and over-arching history of Western metaphysics. The Derridean deconstructive agenda, a major part of his overall thought, challenges the ground beneath those monolithic towers that crowd the skyline of Western metaphysics.[2] Like the tower of Babel, these towers, whose structures are so grand and all encompassing, promise to burst through the firmament itself and afford their creators an unhindered glimpse of God. They are immense structures of meaning, such as Western philosophy, that would aim to contain all that is known and knowable within their bounds. The questions raised by Derrida and Derridean deconstruction, however, shake the very foundations of these towers and undermine their solidity and reliability.

While Derrida's thought exceeds what is understood to be the deconstructive agenda (and likewise the deconstructive movement exceeds Derridean influence), deconstruction forms a crucial part of his theoretical history and formation. Deconstructive readings are also the dominant mode with which Derridean thought has appeared in biblical studies until relatively recently. In my own reading, however,

---

1. Unless otherwise noted, all biblical translations are from the New Revised Standard Version.
2. These towering edifices include metaphysics, humanism, history, the book, logic, and rationalism; and the foundations are composed of grounding notions such as Truth, Being, Presence, and Identity.

I will not be undertaking a deconstructive reading of the Markan transfiguration. I am more interested in engaging with those later works of Derrida's that exceed this category. In chap. 4, these later works will be introduced and read alongside the Markan transfiguration. At this introductory stage, however, it will prove useful to look at Derrida's deconstructive work as a way of introducing some of his key ideas, ideas that are just as relevant to his later, nondeconstructive writings.

How does one understand the foundation-shaking consequences of Derridean deconstruction? Numerous introductions to the writings of Jacques Derrida's thought offer varied attempts to pin down deconstruction and, in doing so wrestle with what can uncontroversially be regarded as an elusive and opaque term. This opacity is clouded further by some of Derrida's own comments, such as, "All sentences of the type 'deconstruction is X' . . . a priori miss the point. . . . Deconstruction is not a method and cannot be transformed into one" (Derrida 1990: 271); "The enterprise of deconstruction always, in a certain way, falls prey to its own work" (Derrida 1974a: 24).

If we pay heed to comments such as these, the best method of tracing an outline around some of the basics of Derridean thought may well involve looking at a deconstructive piece undertaken by Derrida himself. Derrida's reading of the Babel story is regarded as one of his most accessible deconstructive efforts, and it is especially relevant to this discussion because of its biblical subject matter (Derrida 2002b).[3] Before any detailed explication of the Derridean approach to Babel is given, however, it will be important to say something of the background and context from which deconstruction has emerged. In addition, some introduction to the conceptual and structural features with which it takes particular issue will be needed.

## I. Structures, Signifiers, and Centers

Derrida's deconstructive project owes a great debt to linguistics, especially the semiological work of linguist Ferdinand de Saussure. The particular part of Saussurean linguistics that interested Derrida can be found in Saussure's argument that the linguistic "sign"[4] is defined not by a particular set of "innate properties" but by the differences that distinguish it from other signs. In a linguistic system, says Saussure, "there are only differences" (Derrida 1974a: 53). For Saussure, the lin-

---

3. J. F. Graham claims "Des Tours de Babel" is "the most elegant and most accessible of Derrida's excavations of the Bible" (*Semeia* 54: 3); Gil Anidjar speaks of "Des Tours de Babel" as "one of Derrida's most significant contributions to a reading and rereading of the bible" (Derrida 2002a: 102).

4. Quite simply, a sign is understood to be a "sign of something," a referent to another "presence." But of course it is not this simple, and much has been written since and following Saussure regarding the theory of signs, semiology. For two different approaches to semiology, one may take, for instance, the work of the American structuralist and semiotician Charles S. Peirce (*Collected Papers*, ed. Charles Hartshorne and Paul Weiss [Cambridge, Mass.: Harvard University Press, 1931–35]) and compare the French literary and psychoanalytic theorist Julia Kristeva (*Revolution in Poetic Language*, trans. Margaret Waller [New York: Columbia University Press, 1984]).

guistic sign has two constituents: the signifier, which is the sensible (acoustic or graphic) constituent, and the signified, which is the concept communicated by the signifier. The signifier is the spoken word; the signified is the concept to which this word refers. The word "cat"—the signifying term—refers not only to a particular animal but also to those sets of properties and characteristics that form an "ideal" cat—that which is signified. In this way, the signifier and the signified become bound together, forming a conceptual couplet, and their mutual orientation toward each other as a pair is seldom questioned—they form their own binary opposition.

While Derrida rejects Saussure's signifier/signified order as any type of solid foundation, he embraces Saussure's claim that language is formed within a network of differences. Although Saussure argues that the signifier and the signified are inseparable—that the word is inescapably linked to its referent—by meditating on the terms that form this same binarism, he opens up the material element of the signifier to something outside the boundaries of the signifier/signified opposition. Saussure goes on to claim the sound of language, the actual spoken word itself, is determined not by its relationship to the concept that grounds its meaning, its *signified*, but by its difference from other spoken words, other *signifiers*. Thus a signifier is aligned not to a corresponding signifi*ed* but to yet another signifi*er*.

For example, the words contained within a dictionary are provided with definitions which are themselves made up of words that, in turn, have their place between the covers of the same dictionary wherein they are attributed definitions made up of still more words, and so on infinitely. For Derrida, the signified, the concept or object, cannot function to stabilize the sign, or word, because the signifier is defined relationally. Consequently, signs come to be understood not by means of their closed signifier/signified opposition but, rather, through their infinite capacity to "mean" regardless of the context in which they are found.

That words cannot claim some direct and "objective" relationship to an underlying concept is demonstrated when it is noted that different languages provide different words for the same concepts. Moreover, the meanings of words can change, as can the concepts to which they refer. In fact, often it is the context that gives a word meaning more than any set of preexisting empirical concepts. Thus, for Derrida, the relationship between signifier and signified is at best a conventional one. Relationality is the only "real" element in the linguistic frame:

> [N]o element can function as a sign without relating to another element which itself is not simply present. This linkage means that each "element"... is constituted with reference to the trace in it of the other elements of the sequence or system.... Nothing ... is anywhere simply present or absent. There are only, everywhere, differences and traces of traces. (Derrida 1981b: 26)

In *Of Grammatology* (1974a), Derrida's investigation of binary oppositions, relationality, and the importance of difference becomes a critique of the foundations of the Western philosophical tradition. Subsequently, when Derrida speaks of Western metaphysics, he speaks of a philosophical system or systems of meaning grounded upon an endless series of opposing terms:

> All metaphysicians, from Plato to Rousseau, Descartes to Husserl have proceeded in this way, conceiving good to be before evil, the positive before the negative, the pure before the impure, the simple before the complex, the essential before the accidental, the imitated before the imitation, etc. And this is not just *one* metaphysical gesture among others, it is *the* metaphysical exigency, that which has been the most constant, most profound and most potent. (1987: 313)

The list of oppositions can be continued endlessly: presence over absence, light over darkness, meaning over nonmeaning, reason over madness, and so on. But the investigation does not end with the identification of these binarisms. Once identified, the way that one term relates to its other reveals another significant dynamic. Derrida demonstrates that, in fact, one term is always privileged over the other: evil is seen to be the corruption of a raised and privileged goodness; nothingness, the absence of being; error, the distortion of truth; and so on. A hierarchy of terms emerges in which priority is given to the one term that soon grows to eclipse what is seen to be its inversion. In fact, as in the above examples, the second term exists more often as a corruption of the first.

Of even further significance is the observation that the privileged term does not appear to have been randomly selected. It becomes apparent to Derrida that the history of Western metaphysics can be characterized by a privileging of unity, identity, immediacy, and temporal and spatial *presentness* over distance, difference, dissimulation, and deferment. Where Western philosophy has frequently attempted "objective" inquiries into the nature of Being, Derrida shows that inevitably there has been a sketching of Being as *presence*. He goes on to argue that the establishment of Being as *presence* has been a major contribution to the continual promotion and reenforcement of a "metaphysics of presence" as the foundation for further theological and philosophical inquiry (Derrida 1978b: 279–80).

Derrida's critique of Western philosophy as a "metaphysics of presence" focuses on one particularly pervasive dichotomy: the privileging of the spoken word over the written word. Within a system of meaning conditioned by a metaphysics of presence, the spoken word is valued for its immediacy, or full *presence*, to both speaker and hearer; idea coincides with word, and meaning is self-evident. "[T]he voice is consciousness itself. When I speak, not only am I conscious of being present for what I think, but I am conscious also of keeping as close as possible to my thought, or to the 'concept,' . . . " (Derrida 1981b: 22). Directly contrasting with this is the written word, an imperfect record but loyal servant of the spoken and, as such, often-absent word. Possessing the ability to exist without the presence of the speaker/author, the written word reveals a less than ideal deferment of communication and a temporal and physical separation of speaker and hearer. So, while the written word separates and confuses, the spoken word is clarity itself, by virtue of its being self-evident to the speaker and the hearer simultaneously. The spoken word communicates an idea without the need for mediation and is the image of perfectly self-present meaning. Because of this, according to Derrida, the spoken word has become the underlying ideal of Western culture. Derrida calls this implicit belief in fully present, self-evident meaning, "logocentrism," from the Greek word *logos*.[5]

Derrida explains that at the heart of any notion of structure is inevitably some sense of center that serves to "orient, balance, and organize the structure—one cannot in fact conceive of an unorganized structure—but above all to make sure that the organizing principle of the structure would limit what we might call the play of the structure" (1978b: 278).[6] Derrida observes that within Western metaphysics this orienting central point is invariably and intimately associated with a sense of presence: "It could be shown that all the names related to fundamentals, to principles, or to the centre have always designated an invariable presence— *eidos, arche, telos, energeia, ousia* (essence, existence, substance, subject) *aletheia, transcendentality*, consciousness, God, man, and so forth" (1978b: 280).

These central terms serve to orient a system of meaning by providing a reliable philosophical construct, an "organizing principle," in relation to which meaning is granted clarity and transparency. Simply put, such a ground allows the interpretation of meaning as such to be consistent and repeatable. For Derrida, this organizing principle limits the amount of *play* of the structure (1978b: 278). In other words, structure, composed around a central, orienting term, is able to control and limit the chaotic tendency of words to have multiple meanings and contexts as well as the possibility for non-sense.

The *play* of signs is opened up again by the orienting principle, but the possibilities for this play are now set within the larger context of a strictly organized and coherent system. However, in order to stabilize the system, the central term must remain definite and self-evident; it is a fixed point and can never participate in the free movement of sign to sign, no matter how conditional this may be. This central term refers only to itself and does not participate in language; it is seen to be both signifier and signified. In this way, the organizing principle is at once present and absent from the system it orients. It is a *transcendental* signified in the sense that it provides the condition that makes meaning possible.[7] Without the transcendental signified, the "domain" of play is extended infinitely, and, consequently, meaning cannot be contained. The transcendental signified serves as a foundation

---

5. The term *Logo-centrism* places the *logos* at the very center of that which undergirds Western culture: the *logos* and its various meanings as speech, logic, reason, and the Word of God (see Derrida 1978b).

6. By "play," Derrida is speaking of the reference of one sign to another in the same way as in Saussure's "network of differences" mentioned above.

7. For further discussion by Derrida of the transcendental signified, see 1974a: 49–50; 1981b: 19–20.

that anchors the free-flowing sign to a determined and reliable meaning. Derrida points out that the history of Western thought, a history formed within a metaphysics of presence, is marked by the powerful and irrepressible desire for the concept independent of language: the transcendental signified (1981b: 20).

In Western metaphysics of presence, the transcendental signified orients a system in which writing remains secondary to speech and is understood in terms of its role as an inferior substitute required only when speaking is not possible.[8] Writers record their thoughts on a page, thus distancing themselves from their own words and delaying their communication. Writing transforms and corrupts thought in such a way that it can be experienced by another at a later time, in a different place, even after the death of the author. Thus writing becomes associated with difference, distance, and death, a series of corrupting terms that expose and threaten self-present meaning to all forms of adulteration that the clarity of immediacy would have prevented.

And so, Derrida finds that metaphysics is supported by a network of oppositions, and, moreover, he notes that these oppositions are ordered according to presence and oriented around a transcendental signified. In taking the next step from this theoretical position, Derrida's critique does more than simply reverse or rearrange the values in this system and say, for instance, that writing ought to be valued over speech. Instead, he challenges the composition of oppositions as such. He typically does this by identifying an impossible alternative that exceeds the bounds of the dominant binary system. When included within the system, this "other" option disrupts, undermines, or else simply reveals the limitations of the system altogether. The task of the deconstructor is to mark "the interval between inversion, which brings low what is high, and the irruptive emergence of a new 'concept,' a concept that can no longer be, and never could be, included in the previous regime" (1981b: 42). The problem for Derrida at this point is how to form a critique of metaphysics when any persuasive argument against metaphysical totalization requires as a precondition the use of a language that would call into question the very effectiveness of the argument (Hart 2000: 135).

---

8. The conception of writing that Derrida is responding to here is quite specific and is limited to an understanding of writing that is a thoroughly phoneticized script. Put another way, writing of this type refers only to the articulated sounds of spoken language. Derrida acknowledges that writing can be more broadly conceived than this. However, alternative conceptions that are not necessarily restricted to a noun or consonant have been repressed in Western script. By contrast, pictographic script, the Egyptian hieroglyph and the Chinese character, do more than simply reference the sounds of speech. Rather than denigrating such nonphonetic writing for its imprecision and its distance from the *logos,* Derrida valorizes the hieroglyph: "Nonphonetic writing breaks the noun apart. It describes relations and not appellations. The noun and the word, those unities of breath and concept, are effaced within pure writing" (1974a: 26). Moreover, Derrida goes on to point out that "a purely phonetic writing is impossible and has never finished reducing the nonphonetic.... 'Phonetic' and 'nonphonetic' are therefore never pure qualities of certain systems of writing, they are the abstract characteristics of typical elements, more or less numerous and dominant within all systems of signification in general" (1974a: 88–89).

## II. Différance

So how does Derrida critique metaphysics without reinscribing a metaphysics of his own? The beginning of an answer to this question can be found in Derrida's neologism *différance*. The word *différance* at the same time names and demonstrates that which forms the (non)center[9] of the Derridean critique of the Western metaphysics of presence. Derrida draws from the French *différer*, meaning both "to differ" and "to defer," but what one notices initially about this word is the curious substitution of an "e" from the original *différer* with that of the "a." In terms of French pronunciation, such a substitution is "written but not heard," and for Derrida, this is precisely the point (1981b: 8). *Différance* to some extent foils the metaphysical privileging of presence by being known in its written form as distinct from its spoken form—indeed it is "unknowable" in speech. In this case, the written word is no longer a falling from speech, an imperfect corruption of the fully present union of thought and word. *Différance* demonstrates that the written word is no longer the outcast child: "Plato said of writing that it was an orphan or a bastard, as opposed to speech, the legitimate and high-born son of the 'father of logos'" (1981b: 12).

By not finding its origin in speech, *différance* demonstrates a lack within speech itself. *Différance* is an instance where the written word effectively sidesteps speech's monopoly on presence. More than that, *différance* indicates a "fault" that infests the sign but which is at the same time the condition of possibility for the sign. *Différance* refers to no "thing," no "presence," and yet, as a word, it is still a sign like any other. While the "a" is pronounced, its *difference* cannot be. This demonstrates that although this word is by definition a sign, it refers to "referral" itself and to "difference" as such. Of particular importance is the way *différance*, by definition, does not refer to any "positive terms": "*différance* refers to the (active and passive) movement that consists in deferral by means of delay, delegation, reprieve, referral, detour, postponement, reserving" (1981b: 8). As a word that is not able to be adequately "present" to speech, *différance* comes to demonstrate in itself precisely what it is held to mean: deferral and difference inhabiting the core of unity and presence.

In this way, *différance* signifies no "thing" at all, but rather, it signifies the condition that precedes and enables meaning. Derrida sums up these characteristics in the following paragraph:

---

9. Keep in mind, however, that Derrida is not trying simply to create an "alternative" to the metaphysical system he is dismantling. An alternative, with a new "center" or transcendental signified, would be just as "metaphysical" in this theoretical sense. To offer an alternative would just be a matter of rearranging the terms, while the same structural framework remains intact and unchallenged. Derrida therefore seeks to subvert the present metaphysical order from within, turning its own terms in on itself: "The movements of deconstruction do not destroy structures from the outside. They are not possible and effective, nor can they take accurate aim, except by inhabiting those structures. Inhabiting them *in a certain way* . . ." (1974a: 24).

*[D]ifférance*, then, is a structure and a movement no longer conceivable on the basis of the opposition presence/absence. *Différance* is the systematic play of differences, of the traces of differences, of the *spacing* by means of which elements are related to each other. This spacing is the simultaneously active and passive (the *a* of *différance* indicates this indecision as concerns activity and passivity, that which cannot be governed by or distributed between the terms of this opposition) production of the intervals without which the "full" terms would not signify, would not function. (1981b: 27)

*Différance* encapsulates the seminal insights that Derrida has taken from Saussure's investigations of language systems as systems founded on differences. *Différance* demonstrates how language is already constituted by the very differences and distances it seeks to overcome. "As soon as there is meaning there is difference" (Derrida 1981a: ix). Consequently, Derrida comes to view *différance* as preceding language and meaning and concludes the above paragraph with this point: "It [*différance*] is also the becoming-space of the spoken chain—which has been called temporal or linear; a becoming-space which makes possible both writing and every correspondence between speech writing, every passage from one to the other" (1981b: 27).

Derrida demonstrates with this word that, in fact, difference lies prior to and at the very heart of immediacy and presence. Difference, mediation, and deferral may be the unfavored and repressed elements of a hegemonic metaphysics of presence, but Derrida goes on to pry open metaphysics and to demonstrate that it is just such conceptions as these that inhabit and indeed can be shown to precede the "ground" of metaphysics itself.

The emergence of *différance* is not simply the overthrowing of "presence" in order to replace it with its inversion: a situation noted earlier in which one metaphysical system replaces another. If more care were to be shown, it would prove more appropriate to cross out the word *différance* altogether. For only when it is "under erasure" does its double nature become apparent. Here Derrida refers to Heidegger and his own crossing out of his term "Being" (*Dasein*) to imply the fault with speaking about something that, to a large degree, becomes something it is not through the very act of naming. On the one hand, *différance* is a challenge to systems of totalization—such as the metaphysics of presence—and, on the other hand, as a sign among other signs, there is always the possibility that one could make it function as a transcendental signified and find that it has become a new "center." When crossed out (*différance*), there is some recognition that even though metaphysics is necessarily tied up with any use of signs, the focus on determined meaning and structure remains under question and is self-consciously marked as problematic. The word is crossed out but all the same remains legible. A kind of paradox exists here: a challenge to metaphysics that is aware that the demise of metaphysics involves the demise of the challenge itself. The purpose of this paradox is to reveal language as language rather than as meaning. Speaking of the constructive implications of erasure to illuminate language, Derrida explains: "That deletion is not, however, a 'merely negative symbol.' That deletion is the final writing of an epoch. Under its strokes the presence of a transcendental signified is effaced while still remaining legible, is destroyed while making visible the very idea of the sign" (1974a: 23).

The erasure of the word makes legible the structures of language and the conditions of meaning. *Différance* becomes a new word that is also the oldest word, the word that comes before meaning. *Différance* allows language to surface as language, and clarity of meaning is replaced by the clarity of those structures of meaning that rely first and foremost on *différance*. With an eye toward words and meaning, toward text and textuality, and toward the ways in which we read, Derrida is able to move closer to something that resembles deconstruction.

## III. Foundations of Sand

Derrida demonstrates with his investigation of Saussure and the foundations of language that the apparently solid and sure foundations of metaphysics are ultimately illusory. Furthermore, dualities that favor presence over absence and that exhibit a nostalgia for full presence in turn belie a dread of insecurity. The Babelians, treasuring their single language, set about constructing an awesome fortress to safeguard and affirm this unity, the power behind its creation. At the same time, in the very act of building, of uniting stone with stone, they also sought to stave off their underlying fears of dispersal. But Derrida shows that homogeneity and the apparent success in controlling words and meaning can never amount to more than wishful illusion. The tower of Babel was doomed to failure before it was even begun. Such a tower has no solid foundation and can never be completed. The building blocks of language themselves are not permanently set on specific foundations of meanings but instead on the shifting sands of language itself: words are given meaning not so much by what they refer to as by how they differ from other words. Difference rather than identity is the prerequisite for meaning.

Babelian dichotomies such as unity vs. dispersal and power vs. helplessness are shown to be overly simplistic distinctions. When read more closely, one finds that dispersal in fact lies in the very heart of unity, and helplessness lies deep within any notion of power. The *de*struction of Babel lay in the very heart of its *con*struction, and the dispersal of language and peoples is an inevitability of this unity. Structure, be that linguistic or architectural, takes one only so far in controlling the "play" of meaning. The Babelians discover soon enough that their ability to build the tower, regardless of its miraculous design, falters, and their plan to reach heaven is abandoned (see Gen 11:8).

How can we pose such a critique of the Babelians when with our own arguments we inevitably begin building towers of our own? The science of deconstruction is mindful of this circularity. How are we to "define" deconstruction, when definitions themselves are all about making present meanings: clarity dispelling ambiguity? All the same, some working definition is needed lest we become paralyzed, unable to find a way through an insistent metaphysics of presence that undergirds our every word.

Derrida demonstrates that what may seem like clearly defined boundaries separating text from author from context from critic, although they are in some ways necessary in themselves, are more or less arbitrarily drawn. Derrida redraws the boundaries that contain the text and in doing so redefines a notion of textuality that encompasses a much broader account of experience. Rather than being exclusively based on fundamental grounding tenets such as "Truth" and "Being," experience is seen instead to be a collection of radically "open" texts intersecting at innumerable points, often in quite unexpected ways.

The notion of text here goes far beyond the simple understanding of a text as a contained, concrete entity with a singular history and meaning. In fact, the *reader* becomes thoroughly implicated as yet another intersecting text. With the boundaries of the text redrawn, Derrida investigates the way "the text" works both with and against any single attempt to offer a unified reading. Derrida uses the philosophical tools available to him, but changes the stakes so that his readings yield quite unexpected results—results that challenge the tools, indeed the very toolbox.

Deconstruction can be viewed as a critique of "ground," implicit or explicit, within any system of totalization. Logocentric systems, for instance, preordain a unified, *objective logos,* or "being," and as such, notions of "presence" are promoted while more fluid or rhizomatic notions are suppressed. Challenging the relationship between the primacy of speech and the subservience of writing within these systems, Derrida extends the bounds of the text to encompass speech and voice. He disrupts the full presence of the logos through his investigations of the subversive, fragmentary qualities of the deferral and differing of meaning so prevalent within the structure of writing.

## IV. Derrida and the Tower of Babel—"Des Tours de Babel"[10]

Derrida's reading of the Babel story is not a traditional biblical studies reading. Derrida dislocates the text from its traditionally prescribed boundaries, removing its necessary connection to particular structural parameters and allowing the free "play" of meaning to lead interpretation where it will. This deliberate sidestepping of traditional scholarship explains why Derrida's reading is not so concerned with historical, authorial, or contextual issues.

---

10. The title of Derrida's treatment of the Babel story provides a summary of the sorts of themes he goes on to explore. "The title can be read in various ways" as the translator of Derrida's essay, Joseph F. Graham, explains. "*Des* means 'some,' but it also means 'of the,' 'from the' or 'about the.' *Tours* could be towers, twists, tricks, turns, or tropes, as in a 'turn' of phrase. Taken together, *des* and *tours* have the same sound as *detour*, the word for detour" (Derrida 2002b: 134).

This is not to say, however, that Derrida's respect for this biblical text is any less sincere. His respectful approach is apparent in statements such as "from its height Babel at every instant supervises and surprises my reading" (2002b: 117). What he does with his deconstruction of Babel is to read it as a literary fable, a myth, and he examines the implications of this story for understandings of translation and finally of language itself. Derrida summarizes his initial thoughts early on in his reading and explains that the story of Babel is

> Telling at least of the inadequation of one tongue to another, of one place in the encyclopaedia to another, of language to itself and to meaning, and so forth, it also tells of the need for figuration, for myth, for tropes, for twists and turns, for translation inadequate to compensate for that which multiplicity denies us. In this sense it would be the myth of the origin of myth, the metaphor of metaphor, the narrative of narrative, the translation of translation and so on. (2002b: 104)

Derrida's reading of the Babel story is not just about the dispersal of a oneness into an irreducible multiplicity. It is simultaneously a comment on the impossibility of totalization as such: the workers could never finish building their tower—their monumental language. Translation tells us about language that there is always something that remains outside, something untranslatable that is left behind.

Developing this point, Derrida turns to the name "Babel" with all its definitional ambiguities.[11] He is particularly interested in its qualities as both proper name and common noun: "Babel" is used both as the *name* "Babel" and also as the *word* for "confusion." As a proper name and therefore a reference to a singular being, the name "Babel" is essentially untranslatable. As a common noun, however, the word "babel" means "confusion" and is related to the generality of meaning and therefore *is* translatable, but with this translatability comes further ambiguity. The translation of the word "babel" as "confusion," an association almost too convenient for Derrida's argument, is itself further confused by having at least two additional meanings: the confusion of tongues; a state of confusion: "The signification of the word 'confusion' is itself confused" (2002b: 105). Thus, Derrida introduces a double bind and focuses in on a word that is simultaneously untranslatable and translatable. This, in turn, leads him to an investigation of the meaning and implications of both the word and work of "translation."

On the one hand, proper names are necessary to language, because words need some tie with a particular referent in order to have a meaning that can be shared; God provides this gift in his bestowal of the name "Babel" (Gen 11:9). But at the same time, this name is the means by which the possibility of a univocal language is destroyed. As was shown earlier, Derrida draws on Saussure to argue that words

---

11. Derrida quotes from Voltaire's *Dictionnaire philosophique*: "*Ba* signifies father in the Oriental tongues, and *Bel* signifies the city of God, the holy city. The Ancients gave this name to all their capitals. But it is incontestable that Babel means confusion, either because the architects were confounded . . . or because the tongues were then confounded . . ." (2002b: 105).

gain meaning by their references to other words, rather than their associations to particular things in the real world. At the moment of naming, the tower is abandoned and civilization scattered. Here Derrida plays upon the word "gift" with its German meaning in mind, when he speaks of a God who allows the creation of language but who "also sows destruction and 'poisons the present' (Gift-gift)" (2002b: 105).

But why does God punish them with his name? Derrida explains that the "Shem" crave words and a language that is transparent to a set of shared and constant meanings. It is from this longing that the Shem want to make a name for *themselves*. Derrida interprets God's move to name as an act of resentment where, in the act of naming, he makes translation both necessary and impossible; indeed the story tells of translation's necessity *as* impossibility (2002b: 108).

Derrida speaks of proper names as not properly "belonging" to language. They are not part of the free flow of signification and as such are not "translatable" even within the language from which they arise. For instance, it is in translation that the Babel story is most often read, and the name "Babel" stands essentially untranslated in this context. There is an interplay between meanings because "confusion" becomes a proper name as well as a common noun, and so too "Babel" becomes a common noun as well as a proper name. But the two meanings can never become identical: a proper name by definition can never be confused with a common noun. God's act foils the Shemites' attempts to make a name for themselves: "He imposes his name, his name of father; and with this violent imposition he opens the deconstruction of the tower, as of the universal language; he scatters the geological filiation. He breaks the lineage. He at the same time imposes and forbids translation" (2002b: 107).

By attempting to create their own name, the Shemites have sought to universalize their idiom, creating a "peaceful transparency of the human community" (2002b: 111). This attempt at absolute homogeneity holds as its goal an idealized, unified system of meaning—a system that seeks to dispel confusion and ambiguity by relying on rational transparency. But God disrupts what can also be seen as a form of colonial violence or linguistic imperialism and destines them to translation. In his naming, God subjects the Shemites to the law of a translation both necessary and impossible. The name God gives ruptures the Shemites' idealized linguistic union.

With his name, God ushers in a language of tongues (of lips),[12] a language based within itself rather than around some idealized, yet unattainable, reality. Derrida looks to the "truth" of language; and instead of finding this in a transcendental "reality," he finds it in the simple fact or possibility of utterability—a notion that is always prior to any prescribed or attributed meaning. Rather than a transcendent language to which all languages refer, a promised kingdom to which translation edges closer through the reconciliation of languages, Derrida's concept of

12. "Come, let us go down, and confuse their language (*śāpāh*, lit. 'lip') . . ." (Gen 11:7).

translation, as drawn from the Babel story, is more of a unity without any self-identity.[13]

And so Derrida uses the Babel story to develop insights into the relationship between structure and otherness in language itself. He develops two models of language: that desired by the Shemites and that enforced by God. The two are intimately bound, not in the sense of their being clearly opposed, as would be the case of a classic binary relationship, or in the sense that one term takes priority over the other. They interrelate and co-inhabit each other as two irreconcilable elements of the same experience. One model becomes the condition of possibility for the other, and it is not always possible to see where one ends and the other begins. Language requires translation. In other words, we are compelled to ask the question "What does it mean?" And yet at the same time, language eludes this search for meaning because the answer to this question can never be exhaustive.

The structural traits of the sign (or the conditions of possibility for a sign) are twofold: first, a sign is capable of infinite meaning, and second, this possibility of potentially limitless meaning exists regardless of context and intention. Consequently, translation can never exhaustively account for the meaning of any sign, word, or sentence. Because of this, translation is always in a very real sense limited and incomplete.

Derrida is responding to (and arguing against) the idea that translation draws languages together with the purpose of approaching an ideal that he terms "pure language." The imminence of pure language is further evoked the more translation succeeds in uniting individual languages that are considered impoverished in their isolation from one another. When united by the power of translation, these languages exhibit a "growth" toward a completion, or an end, achieving a further closeness to the fullness of meaning. This envisaged fullness of language is in effect a "transcendental language," an ideal that is not itself presentable. But this distant point of fullness beckons from afar and orients those efforts to accumulate and combine differences between languages, promising that all differences can be resolved in a manifested totality of meaning.[14]

For Derrida, however, this ideal does not exist. Translation shows instead that the "truth" about language lies not in its reference to an idealized transcendental discourse, but rather that language is both meaningful and meaningless; meaning

---

13. Here we see Derrida's notion of *différance* coming into play. *Différance* does not mean any "thing"; it has no self-identity and is on the cusp of both presentability and nonpresentability.

14. Here and elsewhere Derrida is responding to the writings of Walter Benjamin, which he reads closely in "Des Tours de Babel" and which prove highly influential on his thoughts on translation. Benjamin's influence looms large in Derrida's thought; and considering his relevance to the themes explored in this book, particularly his work on translation and the fragmentary, he would no doubt make a valuable conversation partner. However, despite Benjamin's long shadow, I have opted to engage with the thought of Maurice Blanchot, another thinker who is mentioned by Derrida in "Des Tours de Babel." In chap. 5, aspects of Blanchot's thought are taken up in more depth, specifically his exploration of a literary notion of "sacredness," which will prove important for considering certain theological implications.

is conveyed while it is simultaneously prevented. The "truth" of language lies in the text *before* it is translated, the moment when it is still "to-be-translated" and therefore still essentially indecipherable. It is at this point that meaning is yet to be attributed and that the text is accorded its fullest potential; the text is simply transferable as such, but not yet translated. For Derrida, this is the most sacred moment for the text and in effect the moment of truth—the moment at which the text insists on being translated, and yet at the same time foils any attempt. This is what is named in Babel: "[T]he law imposed by the name of God who in one stroke commands and forbids you to translate by showing *and* hiding from you the limit" (2002b: 132–33). The sacred text marks this "limit," and as such it marks the occurrence of a *pas de sens* (2002b: 133)—a *pas de sens* that is both obscurity and clarity, and is at the same time "non-sense" and a "step of sense." The "sacred" text reveals meaning as language and literature as literality as it holds in balance the devotion of the sacred to translation and translation to the sacred.

## V. A Question of Method

Derrida is reluctant to propose a definition of deconstruction; but what can be said of deconstruction in light of Derrida's reading of the Babel story? One way of attempting an answer to this question is to say what deconstruction is *not*. For one thing, deconstruction is not a form or mode of analysis that helps to fill in gaps, smooth over rough textual patches, and lead to the positing of a more "solid" reading. At the same time, however, deconstruction is not a method of stripping back texts in a destructive way, emptying them of meaning and tossing them aside: "[J]ust as the tower is not destroyed in the Genesis story, so the deconstruction of metaphysical discourse is in no way a destruction of it" (Hart 2000: 110–11). Neither is it a dismantling of a text in order to simply reassemble it differently, for "to remain in this phase is still to operate on the terrain of and from within the deconstructed system" (Derrida 1981b: 42).

Deconstruction can be viewed as a challenge to systems of totalization: "Whether Derrida fastens upon 'reason,' 'truth,' 'arche' or 'ground,' his point is the same: a discourse's condition of possibility is also, and at the same time, its condition of impossibility for being totalised" (Hart 2000: 132). Even the most acute criticism of a text, a probing inquiry into the origins of language and thought, which presents findings that shatter previous conceptions, cannot be considered deconstructive if it involves the affirmation or reinscription of the metaphysical structures that it may have so cleverly dismantled.

However, this problem of how to theorize about the end of metaphysics from within metaphysics remains. How can a deconstructive reading, if understood as a critique of totalization, evade its own metaphysical reinscription? In other words, how can a criticism of totalizing systems such as metaphysics escape what seems like the inevitability of creating or relocating to new grounds?

Derrida comes some way toward answering this question in his reading of the

Babel story. He succeeds in demonstrating that when reconsidering the role of the "play" of meaning, the word "Babel" differs from itself and is thereby groundless. By refusing to resolve the heterodox nature of the word "B/babel," he shows that meaning and nonmeaning are revealed to be intimately related, neither term prior to or privileged over the other, and neither term able to stand on its own as distinct from the other. In this way, Derrida succeeds in locating an interpretive position, an opening in textual meaning, that does not fit into the old (metaphysical) order. Derrida finds that what is vital to the word is not its "true" meaning or resemblance, but its "truth" as difference—as *différance*.

## VI. Philosophy and de Man

There are many fine introductions to both Derridean thought and deconstruction, and the above discussion is by no means meant to be judged by their standard.[15] Having sketched something of an introduction to Derridean thought and deconstruction, some points need further consideration. For one thing, the scope of deconstruction and of Derrida's thought presented here is meant only to set up some basic parameters from which to work. Although Derrida and deconstruction have been closely associated, it would be far from accurate to equate Derridean theory with the "deconstructivist movement." In need of clarification is the fact that Derrida's work goes well beyond notions of deconstruction just as deconstruction well and truly exceeds Derridean thought. This is an important observation when we consider that this is a book that proposes a Derridean reading as distinct from a "deconstructivist" reading of the Markan transfiguration. Whereas "deconstruction" is a term that arises from Derrida's own writings, the particular character of deconstruction as a movement owes more to its development in the context of the Yale School and, more specifically, to the work of Paul de Man.

Another issue to be considered here is the academic reception of Derridean theory. Deconstructive criticism as a mode of textual reading has been followed by a certain amount of controversy over the past few decades. This controversy has been well documented and the arguments are ongoing.[16] Aside from this more general issue, however, there has also been a certain amount of criticism that focuses more specifically on Derrida's work as a philosopher and less on his part in a literary movement. The critiques from analytic philosophy, for instance, have been both scathing and dismissive. Before examining the application of his theory in biblical studies, and in order to provide another perspective, it will be worth pausing for a moment to catch a glimpse of how Derrida's "home" discipline of philosophy has attempted to come to terms with his work.

---

15. See, for example, Culler (1982); Leitch (1983); Norris (1987); Bennington and Derrida (1993); Rorty (1995); Caputo (1997).
16. See Ellis (1989); Tallis (1995); Mouffe (1996); Rorty (1992; 1995); Wheeler (2000).

North America in the 1970s saw the meteoric rise of deconstruction within the field of literary studies, where it was embraced as a startling new way of approaching texts and textuality that broke the choke hold of metaphysics and the hegemonic strictures of New Criticism (Davis and Schleifer 1985: vii). But a discussion of deconstruction, no matter how limited in scope, is not complete without mentioning the debt owed to Paul de Man. Whereas the name for this movement may have emerged specifically from Derrida's writings,[17] the formation of this movement and the development of a deconstructive strategy for reading emerged largely from the example of Paul de Man (Rorty 1995: 167). Derrida's, but more especially de Man's influence over a Yale School of literary criticism,[18] shaped the way deconstructive criticism was developed and practiced, transforming literary criticism in the United States by redefining the types of questions that can be asked of language, literature, and culture (Davis and Schleifer 1985: vii). When set side by side, however, the styles of these two thinkers can be seen to be quite distinct. De Man's work takes on a certain melancholy and angst when compared to the wit and playfulness exemplified in Derrida's writings:

> Perhaps the greatest difference between the two men is that Derrida resists both the "existentialist" pathos of early Heidegger and the apocalyptic hopelessness of late Heidegger, whereas de Man exhibits both. . . . [Compared to de Mann, Derrida] seems to be commending, and exemplifying, an attitude of playfulness. . . . [Moreover,] Derrida is frequently witty, and even frivolous, in a way that de Man almost never is. (Rorty 1995: 180–81)

In the last few decades the deconstructionist movement that began with the Yale School has roamed well beyond the bounds of literary theory and has had significant influence on disciplines as varied as political science, law, history, and even the sciences. In more recent times, however, deconstruction has seen some decline and within literary studies, has been superseded and reformulated by a "cultural critical" approach to reading texts.[19] This approach draws more heavily from the influence of Michel Foucault, who like Derrida and de Man, was a prominent figure behind the emergence of postmodernism. Foucault was an equally influential figure whose work was eclipsed for a time by the rise of deconstruction (Rorty 1995: 166). It could also be said that Derrida's work has, to some extent, also been

---

17. Specifically, "deconstruction" is Derrida's translation of Heidegger's *Destruktion* (from *Being and Time* [1962]), and in it he seeks to capture the sense of Heidegger's term as a "freeing up" of the hold metaphysics has had on thinking: a type of "de-structuring" (Cutrofello 1998: 897).

18. A group of scholars that also included Harold Bloom, Geoffrey Hartman, Barbara Johnson, and J. Hillis Miller. It is difficult to group all these scholars under a deconstructionist banner because their work varied widely from individual to individual and cannot all be described as deconstructive per se (see particularly the work of Hartmann and Bloom). Imre Salusinszky presents a series of fascinating interviews with these influential scholars in his book *Criticism in Society* (1987).

19. David Lehman points out, however, that despite deconstruction's decline in literature departments the subsequent rise of "the 'Age of Theory' was largely defined by deconstruction" (1995: 141).

eclipsed by deconstruction, a term with which he has never been totally at ease (Derrida 1996). Derrida's work clearly developed beyond the deconstructive program outlined in his earlier writings, and his thought continued to evolve in what were highly original and often baffling philosophical writings (Rorty 1995: 167).[20]

This book will engage, to some extent, with works from both ends of the Derridean theoretical spectrum. For this reason, the work to follow cannot be confined within what constitutes a deconstructivist approach and therefore will not specifically engage with the reading techniques exemplified in the work of de Man or with the traditions begun at the Yale School. The focus in what follows will be limited to the theoretical work of Derrida. When this book does engage with deconstruction it will be less in terms of a strategy for reading texts and more, in the Derridean sense, of "a way of approaching the 'wholly other' and of attempting thereby to conjure 'an experience of the impossible'" (Cutrofello 1998: 897).

The second point to be made here pertains to the fact that Derrida's contribution to academic thought has not been received without controversy. Although Derrida's thought has found its most welcoming and hospitable home within the field of literary studies, there have nonetheless been some critics that have considered deconstruction a less-than-welcome house guest.[21] The trend in critique directed toward Derrida follows difficulties with his nonfoundationalist approach to language and his less-than-conventional methods. These criticisms are most pertinently expressed by those who criticize Derrida in his capacity as a philosopher, an identity and tradition he would certainly not shy away from.

Derrida's philosophical influences are undeniable, and it is clear that his philosophical beginnings shaped his intellectual trajectory and development.[22] But the championing that deconstruction received in the field of literary studies has not necessarily been shared by British and American philosophers. This has particularly been the case within analytical philosophy, where, generally speaking, Derrida received far-from-glowing reviews from those who view his playful techniques and his obscure style as antithetical to their explicit approach and linear exposition. Richard Rorty explains as follows:

---

20. Gregory Ulmer notes that in one of the more important introductions to deconstruction, *On Deconstruction* (1982), Johnathan Culler excludes from his consideration such Derridean works as *Glas*, *The Post Card*, and *The Truth in Painting*. Culler concentrates instead on what Yvonne Sherwood speaks of as "vintage Derrida" (Sherwood 2000: 69; referring specifically to *Of Grammatology* and *Writing and Difference*). For Ulmer, these later more experimental readings of "art texts" represent a second phase in Derridean thought and one where "[w]riting, as Derrida practices it, is something other than deconstruction, the latter being a mode of analysis, while the former is a mode of composition" (Ulmer 1985: xi).

21. Notably John Ellis in *Against Deconstruction* (1989).

22. In his introduction to Derridean thought, Cutrofello observes that "to identify all of the philosophical problematics at stake in Derrida's writings, it would probably be necessary to have some familiarity with works of Kant, Hegel, Marx, Nietzsche, Husserl, Heidegger, Levinas, Saussure, Lévi-Strauss, Austin, Foucault, Freud, Lacan, Nicolas Abraham and Maria Torok" (1998: 897).

For many of these philosophers, heirs of a tradition which began with the logical positivists' opposition to metaphysics (not in the wide Heideggerian sense of the term but in a narrower sense in which "unverifiable" metaphysical, theological and moral claims are opposed to "verifiable" scientific claims) Derrida's work seems a deplorable, frivolous, wicked, regression to irrationalism. (Rorty 1995: 174)

The critics to whom Rorty refers see Derrida not as a literary critic engaged in close textual work that calls into question ways of reading and conventional notions of the "literary," but as a post-Heideggerian philosopher who challenges the dominance of a language of metaphysics in philosophical discourse.[23] Some object to his idea that language does not correspond to the nonlinguistic, to the "real" world. Others find a milder criticism in the Derridean claim of a self-contained language which, although not necessarily wrong in itself, has been expressed in such an extravagant "hyperbolic" way that it has led to the extrapolation of "silly" consequences (Rorty 1995: 176). In other words, challenging the metaphysical hegemony within philosophical discourse is one thing, but it need not extend to the dissolution of everyday distinctions where certain words are used in either relatively univocal or relatively ambiguous terms (Rorty 1995: 176).

In his attempt to find some common ground between analytical philosophy and Derridean theory, Samuel Wheeler compares Derrida with Donald Davidson and finds that they both reject what he describes as a "magic language":

> The magic language is the language in which we know what we mean, think our thoughts, and form our intentions. There is no question of interpreting sentences in the magic language, since the magic language is what interpretation is interpretation into. Furthermore, there is no question of discovering what the terms of the magic language mean, since the terms of the magic language are nothing but the meanings expressed by words of natural languages. (Wheeler 2000: 3)

This is the type of language Derrida challenges when he speaks of logocentrism and metaphysics of presence. What differentiates Derrida from Davidson and other analytic philosophers is that he believes the philosophical concepts he deconstructs have in fact thoroughly structured the entire language and therefore also the theoretical tools that challenge them. In other words, "anyone who says something like 'I must repudiate the entire language of my culture' is making a statement in the language she repudiates" (Rorty 1995: 172). This being the case, he sets about approaching philosophical critique in ways that circumvent this problem by using unconventional means. The results of this are that Derrida's work does not resemble the style of analytical philosophy, even though there are some stark similarities (Wheeler 2000: 3–4).

---

23. This, of course, is an oversimplification because the complexities of Derrida's reception in philosophical as well as literary spheres are both enormously varied and complex (see, for instance, David Wood's introduction in Wood 1992: 1–4). It is enough, however, to show at least something of his regard in his "home" discipline of philosophy.

Rorty explains that certain philosophers have difficulty with Derrida's unique style of "philosophizing" and consequently label him oracular or poetic rather than reflective and argumentative, as a philosopher should be. Rorty corrects this distinction, pointing to examples of philosophers such as Aristotle and Russell, who he acknowledges are well categorized as argumentative problem solvers, but he also mentions Plato and Hegel, who he finds are better described as oracular world disclosers (Rorty 1992: 239). Rorty further observes: "Poetic world-disclosers like Hegel, Heidegger and Derrida have to pay a price, and part of that price is the inappropriateness to their work of notions like 'argument' and 'rigour'" (Rorty 1992: 239). This quality of Derrida's thought is recognized by Rorty in his latter writings more than his former. Rorty sees in texts such as the "Envois" section of *The Post Card* (1987) a distinct movement away from the academic, "standard rules for philosophy" manner (Rorty 1992: 243).

While Rorty emphasizes points of convergence between Derrida and wider philosophical inquiry, Wheeler recognizes some distinct divergences, particularly between Derrida and Davidson. The major point of difference for Wheeler comes down to their respective positions on the notion of "truth." Since neither philosopher accepts a "given," or transcendental signified grounding a "magic language," the notion of truth needs to be redrawn. Wheeler summarizes their positions as follows. First Derrida:

> [S]ince there is no given, and since what is said is contingent on human decisions, and since many such judgements are indeterminate even within a theory, one may conclude that judgements cannot be objective in the sense of corresponding to being. So truth becomes another fiction, resting on metaphysical misconceptions.
>
> Davidson, accepting the same premises, rejects the book that truth supervenes on being. If truth is absolutely central and basic to the possibility of thought, then the indeterminacy of truth relative to all other phenomena just means that truth is irreducible and that there are unknowable truths. (Wheeler 2000: 8)

The consequences of Davidson's insights for Derrida are twofold. First, even though every system of meaning, by virtue of being systematic, is open to being deconstructed, such a movement does not necessarily render a system "defective" in a derogatory sense. Second, and following from this first point, recognizing that systems are "faulty" is not necessarily to say they are unusable, either as a practical device "for directing space ships or computer hardware" or even for purposes of intellectual inquiry (Wheeler 2000: 228). Wheeler concludes that everyday distinctions are not distinctions "in the order of concepts" and so need not have the kind of precision important in philosophical analysis and scientific discourse. Although he acknowledges that positing an "everyday" as distinct from a "philosophical" realm is ripe for deconstructing, he nonetheless argues that it is still of benefit. Even if it is not possible to distinguish with precision, it is still possible to separate the everyday from the philosophical in a rough fashion whereby a distinction can be maintained that would allow for these situations to more or less work.

Derrida's reception within academic philosophy has been introduced as a way of raising a number of pertinent theoretical points of difference. The warm reception of Derrida's work within literary theoretical circles contrasts with the more wary response given by philosophers. That said, Rorty and Wheeler reveal Derrida to be an unconventional philosopher whose methods are different from but not completely incompatible with what is generally expected in their field.

Although the debate as to the validity and institutional acceptance of Derrida's thought continues within philosophical circles, it will not be necessary to completely justify Derrida's approach in order to make use of it in this book. Although not prolific, the uses of Derridean theory within biblical studies are already many and varied. In chap. 2 I will look at a select number of these applications. Several themes to emerge from these readings will be particularly useful for my own reading to come in chap. 4.

## Conclusion

This chapter has had an introductory purpose. It began with the introduction of some key Derridean terms such as *différance*, metaphysics of presence, binary oppositions, and the transcendental signified. Once the association between deconstruction and Derrida was acknowledged, Derridean thought was further introduced through the exposition of his reading of the story of Babel, "Des Tours de Babel" (2002b). In this reading, we saw that Derrida concentrates on the problems of translation, paying particular attention to the name "Babel," a word with multiple meanings as both proper and common noun. The reading ends with an account of the sacred "limit," that *pas de sens* where meaning is both obscurity and clarity.

Armed with a better sense of reading deconstructively from Derrida's example, I briefly explicated the distinction between the deconstructivist movement and Derridean theory. Here, something of the controversy behind Derrida's reception in philosophical circles came to the fore. The particular controversy appears to be centered on questions of method and style. Derrida's obscure methods and playful style have been considered to be at odds with the more linear approach of analytical philosophy. Richard Rorty attempts to answer this charge by comparing Derrida to Plato and Hegel, whom he views as "oracular world-disclosers" and quite different from "argumentative problem-solvers" such as Aristotle and Russell. Within this classification, Rorty has been able to embrace Derrida's movement away from the conventional philosophical approach, although he admits that it remains controversial. On another issue, Samuel Wheeler compared Derrida and Davidson, noting their differing conceptions of truth. As a possible solution he proposed that despite Derrida's challenge to fixed meanings and grounds within philosophical systems, it is possible and indeed necessary and acceptable to function within these "faulty" meaning systems on an "everyday" basis.

In the next chapter, a different set of issues will emerge as my attention focuses more specifically on the reception and practice of deconstruction within the field of biblical studies. I will present a number of examples of implementing Derridean theory within this academic field as a way of demonstrating something of the range of applications. Moreover, I have selected examples that will help to position and foreground the work to come in chap. 4.

In chap. 4, I propose to read again, to "reread" the transfiguration narrative in light of Derridean theory. In this instance, it will not be the earlier Derridean material that I have just discussed that forms the primary emphasis of my analysis. Instead, I turn to his later works, in particular *The Post Card* and *The Gift of Death*. A number of key images and concepts from these texts will be explored in tandem with the images, problems, and puzzles of the transfiguration story.

Chapter 2

## The Critical "Other":
## Derridean Theory within Biblical Studies

### Introduction

Having introduced Derridean theory in the first chapter, I now narrow the focus and look to the reception and application of Derridean theory within biblical studies. Through the course of this chapter it will become clear that the issues that arise between biblical studies and Derridean theory differ from those faced by philosophy. Because the majority of biblical studies' readings that draw on the writings of Derrida fall under the banner of deconstruction, I will survey a number of examples of this type of approach. This survey will be guided by two interrelated questions. The first question asks about the relationship between critic and text and explores the impact and consequences of employing Derridean theory in the critical process. A second question asks how deconstructive readings in biblical studies have engaged with a sense of textual otherness. There will also be some attention given to the critical implications of such an encounter. I should also state from the outset that what follows is not a neutral and representative survey of deconstruction in biblical studies (if such a thing were possible). I have deliberately selected a limited number of examples in order to develop and illuminate the questions outlined above, and I have also chosen them in order to provide context, to foreground and to position the specific trajectory of my own Derridean reading of the Markan transfiguration.

### I. The Self and the Other

Derrida's appearance in biblical studies can be seen as early as the early '80s with the publication of *Semeia* 23, *Derrida and Biblical Studies* (1981).[1] Deconstructive readings of biblical texts have dotted the academic horizon ever since, as have numerous introductions and theoretical conversations attempting, variously, to promote, clarify, undertake, and vilify Derrida's theoretical contribution. In chap. 1,

---

1. Derrida's influence in biblical studies predates this edition of *Semeia*, however. For instance, John Dominic Crossan, one of the editors of this edition of *Semeia*, had published *Cliffs of Fall* (1980) the previous year. In this work, he looks to the Gospel parables, engaging with Derridean theory in the process.

a distinction was made between deconstructivist theory and Derridean thought, and Derrida's discomfort with the former was noted. While it is true that deconstruction is an important aspect of Derrida's thought and he is still considered by many to be a major proponent, his later works move beyond the scope of what has become known as the deconstructive approach. However, the majority of applications in biblical studies of Derrida's thinking appear in the form of deconstructive readings. Therefore, although wary of reducing Derridean theory to the deconstructive enterprise, this chapter will primarily examine deconstructive work in biblical studies as a means of charting the application, incorporation, and development of his wider theoretical interests within this discipline.

The survey to follow will take up two related questions that will have bearing on the reading to follow in chap. 4. On the one side is the question of method and style. What type of approach have commentators used in applying Derridean theory to biblical texts? What does their style reflect about their own self-conception as critics and has this had a corresponding effect on the way they approach the text? Examples of deconstructive readings with styles ranging from the traditional to the experimental will be drawn from the work of David Clines, Edward Greenstein, David Seeley, Wallace Bubar, and Stephen Moore. All these critics demonstrate in differing ways this question of the relationship between critical style and self-conception within the process of interpretation. Particular emphasis will be placed on the work of Moore, not only because of the number of examples he provides but because his stylistic example will be the most useful for setting up my own reading in chap. 4.

The second question is one that emerges from the fruits of a deconstructive reading. In what ways has Derrida's theoretical work gone beyond what can be strictly termed deconstruction? Moreover, what ways do critics go beyond the deconstructive process of uncovering metaphysical preconceptions? It is this sense of a "beyond" as it has occupied the critics that is dealt with here. How is a "beyond" to be conceived of when the structures of metaphysics are no longer sufficient? The various ways in which critics engage with this sense of a "beyond" as a notion of "otherness," and the implications of such an encounter will reveal how my own reading in chap. 4 is rooted in work that has already begun in biblical studies. Deconstructive readings from the work of Yvonne Sherwood, Terence Keegan, Patrick Counet, Gary Phillips, and once again, Stephen Moore, will be examined, as will the various ways they respond to this elusive notion of "otherness."

Finally, I will look to the more poetic approach of Francis Landy, a biblical scholar whose poetic style and theoretical approach represent something of the middle ground at which I am aiming. Landy's individual style is an example of incorporating Derridean theory while going beyond the deconstructive agenda. His work draws more on Derrida's later writings to produce readings that engage with literary notions of death, fragmentation, and the profoundly contradictory experience of language and meaning.

This is by no means an exhaustive account of either Derrida's impact on biblical studies or the practice of deconstruction in this field.[2] The intention is merely to provide a survey, or sample, of Derrida's impact for purposes of orientation and contextualization. This will help to both further clarify some elements from the previous chapter as well as foreground my rereading of the transfiguration scene.

## II. Reading Critically and Critiquing the Reader: The Evidence of Style

Within biblical studies, David J. A. Clines is an influential literary critic who has utilized Derridean theory to produce a range of deconstructive readings over the past fifteen years or so (see Clines 1990, 1993, 1995, 1998). Some degree of his influence can be gauged in two recent reviews of the first volume of his two-volume work *On the Way to the Postmodern* (1998). The first reviewer writes: "This volume is an excellent source for one who wants to see how a deconstructionist works and what principles underlie this approach to texts, as well as the strengths and weaknesses of the postmodern" (Franke 2000). A second reviewer speaks of Clines's theoretical expertise in all things postmodern, claiming that these two volumes "show that the author masters various ways of interpretation—formalist, intertextuality, genre, feminist, materialist, deconstruction, and psychoanalytic interpretations—and uses them freely with any written artifact." Furthermore, he speaks of Clines's work as "show-windows of contemporary biblical studies" (Lee 2000).

In his deconstructive readings, Clines appears to approach the text with a strong sense of the critic as standing apart from the text. This being the case, there would be no need to challenge the style of criticism, because such a challenge would appear to have no bearing on the results of interpretation. Clines's deconstructive readings do not call into question or seek the implications of the relationship between scholar and text. Consequently, elements of Clines's deconstructive readings are problematic from a deconstructive perspective. In a deconstructive reading of Job (1990), Clines makes comments that posit a clear division between reader and text.[3] In his introduction, Clines poses the following aim: "In this paper I shall be arguing that the book [Job] does indeed deconstruct itself in several fundamental areas. I shall try to distinguish these deconstructions from simple incoherence, and suggest that its rhetoric inoculates it against its deconstructibility" (1990: 65).

---

2. There has been a recent proliferation of work using Derrida's later theoretical ideas, particularly since his presence at the 2002 AAR/SBL Annual Meeting in Toronto. Chief among the volumes produced as a result of this encounter are *Derrida's Bible* (Sherwood 2004) and *Derrida and Religion* (Sherwood and Hart 2005).

3. The reader is positioned opposite the text as the accomplished wielder of deconstructive techniques. This is evident in Clines's use of such phrases as "in which we may see the book of Job deconstructing itself (or, we might prefer to say, in which it is open to deconstruction by the reader)" (1990: 66).

Although it is true that Derrida believes a text contains the seeds of its own deconstruction, the repetition of this view throughout his reading gives the impression that Clines sees deconstruction at work only in the text and not within the critical process. This view is seen again in "Ethics as Deconstruction," an article in *On the Way to the Postmodern*, where Clines tackles a number of texts—Deut 23:15–16; Gen 9:5–6; John 8:3–11—concentrating on moments of ambiguity and contradiction that make settling on one "correct" reading difficult. Every now and again in Clines's deconstructive reading, certain phrases stand out awkwardly. Phrases such as the following: "I shall look at some biblical texts where an ethical idea or prescription or hint seems to be founded on a deconstruction" (Clines 1998: 95); "This deconstruction rubs against the grain of the text . . ." (1998: 106); "That is quintessentially the outcome of a deconstruction . . ." (1998: 111).[4] Championing incoherence and fragmentation may well be a deconstructive technique, but Clines does not appear to be at all critical of the fragmentation of readers themselves. It would appear that Clines seeks to undermine the "text" from his scholarly position, a unified and reliable viewpoint which is always situated outside the text. Thus he comments that he is looking at how the "book does indeed deconstruct itself" (1990: 65), while paying little attention to his or any reader's part in "creating" and continually "re-creating" this same "book."

By not challenging his own scholarly perspective, Clines is in danger of appropriating deconstruction into a fairly traditional scholarly framework. Thus, after "deconstructing" the passages from Deuteronomy, Genesis, and John, Clines can still make comments such as "I cannot bear to be kept in the dark about something that is the case . . ." (1998: 122). Despite his efforts to read deconstructively, it seems that Clines refuses to abandon his own logocentric impulses, his need to read structures as inherent and self-evident, and his thirst for "presence" within texts. This may well be a part of a reluctance to challenge an established approach to scholarship that values these same qualities—such as clarity of expression for instance. A telling moment comes when Clines comments on the opacity of J. Hillis Miller's writing style, which he regards as excessively convoluted: "I feel sure it must be possible to make the point more lucidly without losing any of the subtlety; I also feel sure that if I cannot understand something after I have read it five times the fault is probably not mine" (1998: 119). Ironically, the particular passage Clines uses as his example is a part of a discussion by Miller about why there is a need to challenge traditional approaches to scholarly inquiry. Clines quotes Miller:

> It is not because stories contain the thematic dramatization of ethical situations, choices, and judgments that they are especially appropriate for my topic [the ethics

---

4. Other giveaway phrases include "Here is the concept of voluntary slavery, which is deconstructive in the alternate mode" (Clines 1998: 99); "the second pair of deconstructions" (101); "But if a deconstruction is a . . ." (110); "A text that professes to give a reason for paying taxes but does not deliver on its promise is a deconstructive text" (115).

of reading], but for a reverse reason, that is, because ethics itself has a peculiar relation to that form of language we call narrative. The thematic dramatization of ethical topics in narratives are the oblique allegorization of this linguistic necessity. (Clines 1998: 119)

Miller is making a point about being careful not *only* to look for ethical structures or systems at work within narrative texts. The tendency for scholars to identify ethics with the narratives in which they are expressed is easy to fall into because, for whatever reason, ethical systems have "a peculiar relation" to narrative structure or form. Miller goes on to make the point that by closely and unquestioningly binding together narrative and ethics in this way, one is in danger of forgetting the structures and preconditions of language itself which allow for such a congenial union. These structures and linguistic patterns which draw ethics and narrative together *themselves* become the subject of further analysis, the limitations of which deconstruction is always at pains to point out.

Clines locates deconstruction within a text as a textual trait. He refers to finding deconstructions within texts in such a way that he distances the text from the reader: "The deconstruction is then an aspect of the text, something that one knows about the text, as one knows about its language and its rhetoric and its context and so on" (1998: 123). But of course deconstruction brings these "givens" that Clines lists into radical doubt. In Clines's deconstructive readings, attention to his own structures of thinking is given no critical attention, and he emerges from a deconstructive encounter with his theoretical structures and systems seemingly intact. Establishing a deconstructive reading, rather than, as Clines puts it, "identifying a deconstruction," is not a case of establishing yet more "facts" (1998: 123) about a text.[5] For a text (and this notion of text needs to be more broadly based so as to include the reader, for instance) has meaning regardless of the context. In other words, change the parameters, and the text continues to have meaning. Maybe not the intended or original meaning, but a potential that always exceeds (even precedes) any specific set of contextual or intentional parameters. Consequently, texts always go beyond what we "know" at any one time about the specificities of language, rhetoric, context, etc. Traces of meaning erupt from within and refer beyond the space between reader and text. In this way, a Derridean "text" is always an "inter-text"; always a collection of texts only partially visible to and which include the reader. Clines attempts to set himself outside of the notion of textuality by locating deconstruction as one factor among many within the "text"—a remote and solid object present before him.

Clines's criticism of Miller raises the point that expression that is too convoluted serves to alienate rather than illuminate. However, this objection to the potential

---

5. Clines speaks of the results of a deconstructive reading as being factual, forgetting that these results themselves are subject to deconstruction: "But if it can be shown successfully to a reasonable number of people that a text deconstructs itself, that is for me a *fact*" (1998: 123).

problems of theoretical opacity does not necessarily translate to the uncritical acceptance of one's own scholarly position. In addition, it does not mean that appropriation of Derridean theory to one's own approach necessarily renders one's scholarly style convoluted or opaque. This latter qualification appears to be a concern of others who have attempted to integrate Derridean theory and deconstruction into their critical approach.

In his introduction to deconstruction, Edward Greenstein agrees that the playful and ironic style ought to be part of deconstructive readings. Greenstein observes that

> To write continuous, straightforward prose would be to deny or suppress the kaleidoscopic character of our knowledge.... Derrida seeks to de-centre and liberate from (always superimposed) structure on the one hand and to underscore the dynamic play within language on the other by expressing himself in unconventional form and rhetoric. A new way of thinking prompts a new way of writing. (1989: 44–45)

Speaking of his own method, Greenstein goes on to say:

> Though hardly going all the way, I have attempted to incorporate certain aspects of this quite earnest provocative mode of discourse into the present essay. The style is not intended to distract but to call attention to the question of how we make meaning and how all discourse is in a real sense a composite—what Derrida terms a "bricolation"—and echo of prior discourse. (1989: 44–45)

It comes as a disappointment, then, that Greenstein's subsequent deconstructive reading falls short of what he promises, or at least, it does not go quite far enough. Despite his awareness of the need to discover new "ways of writing," when he tackles the story of how Aaron's eldest sons die (Lev 10:1–5), although using some characteristic deconstructive devices,[6] his reading fails to reach the places he has described in the paragraphs quoted above and in his earlier introductory sections. There is not much sign of "unconventional form and rhetoric." And whereas it is certainly "a new way of thinking," in Greenstein's case, this hasn't translated into an especially "new way of writing."

Greenstein concludes that the undecidable reigns in Lev 10:1–5: "the very strangeness of the episode undercuts its susceptibility to rational explanation" (1989: 64). And this ambiguity contributes to a sense of the sacred, to an ineffable and unpredictable Yahweh to whom we, driven by our own need for security and comfort, attribute order and design. Such a conclusion is of interest when considered alongside Greenstein's comments about deconstruction. Earlier he states with apparent confidence that

---

6. For instance, Greenstein "plays" with words: bracketing letters which provide interesting and unexpected references; using slashes to provide alternative words equally valid although with differing implications; and the honing in on ambiguities in the text and on how they have been interpreted.

> Ambiguity is characteristic of language itself, the dynamic play in the scene of reading. While other critical approaches attempt to solve the puzzle, deconstruction denies the objectivity of order and "renounce[s] the ambition to master or demystify its subject (text, psyche) by the technocratic, predictive, or authoritarian formulas." Meaning is always indeterminate. (1989: 57)[7]

Could it be that Greenstein harbors a certain unease about his project? Earlier he states: "To deconstruct the Bible would reduce it to the same nothing to which other texts have been deconstructed" (1989: 54). It is doubtful whether Derrida would consider deconstruction as doing this at all. Derrida professes to deconstruct texts he loves, not in an effort to "destroy" them, but, rather, more out of respect for these texts. The role of deconstruction is not to strip everything away, leaving an empty hole in its wake. It is possible, however, that this thought is a threatening one to Greenstein, especially in light of another telling comment: "Deconstruction must blow away the cloud of God's presence that hovers over virtually all biblical narrative" (1989: 55). It is as though Greenstein is pitting deconstruction against notions of God and holiness in an antagonistic sense. While deconstruction may well be useful in revealing the metaphysical elements that pervade such a conception of "God's presence," this does not necessarily involve "blow[ing] away" this cloud of existence altogether.

Greenstein then sets out to "deconstruct" the Leviticus passage; however, he goes on to reinvest it with God's "presence," but "presence" as ambiguity rather than as "facticity."[8] Thus, although he attempts to be deconstructive, Greenstein ends by reasserting the metaphysical frames of reference he seeks to do away with. To be fair, it could be argued that this is an inevitability that accompanies any deconstructive reading. The mistake is not Greenstein's assertion of an alternative interpretation of this passage, but a desire to replace one with another. Although his alternative is not based on the facticity he is concerned to deconstruct, by *replacing* facticity, order, and certainty with ambiguity and unpredictability, he is unavoidably replacing one metaphysical system with another; the values may have changed but the structure remains. Greenstein's mistake is believing, as he puts it, "Derrida's clearing the [metaphysical] ground ... might allow for some other, non-metaphysical constructive theology ... in place of the descriptive theologies that have typified Western religions" (1989: 54). This prospect does not seem to please Greenstein, and he regards it as "out of sympathy with the Bible's own outlook" (1989: 54). As such he appears to adapt his deconstructive reading, tailoring it to allay his own fears of nihilism and avoid the threat of ending "with a Nietzschean vision of the void" (1989: 54), by offering an alternative that does not take him too far at all from the one he criticizes.

Greenstein ponders the "imponderable *mysterium tremendum*," and finds something about this mystery truly frightening. Rather than explore the results of chal-

---

7. Here, Greenstein is quoting a member of the Yale School, Geoffrey Hartman (Hartman 1980: 41).
8. "One service of deconstruction ... is its capacity to break facticity" (1989: 63).

lenging metaphysical conceptions of the divine, he covers over the hole he sees as having been opened up by deconstruction with a vision of an "absent" God, no less metaphysical than a God fully "present." Although Greenstein aptly demonstrates how a text can be deconstructed from within, it seems clear that he is wary of altogether relinquishing a certain notion of textual presence.[9]

In *Deconstructing the New Testament* (1994), David Seeley tours through New Testament texts, casting a deconstructive gaze at the Synoptics and John as well as at the letters of Paul. Asking the question "Why employ the thought of Jacques Derrida to read the New Testament?" (1994: 1), Seeley answers with an assertion that biblical historical critical scholarship and Derrida's work share a "surprising kinship," Derrida lending a "new sharpness and clarity" to what has long been of interest to biblical scholars (1994: 1). Referring to Moore's work,[10] Seeley speaks, by contrast, of his own approach: "What I hope to do here is to present a more staid examination of New Testament texts, but using Derridean presuppositions. . . . Indeed the style should be quite familiar to biblical scholars" (1994: 2).

Seeley traces a summary line through Derrida's analysis of a history that has privileged speech over writing, and looks particularly at Derrida's analysis of Levi-Strauss and, to some extent, Rousseau. Then Seeley charts a similar history through the tradition of biblical interpretation going back to Irenaeus and Tertullian, with a particularly enlightening reading of Augustine's conversion. He ends with the more recent work of Rudolf Bultmann and Burton Mack.

This parallel reading of the history of metaphysics alongside the development of biblical interpretation leads Seeley to conclude that the acceptance of a fragmented mode of reading encouraged by the deconstructive understandings of Derrida is similar in spirit to new trends in biblical scholarship:

> Derrida is not as foreign to biblical studies as might have been expected . . . taking Derrida seriously does change the way one practices exegesis. One becomes much more comfortable with tensions in the text, even if they threaten the latter's unity or coherence. . . . One can relax and enjoy tracking different view-points within a text as they mingle, contend, battle, or otherwise interact. There is no longer an urge to reduce this process to a single voice, for one knows that whatever voice might be heard in, through, or behind the text would itself be multiplex. (1994: 19)

Seeley's deconstruction of Mark is a broad-based investigation into the reasons Mark gives, or more accurately doesn't give, for Jesus' death. Seeley's reading roams through the text, honing in on a number of problematic passages with his

---

9. It is only fair to add that these observations about Greenstein's writing in 1989, and any fear that he may have had then, have been more than ably come to terms with since. See particularly his parallel readings of Job's encounter with the whirlwind in Greenstein 1999: 301–17.

10. Seeley quotes Moore: "Sometimes my composition has taken the form of a collage—a surrealist collage, to be precise" (Moore 1992: xvii) and "the Derrida of my own text will be an inventive writer first and a philosopher second" (Moore 1992: 4).

new "deconstructive eyes" and hoping to make new sense of old problems. For Seeley, deconstruction seems to have allowed him to ask new questions and to treat the text a little differently in obtaining his answers, but his approach remains firmly in the mold of traditional biblical studies.

In the end, Seeley comes through with what he promises at the outset of his project and does not really stray too far from the style of contemporary scholarship. He seems content to ask questions of the text more than of traditional approaches to interpretation. In his conclusion, Seeley states, "This book has shown that deconstruction can be usefully placed at the service of biblical studies" (159). The value of deconstruction for Seeley is to provide ways of approaching texts that aid in uncovering and dealing with what have become traditional glosses and omissions. He ends his deconstructive tour of the New Testament by saying that his study has "yielded one clear result which must be considered in any assessment of Christianity: in the beginning was diversity" (178). His attempt to place deconstruction "at the service of biblical studies" appears to involve a certain domestication of deconstruction for use as one of the many tools of traditional biblical studies methodologies. The risk of placing deconstruction at the disposal of traditional biblical studies is that the "parent" methodologies, according to their status, may find themselves above and beyond close scrutiny and critique.

In this way, Seeley is not as rigorous in examining the tools of his own discipline and appears to drive a wedge between text and criticism, happily scrutinizing the former while subordinating deconstruction to the latter. Deconstruction's chief contribution to biblical studies, according to Seeley, is its ability to "highlight differences between and within biblical texts—differences which, for one reason and another, have often been glossed over or ignored" (159). Seeley's willingness to conform to established scholarship is revealed when he goes on to explain,

> This ability answers the question posed by one scholar who read these pages before their publication. He stated that he was still uncertain how this method advances the discipline, and asked: "Is it that one finds in the tensions the keys to understanding a text, or that they demonstrate that finding a single, coherent understanding of a text is impossible . . . ?" (159)

Although Seeley is right to comment on the inability of any one interpretation to contain all the potential meanings of a text, the question must be asked at this point about Seeley's cooperation with notions of disciplinary "advancement." By looking toward the further evolution of the field without any necessary question of its foundations, is Seeley consolidating a framework that looks toward the possibility of including everything within itself? He may use deconstruction as a way of reading texts, but by not scrutinizing his approach, the same logocentric features that he identifies at work within texts will be allowed to reign unchecked, with only a few exceptions, within the structures of analysis that define and make possible the traditional biblical scholarship he seeks to retain and maintain.

Seeley's reading of Mark's literary attempts to unite a diverse readership in some ways mirror his own attempts to unite deconstruction with biblical studies. Unfortunately, Seeley's attempts at unification thwart a benefit of deconstruction he often refers to: the acceptance of diversity in interpretation. By "uniting" deconstruction with biblical studies, Seeley may be attempting to promote the possibility of multiple, coexisting interpretations, but he also (inadvertently) promotes a sameness of scholarly endeavor and reestablishes a certain narrowness to the biblical studies theoretical repertoire.

Like Seeley, Wallace Bubar also takes Moore's deconstructive work as his model. After quoting Moore's image of the ending of Mark's Gospel "saw[ing] through the branch on which the book is perched" (Bubar 1995: 146), he poses a similar metaphor illustrating his own intention: "I shall explain how the ingredients in Matthew's slimmering [sic] brew spill over, eroding the very foundation upon which the book rests—that is the church" (146).

Bubar takes Peter's role in Matthew's Gospel as "cornerstone," the "πέτρα upon which the church is founded," and demonstrates how these images contain the "seeds of their own deconstruction, as well as the seeds of Matthew's deconstruction" (150). Bubar reads Peter more as "stumbling block" than "foundation stone," an aporia in the sense that Derrida uses this term—a point of impasse where ambiguity and contradiction are unable to be clearly resolved.[11] In the light of his deconstruction of Peter's role here as "rock" of the church, Bubar makes some more political observations on the history of the church and the state of contemporary exclusion of certain minorities: "The unfortunate history of the church, with regard to the acceptance of gentiles, women, people of color, divorcees, gays, lesbians, and countless other groups, is one giant perpetuation of Peter's sin" (152).

Bubar's deconstructive style stays very much within the field of traditional biblical criticism and within the text he is examining. But he seems to aim for the "destruction" rather than for the "deconstruction" of Matthew's text. This ambition is given away in the title of his paper, "The Utter De(con)struction of Matthew and His Church." While deconstruction can be seen to destroy monolithic methods of reading, demonstrating the polyvalent meaning of any text, it does not necessarily "destroy" or even reject traditional criticism as such.[12] While Bubar concludes that he has "depicted both an institutional church in ruin and a Gospel in the process of self-deconstruction" (157), he does not seem to have turned a deconstructive

---

11. Bubar cites Christopher Norris (1983) who comments on the aporia or "unpassable path" in terms of its use in deconstruction: "Language often runs onto blind-spots of paradox—aporia in Derrida's Aristotelian terminology—which prevent it from effectually meaning what it says, or saying what it means." He goes on to say that the isolation of an aporia within a text means looking "for the place(s) where the text contradicts itself, creates it own impasse and thus unwittingly reveals the validity of the deconstructive argument . . ." (Bubar 1995: 19).

12. Danna Nolan Fewell expresses this point succinctly when she writes, "Method plus text always equals a surplus of text" (1995: 141).

eye to his own field of criticism, and one wonders how far he is willing really to challenge and test the bounds set for critical inquiry. Given the examples cited above, it would appear that not being aware of their own critical perspective and the extent to which they participate in their readings is a factor that unites Clines, Greenstein, Seeley, and Bubar.

Although held up as an exemplar by both Seeley and Bubar, Moore's work remains something of an anomaly within biblical studies. Moore's imaginative and unconventional deconstructive style, although appreciated, has not been widely adopted. Moore noted the landscape at the time of writing *Mark and Luke in Poststructuralist Perspectives* (1992), and referred to biblical scholarship as still in the "before" stage. This is despite deconstruction's challenges to traditional modes of reading, despite critics outside biblical studies having engaged with biblical texts, and despite the theoretical movement toward the "beyond" stage especially evident in American literary studies (1992: xv). Moore points to an element of Derrida's work that had not yet found its way into biblical studies:

> Derrida not only reads philosophy, he has apprenticed himself to modernist and postmodernist writers (as in *Writing and Difference* [1978a], *Dissemination* [1981a], *Glas* [1986a], *Signsponge* [1984], and *Ulysses' Gramophone* [1992b]) and visual artists (in *The Truth in Painting* [1985]), not deconstructing them as he does the philosophers but culling strategies from them instead. (1992: xvii)

It seems it is with this observation in mind that Moore describes his own method:

> Graphic imagery, creative anachronism, sustained wordplay (wordwork, rather), and surrealistic stories of reading make up my method in this book. . . . I am eager to reply to the Gospels in kind, to write in a related idiom . . . to respond to a pictographic text pictographically, to narrative text narratively, producing a critical text that is a postmodern analogue of the premodern text that it purports to read. (1992: xviii)

Later, Moore adds to this description: "As my reading proceeds, I shall be shuttling from convention to invention, from conventional criticism, whether Marcan or deconstructive . . . to some of the stranger critical outworlds opened up by Derrida's writing" (1992: 4).

Moore is opening up an important distinction here, not only between conventional criticism and deconstruction but between that of a deconstruction more philosophical in character, resembling Derrida's earlier work, for instance, from *Of Grammatology* (1974a) and *Writing and Difference* (1978a), and a more literary, inventive, playful approach demonstrated in Derrida's later works, particularly *Glas* (1986a) and *The Post Card* (1987). However, Moore is quick to qualify this distinction, and at the same time he furthers his point, when he observes that Derrida has "smudged the line" between that of inventive writer and philosopher (1992: 4). Thus, the distinction between conventional criticism and criticism informed by Derridean theory is by no means clear-cut and absolute. Moore raises awareness of the fact that deconstruction is more than simply a reworking of philosophical boundaries, or even a challenge to these same boundaries. There is an element of play associated with deconstruction that is especially evident in some of Derrida's later works but which does not seem so prevalent in biblical deconstructive readings that are more conventional in style. In *Mark and Luke in Poststructuralist Perspectives*, Moore offers deconstructive readings of both these Gospels, and, in the process, deconstructs conventional scholarly approaches to these texts.

For example, Moore looks at the ending of Mark's Gospel—"Mark is a lion with four or more tails" (1992: 5)—and comments on the general reluctance to allow the contradiction found here to stand without seeking resolution:

> Mark incorporates contradiction into the body of its diction where, like some vital internal organ, it sits undigested and unexpelled. Yet legions of Marcan scholars, able to construe contradiction only as blockage, have been only too eager to help the Lion complete its "unfinished" business—to unstop its blockages, cause the streams of sense to flow, give this Gospel of enigma an enema. (1992: 27)

In addition to the problem of multiple endings, Moore also investigates other problematic Markan passages.[13] In the scene of the young man who runs off naked (Mark 14:51–52), Moore comments on the work of traditional scholarship:

> Clearly scholars have one thing on their minds. They are always eager to undress a work—to expose an original content concealed beneath secondary revisions for example, as in their handling of Mark's (rear)ending. But Mark cannot be stripped with ease, and that has been the tease for so many Marcan scholars. Mark has never failed to send the ink coursing through their pens. Sacred scripture as "secret stripture," Mark has been invigoratingly hard to pen down. (1992: 32)

Moore continues his reading of Mark, dipping his own pen into a variety of Derridean works from *The Post Card* (1987), to *Signsponge* (1984) and Derrida's work with psychoanalytic theory. He allows these texts freely to engage with Mark, demonstrating how pervasive and powerfully disorienting Derridean theory can be. In the end, Moore looks at Mark as Derrida looks at Joyce's *Finnegans Wake*:

> [W]e can say that Mark is at least close to dreamwork, the hieroglyph, the illuminated manuscript, or the Joycean experiment as to the scholarly commentary or monograph. In consequence, Mark can just as easily be approached through a postcritical writing that would attempt to match its concrete parabolic style by miming it, as through a critical reading that, in getting Mark right (in putting down the riot), would rewrite it altogether in colorless academese. (1992: 83)

Moore achieves this goal to a varying extent. His style in the first section on Mark, although undoubtedly distinctive, is more recognizably written in academese

---

13. Moore also investigates the obtuseness of the disciples (1992: 11ff.) and the parables (1992: 21ff.).

than what follows in his reading of Luke. In his reading of Mark, Moore seems to be taking much more time to interact specifically with and go some way to clarify Derridean theory. It is as though Moore's work with Mark and Derrida is in preparation for what is to come in his reading of Luke-Acts. In his analysis of the latter, Moore goes into his reading of this text with the problem of the classic dichotomies of presence versus absence and whether or not traditional readings of Luke collude in what can be described as a "repression of that which threatens presence and the mastering of absence" (1992: 89).[14]

Soon, however, Moore allows himself to be swept away in a theme of embodiment that draws on numerous areas of Derridean thought. What follows is an intensely original reading of a thoroughly corporeal Luke-Acts, a text that soon takes on the characteristics of "[a]n obese androgyn," a textual body that "repels and fascinates. It seeks to arouse us from our Platonic fixation with its ideal, aerated body to have us explore, in graphic detail(s), its sensuous materiality" (1992: 157).

Aware that "scholarship can sometimes be too s(t)olid,"[15] Moore's technique involves extensive use of wordplay and punning, while also making effective use of unexpectedly vivid imagery to take his own scholarly investigations into the realm of language itself.[16] As such, in Moore's work, one encounters the boundless intertextuality of language as an often chaotic web of meaning. Indeed, by comparison to the style of traditional scholarship, the creative freedom Moore allows meaning in his readings is as though he has set the bird from its cage. Let us take a few examples. In this first excerpt, Moore, quoting Richard Dillon, latches onto the word "echo" and segues into Derrida:

> "But a story [Acts] which went on to document how those witnesses actually echoed the Master's speech in founding the churches could instill it incomparably better" [quoting Dillon]. Yet what is an echo if not a sound that, in self-dividing, severs and distances itself from its origin? An echo is sound in flight from itself, an earwitness to that irreducible self-differing that hollows out every speech act, however immediate-seeming, the Speech Acts of the Apostles being no exception. Thus, we find ourselves in "a labyrinth which is, of course, the labyrinth of the ear. Proceed, then by seeking out the edges, the inner walls, the passages" [quoting Derrida]. (1992: 95)

In a section entitled "A New Taste-ament," Moore looks to Derrida's experimental work *Glas* (1986a) for inspiration and draws also from the work of Roland Barthes:

---

14. Moore is quoting Derrida here from *Writing and Difference* (1978a: 197). Of particular interest to Moore are the approaches to Luke exemplified in the work of Hans Conzelmann (1960) and Richard Dillon (1978).

15. "Heaviness sets in. Gravity takes over" (Moore 1992: 154).

16. Moore writes: "A good pun is a pun that works, and it works to produce an underpriced brand of knowledge"; "I have tried to scatter semes as Mark's sower scatters seeds, in chance configurations that would yield an unpredictable harvest" (1992: 155).

If text is tissue, *Glas* is fatty tissue—a text that overreads, becoming so obese that it cannot leap up to the level of Idea. *Glas* answers Hegel with its mouth full; "Glas *ist was Glas isst*," it mumbles. "*Edo ergo sum*," it adds, and belches in Descartes' face.

It is not the only one that does, although its table manners are somewhat better than *Glas's*, Barthes' *Pleasure of the Text* wants equally to stick in the gullet. It ends with an apocalips, saying in effect: "One who is more corpulent is coming after me." And there will be heard in its carnal style, when it appears, "the grain of the throat, the patina of consonants, the voluptuousness of vowels, a whole carnal stereophony: the articulation of the body, of the tongue." Made up of "language lined with flesh," the effect of this lubricious text will be "to make us hear in their materiality, their sensuality, the breath, the gutterals, the fleshiness of the lips, a whole presence of the human muzzle." (1992: 109–10)

At times one catches clear glimpses of Moore, the man, in his writings.[17] Drawing on Joyce for stylistic advice, Moore frequently quotes from *Finnegans Wake*.[18] One senses a struggle with a religious upbringing, or at least familiarity with a particular kind of Christian culture, lurking behind his attention to the influence of Catholicism at certain points. Other autobiographical elements are no doubt written on his sleeve, but at the same time they remain hidden to most in what can sometimes be a smokescreen of puns and intertexts.[19] In the final chapter of the work, Moore provides something of a rationale to his approach:

This book... has been a body book, not to say a body bag. I have tried to write a book on the Gospels that would not be bound to the ingested body of a dead Father (Mark or Luke), immeasurably more powerful now than when he was alive, but would be moored more in my own body instead. I have tried to write an incarnate criticism that would say to the (ev)angel(ist), "Be it done unto me according to thy word and not according to thy concept." (1992: 157)

The critical process informs and involves his reading of himself as much as the biblical text. Moore demonstrates that his reading has to do with words, to the qualities of language as language that is reminiscent of Derrida's deconstruction of the Babel story.[20] By allowing the words themselves foremost prominence,

---

17. Moore admits, "I have tried to write a book on the Gospels that would... be moored more to my own body..." (1992: 157).

18. He also mimics its style somewhat: "Finnegans Wake would provide an esplashially voluable slipping stone. It is immersed in the same horrormeneutical problemishes that we face. It presentiments a Joycean intrepidation of the exejesuistical taks. It is a hermetical explosion, and other worryds, with oblicious apperplexicongruity to Much and Gloop, the Godspools under conslitheration. Clearly, it could provide a mudel for babelical scholarship" (Moore 1992: 145).

19. Moore has explored other autobiographical issues elsewhere. See "True Confessions and Weird Obsessions. Autobiographical Interventions in Literary and Biblical Studies," *Semeia* 72 (1995): 19–50; "Revolting Revelations," in *The Personal Voice in Biblical Interpretation,* ed. Ingrid Rosa Kitzberger, 183–200 (London: Routledge, 1999).

20. "There is only letter, and it is the truth of pure language, the truth as pure language" (Derrida 2002b: 133).

Moore encounters the materiality of the text, the text as *différance*. With a focus on linguistic interconnections as his first priority, he pushes to one side the demand to develop ideas, concepts, meanings, and successive interpretations of these texts. In his provocative wordplay, he attempts to elude metaphysical notions of theoretical and ideological progress as well as conventional notions of scholarly form and coherence. In a review of Seeley's *Deconstructing the New Testament* (1994), Moore notes Seeley's reluctance to engage with the impact deconstruction has had on "destabilizing of the foundations of the Western intellectual tradition, including the critical tradition ushered in by the Enlightenment ... of which biblical criticism is a product" (Moore 1995: 730). He goes on to explain: "The foundations of biblical scholarship seldom tremble, and never crumble, in Seeley's book. They do tremble momentarily when Seeley shows how elements in the texts he examines sabotage their author's intentions. But stability is restored every time. He (re)constructs a (hi)story that cements the fragments together in a new synthesis" (730).

Moore displaces the orienting and centering points of scholarly convention, allowing the possibility of play far more scope than is expected. Moore's reading is in many ways the antithesis of Clines's reading in its style and its orientation. Whereas Clines, the critic, is remote from his reading, distantly looking on as the text slowly deconstructs itself, Moore, the critic, is thoroughly implicated in his reading and is deconstructed along with the text. The difficulty with reading as Moore does, with attention to the intertextuality and play of language is that, as Clines feared, the critical exercise takes on a certain opacity. Whereas this is no doubt a part of Moore's approach, to make an impact on conventional criticism as much as textual coherence, the consequences of this approach are that they distance Moore's work from the critical community so that the play of words becomes play and nothing more. A further extreme would be if Moore's work challenged the tradition to such an extent that it became nothing more than an individual display of virtuosity with connections to a small and already "converted" interpretive community. It would seem that for practical purposes, a balance needs to be struck between the positions of Clines and Moore, an approach that compromises so as to incorporate Derridean theory in such a way that still allows participation in certain traditional scholarly goals but without automatically reasserting traditional metaphysical frames of reference.

Possibly with this concern in mind, Moore's next major deconstructive outing represents a reigning in of his style and a more explicit engagement with traditional scholarly concerns than were demonstrated in *Mark and Luke* (1992).[21] In *Poststructuralism and the New Testament* (1994), Moore directs his deconstructive eye toward the passage in John that depicts Jesus' meeting of the Samaritan

---

21. Although, more recognizably traditional in approach, Moore's literary style in *Poststructuralism and the New Testament* (1994) is still far from the "colorless academese" with which he contrasts his work in *Mark and Luke* (1992: 83).

woman at the well. Moore's reading of this work concentrates on how John's text overturns traditional critical approaches to it. Moore surveys work on the passage, noting the different ways it has been interpreted, with the differing figural and literal interpretations of particular interest to him. He observes power structures where inevitably it is the Samaritan woman who is regarded as being taught and Jesus as doing the teaching. Moore speaks of the insights of deconstruction, revealing that "the literary text is capable of deftly turning the tables on the critic who sets out to master it" (1994: 48), and goes on to show that "the critic, while appearing to grasp the meaning of the text from a position safely outside or above it, has unknowingly been grasped by the text and pulled into it. He or she is unwittingly acting out an interpretative role that the text has scripted in advance" (1994: 48). Moore demonstrates this point by looking at the play on literal/figurative interpretation offered to explain this text.

Moore's example is the way the majority of critics determine that the passage in which Jesus mentions the woman's numerous husbands (John 4:18) should be taken literally, and yet criticize the woman for not being able to grasp the nonliteral aspects of Jesus' discourse (1994: 48). Turning the text back on the critics, Moore shows that in 4:18 the critics themselves "become" the obtuse woman they describe, themselves taking Jesus' words with the literal mindedness they criticize in the Samaritan woman.

In elaborating on this observation, Moore adopts a deconstructive style which is very much his own. It is more in the style of conventional criticism and not quite as frenetic as that demonstrated in his reading of Luke in *Mark and Luke in Poststructuralist Perspectives* (1992). With his use of water imagery he draws attention to this theme, not only in the text but also in his own methodology. The search for "living water" runs through Moore's own approach as much as through the texts he examines. A couple of examples will suffice: "The motifs of thirst and drinking well up once again as Jesus hangs dying on the cross" (1994: 54); "Equipped with divining rods, Johannine scholars have combed all relevant fields ... but their findings have been inconclusive at best" (1994: 53); "The believer is more than a mere receptacle for surplus water ... he or she is a channel, or conduit in his or her own right" (1994: 53).

Moore latches onto the ambiguous play between the figural and the literal. "Two kinds of water, literal and figurative, slosh around in the Samaritan woman's head, it would seem, mingling where they should not" (1994: 52). But not content with simply "overturning a hierarchical opposition" (1994: 57), Moore isolates a term that, he argues, resists being integrated, remaining undecidable and ambiguous. This undecidable term is the *pneuma* and Moore finds it flowing as water from the pierced side of the crucified Jesus:

> When water reappears in this gospel from an unexpected quarter, therefore—Jesus' side—following an extended drought, it is an "undecidable" term that fills the literal and figurative categories simultaneously ... in such a way as to flood these hierarchical structures and put them temporarily out of commission. (1994: 58)

The term *pneuma* fits neither into the category of literal nor figurative meaning. "Literality and figurality intermingle in the flow from Jesus' side, each contaminating the other, which is to say that we cannot keep the literal clearly separate from the figurative in the end" (1994: 59). *Pneuma* appears to be both living water, or "spirit," but at the same time actual "well-water" flowing from Jesus' side. Distinctions between figural and literal dissolve in this term, *pneuma,* which demonstrates a more complex, more subtle interaction of distinctions to which these two poles prove inadequate to distinguish. Deconstruction reveals the flaws in monolithic systems of classification and analysis, our own inherited meaning systems, and in language itself by finding moments that call attention to and pry open the gaps in these systems, in the case of Moore's example, the place where it becomes impossible and in fact no longer useful to maintain a clear separation of two categories of figurative and literal.

Moore reads Derrida and then engages with a text, challenging the traditional approach to it and the traditional positing of a scholar that is not affected by the text he or she reads. Ironically, in this reading, Moore's own scholarly approach is more traditional than that of his last deconstructive outing (1992). The punning and intertextuality have been superseded by imaginative connections and twists of plot, but Moore's work is more recognizable to traditional scholarship and resembles other examples of deconstruction in biblical studies.[22]

## III. Beyond Deconstruction: Acknowledging Otherness

In his article "Biblical Criticism and the Challenge of Postmodernism" (1995), Terence Keegan introduces the major differences between Modernism and Postmodernism with some useful parallels from other academic fields, notably, theoretical developments within mathematics and the physical sciences. Keegan notes that postmodern insights bring with them a shift in emphasis. It is a shift that takes the academic from a search for truth with a corresponding monolithic sense of meaning to a more heterogeneous search for meaning*s* and truth*s*. He argues that such a shift will promote openness to the text and to change: "The goal of a postmodern scholar is not to answer the question, 'What does the text mean?,' but to assist the reader to arrive at ever new meanings" (1995: 8). Of interest is Keegan's observation that no logical structure can be complete *and* consistent: "Every text's structure ultimately deconstructs, yielding not a single determinate meaning but a potentially infinite variety of meanings" (3).

Keegan appears to be primarily interested in the political implications of deconstruction. Deconstruction can help reveal the flaws of structure and organization and can thereby dis-empower those who ground their authority within such systems

---

22. Compare, for example, Seeley (1994), Schwartz (1990), and Fewell (1995), and, to some extent, Sherwood (1996).

of meaning.[23] Although Derrida himself appears to be reasonably disinterested in the political applications of his own work, deconstruction has been taken up by many with just such a motivation (see particularly Jobling 1995 and Rutledge 1996; for further discussion, see Rorty 1995). Derrida himself engages with issues such as the place of Judaism in relation to the West, and has maintained a perennial fascination with the various structures and conditions that have subjugated writing to speech within the Western philosophical tradition (see Bennington 1993).

Keegan seems aware of the ability of the text to be a site of polyvalence, undecidability, or a site for "otherness." However, there appears to be little awareness of this "other" in Keegan's own demonstrations of deconstruction at work. In focusing on the political, Keegan is happy enough to dispense with constraining notions of truth and meaning, and seeks a subsequent freeing up of scholarship. But at the same time, he seems to focus on the political dimension of deconstruction in practice, a clear consequence of his mode of reading, but not the only way of reading deconstructively.

In *The Prostitute and the Prophet*, Yvonne Sherwood reads Hosea and finds that the prophetic style of this book has much in common with Derrida's own writings. Sherwood finds a fragmentary, punning intertext full of undecidables that undermine its own hierarchies. "The text appears to be less a presentation of a univocal message than a sustained attempt at punning . . ."—an attempt that disorientates to such an extent that this "eighth-century text is so fundamentally distinct from the conventions of academic discourse that it refuses to succumb to its rigorous demands" (Sherwood 1996: 204–5). Sherwood connects the challenge raised by the seemingly superficial tangle of textual logic and finds implications for this on a deeper, more fundamental level: "The retraction and affirmation of various words and ideas suggests that the text deconstructs itself at a deeper, ideological level" (1996: 204). On this ideological level, Sherwood finds in Hosea a distinct use of overtly sexual imagery, which coincides with the way Derrida manipulates such imagery in his own work. This is a dimension of the text that Sherwood finds understated by commentators, and she notes a similar glossing over of the sexual elements from Derrida's writing that has coincided with his reception in the West. Sherwood attributes this understatement to the underlying belief that "overtly sexual imagery is incompatible with dignified, logocentric discourse" and further notes that "just as few introductions to Derrida focus on his flamboyant use of images of masturbation, so commentators on Hosea tend to omit discreetly or to dilute the association between Yhwh and sexuality" (1996: 205–6).

Sherwood also looks to the seemingly "innocuous rhetorical devices" at work in Hosea, noting how it is from these seemingly benign elements that the text can

---

23. Fewell notes that because deconstruction does not pretend a text can be read in isolation from its politico-historical context; deconstruction inevitably becomes political as soon as the question changes from "what truth is being claimed and what is being suppressed?" to "whose truth is being claimed and whose suppressed?" (1995: 127).

be effectively deconstructed. The question of beginnings reveals that there are a number of elements that distort and corrupt this idealized memory. "Ideologically, the text strives to construct a perfect and innocent beginning, but the rules of language insist that purity and impurity are interdependent, and that the 'derivation' is as necessary and original as the 'origin'" (1996: 209). Not the least of these is the marriage between Hosea and the prostitute, a narrative event that further problematizes this sense of "pure" origins that Sherwood found earlier in the text. Sherwood states, "For Hosea, there is no pure origin and no virginal bride. To use Derrida's phrase, marriage is 'always already' contaminated by promiscuity, and deviation is prescribed in the beginning" (1996: 210).

Hierarchies such as innocence-deviance and faithfulness-infidelity, which rely on a notion of an original, idealized purity for their ongoing rhetorical power, are subsequently deconstructed. Through further investigation of the textual ambivalence accorded to the terms "nakedness" and "wilderness," Sherwood finds that the woman of Hosea becomes a subversive textual site, a "lynch pin of undecideability" that always eludes any systematic attempts to account for it: "As undecideable the woman marks the point of that which can 'never be mediated, mastered, sublated or dialecticized': she is, in other words, the chief element that causes the text to equivocate, flounder and turn back on its own rhetoric" (1996: 212). In this way, Sherwood is positing the woman as a point of "otherness" in the text, the point at which hierarchies are overturned and distinctions become blurred.

Sherwood further illustrates the reluctance of commentators to engage with sexual imagery when she observes how Yahweh is regarded as the a-sexual and legitimate "husband," whereas, by comparison, Baal is cast as his oversexed, depraved, and inferior rival. In challenging this apparently clear-cut opposition between Yahweh and Baal, Sherwood brings to the surface a "repressed but articulate" woman's point of view. The woman's unacknowledged choice of another lover is suggestive of a certain inadequacy in Yahweh. For, as the woman's choice, Baal must have something Yahweh lacks. The woman here is not a voiceless submissive "colonised element of patriarchy" (1996: 309), but a woman with a certain amount of sexual autonomy, and consequently she possesses some level of power to evade male control. Sherwood attributes some of this power to the woman's fertility, a trait that causes this woman to stand out from her more submissive and reliant biblical sisters (Sarah, Rebekah, Rachel, and Hannah) who lack this "power to conceive" (309–10).

In the character of Gomer, Sherwood finds a woman who shares many of the traits attributed to writing in Derrida's system: "'[W]oman' like 'writing,' is a relegated term which cannot be tolerated because it poses a threat to (patriarchal) authority and truth. Whether the relegation is conscious or unconscious, it is, like the dismissal of writing, emphatic, and the text dramatizes the struggle to repress, entrap and systematically exclude the female will" (1996: 308). By naming the woman as the "ultimate undecideable" of the text, Sherwood attributes to Hosea a certain "perversity." Sherwood seems to measure this perversity by the ease with which Hosea accommodates a deconstructive reading. Built around the subversive figure of the woman, Sherwood re-posits Hosea as a text where "the undecideable tensions . . . are central, and essential, to the text" (251). Although wary of describing the "nature" of a text or the "intentions" of its authors, Sherwood nonetheless seems to describe the eager "deconstructive quality" of this text in terms of a new textual identity: "There is dissonance and difference between Western scholarly expectations of a text and the standards by which this particular text operates" (252). The consequences of locating the fruits of her deconstructive reading of Hosea in what she regards as textual attributes would be problematic if Sherwood were implying a solidity to this text and suggesting a correct reading of this text based upon this identity—as though commentators, not having gazed through Derridean glasses, have been blind to these inherent qualities of this text.

Sherwood stops short of making such claims, however, when later in her feminist reading she turns to the relationship between reader and text (254ff.). She goes on to explore the extent to which the woman evades the constraints of a number of violent hierarchies. Sherwood focuses on three such hierarchies: subject-object, accuser-accused, and possessor-possession. She shows how these hierarchies are points of anxiety where the woman's "countervoice" exposes them as unstable, hypocritical, and relative (308–21). When exploring the women's role in these points of conflict and anxiety, Sherwood finds that the text is doubly transgressive: "[I]t audaciously transgresses standards set by the feminist movement concerning the treatment and depiction of women, but more surprisingly, it transgresses feminist definitions of 'the androcentric text'" (298). In finding that the text is resistant to both patriarchal and feminist readings, she is prompted to investigate the relationship between reader and text, and particularly the role of readerly values that are brought to interpretation. The figure of the woman comes to represent that element of the text that exceeds those readerly values, and in doing so reflects back to the reader an altered image of subjectivity that is "redefined not as one who observes with detachment but as one who is subjected to the defining pressures of his or her environment" (322). Sherwood deconstructs the power dynamics of gender relations, which, she suggests, are to some extent read into Hosea, and in the sexual ambivalence of the woman, she finds a mode of otherness whose fluidity and interactivity impact on the critical process as much as on textual thematics.

In a recent application of deconstruction to John's gospel, Patrick Counet seeks to develop a deconstructive reading strategy for biblical studies. He looks to Derrida's early works for the outline of this strategy and then investigates its subsequent development, particularly by North American critics, and its application in biblical studies. Counet investigates a range of Derrida's key ideas, contrasting them with other contemporary approaches to interpretation (for example, Gadamer's hermeneutics). He develops the notion that deconstruction is a method of reading for textual "otherness," and as such recognizes the simultaneous presence and absence of the apophatic in every text (Counet 2000: 171; see especially chap. 4, 143ff.). Consequently, Counet speaks of deconstruction as a kind of "apophatic philosophy" (142) or "negative exegesis" (171): a way of reading that affirms "otherness" without making it "present."

Counet investigates the flesh (σάρξ) metaphor in John's Gospel, focusing particularly on Jesus' offer to eat his flesh and drink his blood in John 6:54, 56, and reading this through John 13. He questions the metaphorical nature of σάρξ: is it to be understood as "flesh" or as flesh? In this way, Counet's investigations of the σάρξ image is about the irresolvable literal/figural ambiguity that is a part of metaphorical language: "The word has become flesh, but the flesh itself has again become word" (237). This impasse prevents translation, interpretation, and the allocation of meaning to Jesus' presence in the Fourth Gospel. In the ambiguity between the figural and the literal, Counet finds that a reading of this metaphor has implications for the reader as well as for the text:

> To obtain spirit and (eternal) life, one must allow Jesus' words and one's person to become one (the word has become flesh). But at the same time, one should not see the incarnation as absolute: the word does become flesh, but the flesh is nothing, it does not become word again: the flesh must not become language or doctrine, but spirit and life. (235)

Counet follows the implications of this incongruity to the end of John's Gospel and finds in the final lines of chap. 21 evidence of a double movement. In vv. 24–25, he identifies two conflicting voices: those of the implied author and the explicit narrator (336). He combines his deconstructive approach with a reader-response approach in such a way that the coherence of the "implied reader" is brought into question. For Counet, the experience of reading John (as a postmodern implied reader) is to be caught between these two incommensurable modes of fragmentation and coherence: "I see how the text invites me to a so-called negative Christology, a deferment in meaning. The value, which is implicitly given, demands annihilation and surrender of the self to something, to the other, beyond one's control. The support which is offered is only valid under the suspending condition of loss of the self . . ." (335). The text is presented by Counet as a kind of fragmentary coherence that finally questions the very coherence and unity of the reader (334–36).

There are two points to be made about Counet's deconstructive reading of John. The first relates to Counet's methodological approach. His approach is admittedly deconstructive, and although it engages with a broader range of deconstruction's subsequent development as a reading strategy, it does not really extend very far beyond Derrida's early and more traditionally philosophical writings. Maybe this factor has contributed to Counet's reading taking on a recognizably philosophical character, even if the system he applies to the text has nontraditional results. There is no sense of playfulness, a characteristic of Derrida's later writings, which Counet may be using to reflexively challenge the tone of his own approach. That said, with his sense of deconstruction as a kind of apophatic philosophy, Counet extends the bounds of textuality to encompass the effects on readerly subjectivity and sees that the reading of the text is also in some way a reading of the implied reader. Although he does not explore the implications of this for readerly self-conceptions, and by extension, notions of subjectivity, it is still a step beyond merely identifying incongruity and inconsistency within textuality. It moves beyond by recognizing the sense that one approaches and responds to "otherness," a notion that pervades Derrida's writings.

In chap. 3 of Moore's *Poststructuralism and the New Testament* (1994), a chapter entitled "How Deconstruction Differs from Source and Story-Centered Gospel Studies," Moore states explicitly what he has demonstrated, by and large implicitly, up to that point. He speaks of the complex relationship and ultimate inseparability of reader and text. At stake in any act of interpretation are differing philosophies of human identity, just as much as understandings concerning the state of the text (1994: 75). Following the insights of Lacanian psychoanalytic theory, Moore challenges the notion of identity as "'an unchanging essence . . . that permeates the millions of ego choices' that constitute each human self" (1994: 75).[24]

Moore, in contrast, is interested in a notion of subjectivity as demonstrated by the Lacanian "Mirror Phase," whereby the subject is divided and fragmented but necessarily seeks and identifies with a coherent reflection. Just as a child desires and attempts to mimic the unity of its own mirror image, so, too, the critic looks into the biblical text as though into a mirror. Moore comments on the act of reading as involving the engagement of the (fragmented) self with the (fragmented) text. "And it naturally follows that the more unity and coherence the interpreter is able to ascribe to the text, the more reassuring and confirming will be the self-reflection he or she receives back from it" (1994: 80). But there is almost an ethical responsibility on the part of the reader to acknowledge this fragmentation in both text *and* self—to acknowledge that "our texts are no more unified than ourselves" (1994: 80). This is where deconstruction intersects with Lacanian psychoanalysis.

> The family resemblance between Lacanian psychoanalysis and Derridean deconstruction is, of course, striking. Central to each is a necessary inability, the inability to dominate the text (for Lacan, the psyche is a kind of "text"), to unify and centre it through a reading that would harmonise or "totalise" everything that is going on in it. Like deconstruction, moreover, and unlike psychotherapy, Lacanian analysis "does not provoke any triumph of self-awareness. . . . It uncovers, on the contrary, a process of decentering, in which the subject delves . . . into the loss of his mastery." (1994: 80–81)

---

24. Here Moore quotes Norman N. Holland, "Unity Identity Text Self," in *Reader Criticism: From Formalism to Post-Structuralism,* ed. Jane P. Tompkins, 121 (Baltimore: Johns Hopkins University Press, 1980).

Like Moore, Gary Phillips takes deconstruction to the Samaritan woman at the well in the Gospel of John, but with a special interest in the ethical implications of this encounter (Phillips 1994b). Although executed with equal rigor, Phillips's approach differs considerably from Moore's.

Phillips appears to have a very specific notion of what he believes to be the purpose of deconstruction and the corresponding place in scholarship it ought to occupy. Of particular note in Phillips's reading is his interest in the work of Emmanuel Levinas. Influenced by Levinas and by Derrida's own interaction with Levinas, Phillips speaks of a search for the "other" within the text as the prime motivation of a deconstructive reading. Such a search for and cultivation of this "other" has an ethical dimension in that it extends its own demand to be acknowledged.

The practical implications of this ethical demand become clearer when Phillips describes deconstruction as a "double reading," whereby reading is undertaken in a traditional manner using rigorous scholarly means, but turns back on itself, or redoubles, so as to reveal its own "otherness," embracing its own ambiguities and undesirables and leaving them to stand as they are. The common alternative to recognizing jarring elements of the text for what they are would be to seek to gloss them over with illusions of uniformity, as is associated with certain forms of narrative or theological readings, for instance.[25] Phillips observes that in most other readings of this passage, commentators are guilty of a tendency to smooth over the problematic elements of this text, an approach which creates coherent readings but inevitably neglects the ethical demand of this "other": a simple demand that incongruity be recognized for what it is (1994b: 293–94).

Jesus' meeting of the Samaritan woman at the well in John's Gospel is of particular interest to Phillips precisely because this text is regarded as one that "stands out by virtue of its textual difficulties, its narrative and discursive complexity, and its interpretative ambiguities and richness" (292). Phillips quotes Haenchen, who writes that "this pericope is a veritable tangle of difficulties that defies every historical, literary and theological solution" (292). Phillips adds to this that "it is precisely in the ironic tension and textual ambiguities of John 4, however, that deconstruction finds its place to work" (292).

Phillips locates "otherness" in a number of places in this text. He reads the Samaritan woman as the "other." In terms of the story itself, Phillips explains that the Samaritan woman, like this particular text, resists being assumed into an

---

25. Phillips gives the example of Ernst Haenchen, who writes of John as "an adroit story teller *who endeavours to report a coherent story*"; "the narrator . . . knew how to write" (Phillips 1994b: 293; his italics). This claim by Haenchen contrasts with Phillips's observation that "given the difficulties of this text, we might see Haenchen's reaction as a fundamental uneasiness with more than just the narrative style and substance of John 4; following Derrida, I suggest that it is an uneasiness with Johannine *textuality* as such that resists being reduced and explained away methodologically" (1994b: 294). The ethical component emerges here once again as a textual demand to be recognized as incoherent and problematic as much as in any unified systematic way.

exhaustive allegory by persistently being disruptive (299). He also comments on the artificiality of separating reader and text, making a similar point to that of Moore and Sherwood, saying that this particular text challenges the view of the reader as central: "John 4 in this respect proves as hard to tame as the Samaritan woman herself narratively!" (300). In so doing, the narrative informs the way methodological questions develop as much as the opposite.

Irony, for instance, is not only a narrative feature; "irony [is] a deep constitutive element of Johannine *textuality* itself" (300; his emphasis). Phillips speaks of the consequences of this interrelationship between narrative and text as follows:

> The irony of the Johannine text presents us as readers with an ethical challenge—to read for what makes multiple levels of meaning possible, namely the potential of this and every text to proliferate without regard to what readers may or may not like—to read for alterity. The alterity of the Johannine text, like the Samaritan woman herself, comes to us without much forewarning. Indeed, from a deconstructive perspective, like the Samaritan woman's reaction to Jesus' request for a drink, the text appears to show little regard for cultural or critical custom. Like the text, the Samaritan woman is a trembling, unstable presence that in some ways could care less what we think theoallegorically. (301)

Upon reaching this conclusion, Phillips rereads the story, following through on his promise to undertake the double reading that he believes deconstruction involves. What he concentrates on in his second reading is the image of the empty water jar that remains at the well once the Samaritan woman has gone. Phillips finds that efforts to erase the Samaritan woman's ambiguity by "expending enormous methodological effort to ignore or to deny the marks she has left upon the text and reader alike" (306) end in failure when it becomes clear that this woman "is not so easily erased from the text" (306). The water jar remains "and is a sign not of the text's closure and univocity, but of the incompleteness and undecidability that serve as the wellspring that nourishes readers so that they return to the well text to read" (306). In comparison to the "living water" Jesus offers, "the Samaritan text signals an *other* water and bread of life that is neither the literal water of the Samaritan well nor the figurative 'water' that Jesus proposes" (306). Like Moore's work generally, in the interest of demonstrating some complex imagery at work, it is best to let Phillips speak for himself as he makes his final interpretive points:

> One of the responsibilities deconstruction has as a reading practice is to be on the lookout for those overlooked signs of Otherness, those places where the textuality of the Gospel continues to capture readers' attention. The deconstructive reader seats herself by the narrative well and makes use of that jar to dip into the text, to draw new meaning and to challenge masculinist reading practices and institutional structures. Of course the great irony in this heavily ironic text is that with a little deconstructive push the jar can be made to fall into the deep well of the text. Meaning splashes out over the top and douses those exegetes who peer down into the text from their safe

theological dry places. However, more than the reader gets wet. The jar is a rem(a)inder that the text, as Derrida points out, always retains surprise for those institutions responsible for making certain readings possible. (308)[26]

The ethical imperative to respond that issues from otherness is for Phillips a kind of giftedness, an important kind of invitation that in challenging me to respond makes me *me* (310). There are a number of senses of "gift" in this story. There is the gift of God, received through understanding, but also a nuancing of giftedness which alters one's perception of this system of exchange so as to make resistance a necessary part of gift-giving: "The Samaritan woman's non-giving and non-receiving is a narrative sign that the narrative-theological gift-giving and reception can not take place without her" (311). The Samaritan woman provides a point that is always outside (always "jarring") and at the same time an indispensable part, necessary for belief, reading, and meaning to happen (311). The Samaritan woman's refusal of the gift brings attention to the structures of gift-giving, and allows these structures themselves to be put in question. Gift-giving is not necessarily bound to the structures of reciprocity, as a narrative reading may well presume. The incongruous presence of the Samaritan woman shows that gift-giving is linked instead to an otherness that lies beyond, but is only recognizable within, structure. Phillips points out that one cannot do without the "other." Jesus cannot do without the Samaritan woman; the narrative cannot do without the empty water jug; and structure cannot do without otherness (312). Phillips proposes that, in the same way, historical biblical exegesis cannot do without deconstructive reading, as the other to its traditional methodological practices: "The event of reading John 4 deconstructively causes text and institutional reading practices to tremble. The consequence is not the dulling of the Johannine narrative or reading, but a reenchantment of Johannine textuality and with it an intensification of the ethical demand placed upon its readers" (312).[27]

Phillips's understanding of deconstructive theory and its place and application is rigorous, nuanced, and farreaching. His own style may still be more traditional than Moore's, yet his attendance to theoretical issues involved in the reception of deconstruction within biblical studies is a larger part of his agenda. Moore, by contrast, spends less of his time justifying his readings and contextualizing them within the discipline and more time elaborating, experimenting, and pushing critical boundaries.

---

26. Clines is critical of Phillips's interest in the reader's relationship to the "other" and the ethical obligation that arises from this encounter. But Clines's criticisms are limited to taking Phillips to task over capitalizing "*O*therness" and to noting the possibility that Phillips is introducing a religious agenda into literary/biblical studies (Clines 1998: 124).

27. In her deconstructive reading of Judg 1:11–15, Fewell finds a similar point of undecidability that leads her to express sentiments similar to those of Phillips. Fewell's ethical directives amount to being honest about the limitations of any one reading method, and not claiming a monopoly on textual meaning. Fewell's final (almost utopian) wish is that deconstruction may change, for the better, the way scholars interact with the text and with their world (1995: 141–42).

## IV. Beauty and the Enigma

The work that has been presented so far has raised questions concerning the implication of subjectivity in the interpretive process and the encounter with otherness.[28] A final scholar to be considered here, Francis Landy, demonstrates an awareness of Derridean theory within a broader theoretical scene as well as an appreciation of the questions that have emerged from the works discussed so far. These are questions such as the following: What is the relationship and interaction between critic and text? How are the identities and distinctions between these two called into question through their interaction? What are the consequences of encountering a sense of otherness in the process of reading? How ought one respond to this encounter? Landy makes use of Derrida in conjunction with a number of other thinkers (e.g., Barthes, Blanchot, Cixous, Kristeva), so as to read biblical texts in a way that is particularly attuned to the poetic qualities of the text. His interest in the poetic is demonstrated particularly in some of the collected essays of *Beauty and the Enigma* (2001).

In his work, Landy investigates the relationship between text and subject and the corresponding difficulties in distinguishing between the two. Moreover, he sees that this ambiguous relationship is built around a poetic notion of otherness. He draws on Derridean theory at a number of points in his work and reads in a way that is not specifically or only deconstructive. Within biblical studies, Landy's investigations stand out as a particularly provocative application of Derridean theory. In his approach to textuality, he demonstrates something of a challenge to conventional methods of interpretation:

> You will find that I am not a linear writer. I cannot produce a logical sequential argument. That is because the text does not work sequentially. Every point is linked with every other in innumerable ways. There are many possibilities of interpretation, which cannot be arranged in logical order. I attempt to describe the lateral shifts, concomitant meanings and potential import of words and sentences as they unfold, without necessarily knowing where they will lead, what I will find.... Reading and writing is a process, and my work is as much a communication of the process as a description of the result. Every reading is provisional and incomplete. (Landy 2001: 20)

Landy looks to the polyvalence of certain words, milking them of their contradictory resonances. He reads in the conflicts and ambiguities of language profound commentaries on death, divinity, and the impossible. In one example, an essay on the prophetic vision of Isaiah, Landy does more than simply identify irresolvable terms that resist solidity and transparency of meaning. Acknowledging "an immense debt" to Derrida (and equally Blanchot, Cixous, and Kristeva), Landy finds in his reading of the vision of Isaiah strong deconstructive resemblances

---

28. It is important to note that these are questions that are not limited to Derridean theory and are familiar to a number of his contemporaries.

(2001: 30). In grappling with the disorienting imagery of Isaiah's vision, Landy describes his own experience of metaphor, poetic, and prophetic language.[29] Observing that metaphors order the world but also disarrange it, Landy explains:

> Such disarrangement happens when metaphors become complex, contradictory, nested one inside each other, when they disrupt sentences, fragment the wholeness we construct. The poetry of Isaiah is characteristically extremely difficult, violent, dissociative; passages of great poetic virtuosity alternate with others of radical simplicity. Critics have devoted themselves to solving the problems of the text by assigning different sections or verses to different hands, by unraveling it. This, however, avoids the problem, and domesticates the prophet to our expectations. Prophetic language, according to this view, cannot be impossibly difficult. The impossibility of the language, however, may express the impossibility of communicating the vision, the twin exigencies of the desire to speak, to persuade, to heal, and the prohibition against doing so, and hence the mystery from and of which the prophet speaks. The poetry is then an anti-poetry, a making of a poetic world that decomposes. (382)

In other words, Landy seeks to read the contradictory and impossible language of prophecy precisely *as* impossibility—preserving the contradiction of a language that obscures while it elucidates. But rather than pause interminably at this impasse, Landy embraces this undecidability and turns it inward so that the deconstructed terms of poetic language become the terms with which to speak of subjectivity and human experience. Landy reads the biblical text with a style that resembles Derrida's later works, particularly "Shibboleth" (1986b) and *The Gift of Death* (1995).[30] By the end of his reading of Isaiah's vision, Landy reads the point of poetic fragmentation, of "anti-poetry," as a point that serves to illuminate and further nuance the experience of subjectivity. For Landy, the poetic embraces the enigmatic by revealing language as language, in all its conflicted, material beauty. This experience of language as fragmentary and indecipherable, as poetic, mirrors the experience of subjectivity which is similarly an encounter with life and hope as much as death and meaninglessness. With a doubled voice, the prophet speaks of this dialogue between the poetic and the subjective. He also speaks of the inability to respond in a way that can encompass this encounter because "The words of the prophet are on the other side of this lived experience" (387). Whereas the poetic exceeds the bounds of intelligibility, Landy nonetheless attends to it and takes it as a reflection of his own fractured humanity (30).[31]

---

29. "Vision and Voice in Isaiah," in Landy 2001: 371–91.

30. In "Shibboleth" (1986b) Derrida discusses the poetic encounter with otherness where metaphor becomes the password, or shibboleth, that permits one to cross the threshold, exacting a price of either life or death. In *The Gift of Death* (1995), Derrida investigates the (near) sacrifice of Isaac and the notion of responsibility in the face of an experience where no response is appropriate. These ideas and others to come out of *The Gift of Death* will be taken up and developed in terms of my own reading in chap. 4.

31. Other essays in *Beauty and the Enigma* (2001) where Landy takes up similar themes include

Landy challenges conventional approaches to biblical interpretation in his recognition of the poetic moment as the point where language and the experience of subjectivity coincide. Throughout his investigations, however, he nevertheless maintains a connection to the scholarly enterprise of developing textual understanding and knowledge. Landy's experience of textuality is reflected in his scholarly style, but, at the same time, he is concerned always to engage with scholarship in his field.

> Footnotes are very valuable to me, not merely for the sake of my academic credentials, but because they grant me a space in which to think about the work of others, even if it may seem irrelevant to me, and because they help me perceive problems that would not otherwise have occurred to me. They are a sign of respect for the tradition of scholarship. (29)

In positing a reading and searching for further meaning for the text, thus, he remains connected and continues to dialogue with a scholarly community that may not necessarily reflect his theoretical principles. In allowing both types of readings to inform his work, he manages to challenge the structures of meaning that support traditional readings, while at the same he avoids the appearance of dismissing conventional scholarship and traditional approaches as worthless. Is his work that of a biblical scholar, a poet, a philosopher, a rabbi, or a mystic? His work is difficult to classify, but then that may say more about the structures of classification than about the merits of Landy's work and effectiveness of his unconventional approach.

## Conclusion

In this chapter, I sampled Derrida's reception and application in the field of biblical studies with a range of deconstructive readings of biblical texts. These readings raised two related questions, one regarding the implication of the critic in the critical process and the other concerning the emergence of a notion of textual otherness. As was noted earlier,[32] styles and methods can be seen to vary between critics, and the questions about the critical process and the recognition of otherness are dealt with to a varying degree. A number of critics exhibited limited awareness of their own critical participation in the reading process and appeared unaware of the subsequent consequences of deconstruction to their own critical positions. Clines, for example, does not appear to see himself implicated in his deconstructive readings at all and approaches the text from a remote critical position. Greenstein appears more aware of the theoretical implications of Derridean theory but exhibits

---

"Tracing the Voice of the Other: Isaiah 28 and the Covenant with Death" (185–205); "On Metaphor Play and Nonsense" (252–72); and "Ghostwriting" (392–413). Of particular interest is "Ghostwriting," a creative piece in which Landy attempts to write the fracture into a narrative.

32. See section II, above.

a certain level of anxiety over the consequences of such a mode of reading. Seeley seeks to assume deconstruction as a tool among many in the biblical studies' critical toolbox, while Bubar seems more intent on *de*struction than de*con*struction and less intent on his role in the process.

Moore, on the other hand, engages with the text in a way that incorporates a strong autobiographical element. He also provides an example of an imaginative and unconventional deconstructive style. His readings, so brimming with pun and wordplay, expose the text as a chaotic web of meaning and a potentially boundless intertext. Consequently, his work in *Mark and Luke in Poststructuralist Perspectives* is a major challenge to conventional scholarly approaches to interpretation. The difficulty with Moore's approach however, is that at times it takes on a certain opacity and threatens to be reduced to a series of virtuosic displays of wit and creative imagining that, while entertaining, are not necessarily the only, nor most effective, way to read the biblical text as a member of a critical community.

In section II, above, the notion of otherness that coincides with a number of deconstructive readings was explored. Keegan notices that polyvalent textuality is a site for otherness. Sherwood goes further to identify the woman in Hosea as the "lynch pin of undecideability" and notes at this point the impact of this otherness, an impact as much on critical process as on textual thematics. Counet reads for otherness in the Gospel of John, seeing deconstruction as a type of apophatic philosophy. The call to respond to "otherness" is heard by Counet and further developed by Phillips, who views it as a specific ethical demand that has bearing on the critical process.

Finally, in section III, I turned to the work of Francis Landy, who, while not directly associated with that of Derrida or deconstruction, brings together the themes of this chapter in a way that will prove useful to my own reading in chap. 4 and the implications for this reading developed in chap. 5. Whereas Moore's linguistic twists and turns can at times seem exploitative, Landy, with what sometimes seems like melancholic reverence, attends to the conflicted beauty of language. He deals with the poetic within biblical literature, and with this focus he demonstrates a particular regard for the sense of otherness found therein. His response to this otherness is expressed in a way that remains sensitive to the interaction between subjectivity and textuality. Landy's style and method show a particular sensitivity to the consequences of this interaction, and yet he also makes a deliberate attempt to remain engaged with traditional biblical scholarship in a way that is uncompromising but not dismissive. Given the various strengths and weaknesses I have drawn out of the work discussed in this chapter, Landy's work stands out as one to be emulated.

Just as the introduction presented in the last chapter was not intended to be an exhaustive account of Derridean theory, the readings that comprise this chapter have not been chosen because they represent the entirety of Derrida in biblical studies. They were selected for the particular issues they serve to illuminate, issues that further clarify the introductions made in chap. 1, but also issues that will impact on the direction my own reading will take in later chapters. A lesson has been learned from the remoteness of Clines as well as from the potential inaccessibility of Moore. Sherwood and Phillips show that there is a certain obligation to engage with a notion of textual otherness. Moreover, this textual otherness is understood to have a corresponding impact on conceptions of subjectivity.

In the next chapter I will review the biblical scholarship on the Markan transfiguration with an emphasis on how the imagery has been interpreted. Of particular interest will be those elements that have been neglected, overlooked, or simply regarded as problematic. The results of this next chapter will plot a course for my own rereading in the chap. 4.

Chapter 3

THE MARKAN TRANSFIGURATION IN BIBLICAL STUDIES

*Introduction*

To biblical studies scholarship, the meaning of the transfiguration passage is not immediately a problem: The transfiguration reveals the glory of God and affirms the glorious identity of his Son. In addition, the transfiguration passage is often read as a central moment (both structurally and theologically) in the gradual thematic exposition of the fullness of Christ's glorious personhood that occurs throughout the course of Mark's Gospel story. The clarity of this particular scene allows the reader to peer past the surface of the story and catch a fleeting glimpse of a deeper and more profound underlying theology. In this encounter, as most commentators would have it, the complexity of Mark's overarching theological agenda is distilled and elucidated in the vivid spectacle of Jesus transformed. Jesus' true nature is presented to the disciples and the reader by means of this spectacle. His place in God's plan is made apparent, and the disciples' inability to comprehend this vision is condemned; and yet even this condemnation serves to affirm further Mark's unified message. In the transfiguration, Jesus' theological identity is clarified and his purpose situated in terms of Mark's unfolding story.

Viewed in these terms, the transfiguration scene becomes the interpretive key to Mark's Gospel—the light that banishes the shadows of incomprehension and by which the hidden truth finally becomes clear: "The scene functions like a hologram. For a brief moment, the disciples glimpse the truth as divine glory shines through the veil of suffering. It foreshadows the time when God will gloriously enthrone Jesus after the degradation of the cross" (Garland 1996: 343). With light comes truth, insight, and clarity, for in the light dwells the fullness of God's glory: "For a brief moment the veil of his humanity was lifted, and his true essence was allowed to shine through. The glory which was always in the depths of his being rose to the surface for that one time in his earthly life" (Hughes 1989: 15).

There is another side to the Markan transfiguration, however, a side that reveals a story of enigmas and vexing interpretive challenges. For instance, although a vision of glory appears to shine through with vivid clarity, it is not exactly clear in what way Jesus is, in fact, transfigured. Apart from offering a description of Jesus' clothing, Mark provides no actual definition (Hooker 1987: 60). It is also curious that amidst such a spectacular vision of the divine, the word for glory, δόξα, is not actually used. Although there is an abundance of the classic imagery of glory, drawing from the richness of the Hebrew Bible,[1] there are also curious absences, undecidables, opacities, and elements that do not completely fit within, and perhaps even threaten to undermine, the promised vision of glorious fullness to come.[2]

Both the gloriously apparent and the opaque, enigmatic sides of the transfiguration scene will be considered in this investigation. Moreover, in the discussion to follow I will look to the scholarship on the Markan transfiguration as much as to the text itself. Of particular interest will be the various ways in which critics interpret this story as a glorious revelation. In these interpretations, I will look at the picture of glory that emerges from this scene while also noting how critics fit this story within Mark's larger narrative framework. In addition, the following survey will also have an eye toward those problematic and disrupting elements, the embarrassments, the awkward gaps and concealed spaces of the transfiguration narrative. How are these accounted for and what do they reveal about preconceptions that influence the way the story is read?

Before attending to the minutiae of the transfiguration pericope, I first give a brief account of those commentators who view the broader Markan narrative as a gradually developing theological agenda with the transfiguration at its center. It is by observing the larger role attributed to the transfiguration within Mark's Gospel that its general associations with God's glory will become most apparent. Commentators often see in the transfiguration a moment of central significance either as a foretaste of glory to come (the parousia or resurrection), or as a crucial and illuminating step in the gradual development of the Gospel's glorious message. Before turning to the details of the text in part 2, something of the transfiguration's function within the wider narrative will be elucidated. While not all commentators accord the transfiguration such central significance within Mark's Gospel narrative, the commentators discussed below represent the many who see the transfiguration intersecting with the overarching theme of God's revealed glory. For now, the point is not so much which interpretation is more convincing than the others, but rather the way interpretations of the transfiguration tend to engage on two levels. First, they accept this passage as a vision of glory, and usually as an incomplete vision pointing toward future fullness. Second, they regard the transfiguration as a moment of central importance in the development of Mark's broader Gospel themes.

## Part 1. Mark's Glorious Process

George Henry Boobyer's *St. Mark and the Transfiguration Story* (1942) was the first attempt at a redaction-critical approach to this text, and many of his conclu-

---

1. There are numerous references that demonstrate these motifs. Just two examples are "seeing" (Exod 16:7; 33:18; Isa 40:5) and "appearing" (Exod 16:10; Deut 5:24; Isa 60:1).
2. For example, the absence of a reference to Jesus' face in v. 2 (cf. Matt 17:2; Luke 9:29); the mundane image of the bleacher in v. 3; Peter's baffling offer to build three tents in v. 5.

sions remain influential. Boobyer reads this story as a prophetic encounter with the future glory of the parousia: "For Mark then, it seems, the Transfiguration prophesies the parousia in the sense that it is a portrayal of what Christ will be at that day, and is in some degree a miniature picture of the whole second advent scene" (1942: 87). He then turns to the way the evangelist develops the more general theme of Christ's glory through the course of the broader Gospel narrative. Boobyer identifies four distinct stages in what he finds is a gradual disclosure of Christ's glory. These stages are found most prominently in the Apostle's ever-deepening understanding of Christ's ultimately glorious manifestation. Boobyer names four distinct stages: "pre-existence; a life of hiddenness on earth; revelation at the resurrection; and still further revelation at the parousia" (52). Boobyer claims that this revelatory continuum is interrupted periodically by hints of things yet to come. For example, there are a number of occasions where, in the midst of the second stage, the stage of "a life of hiddenness on earth," there are already references to the third stage, "revelation at the resurrection" (see Mark 8:31; 9:31; and 10:34). Boobyer finds that the transfiguration story is just such an occasion, a moment of prediction that points toward the fullest manifestation of Christly glory, that of the coming parousia.

Boobyer's classification of the glory revealed in the transfiguration (as, in this case, the glory of the parousia) provides him with a clue to the evangelist's inclusion and use of the transfiguration scene within the thematics of the broader Gospel narrative. This association of the purpose of the narrative with the purpose of Mark's Gospel, with particular reference to glory, is an interpretive pattern that has emerged many times since Boobyer's influential reading.

Locating a promise of the coming parousia in this scene is by no means the only interpretation put forward by commentators. There are numerous alternatives that claim to have accounted for the significance of this vision. Of particular note is the view of this story as a misplaced resurrection account, an interpretation with a similar picture of glory that has often vied for acceptance with the vision of the coming parousia. A major proponent of the misplaced-resurrection theory was Rudolf Bultmann, who suggested dating the transfiguration six days after the crucifixion (Bultmann 1968: 259–61). For those, such as Bultmann, who advocate for a misplaced resurrection account, it seems curious, even scandalous, that the splendor-filled vision of Jesus transfigured should be revealing such an incomplete picture of glory. This incongruity is one reason commentators have viewed this scene as a resurrection account that has been backdated to the middle of Mark's story. Implicit in such a claim is the idea that as a depiction of the fullness of God's glory, the proper place for this scene ought to be at the end of Mark's Gospel at the triumph of the resurrection (Bultmann 1968: 259–61; Stein 1976: 80–90; Watson 1985: 55; Crossan 1988: 347–51).

These and other interpretations of this scene focus on a particular motif of the story and grant it central importance. Whereas the notions of parousia and resurrection have focused particularly on the vision of Jesus transfigured, other interpretations may concentrate, for instance, on the appearance of Moses and Elijah in v. 4. In this particular case they may posit the central importance of the ongoing Markan motif of Elijah (van Iersel 1998: 66) or else find in Jesus the new Moses (Ziesler 1970: 264ff.). They may even see in these details the developing distinction between Jesus and John the Baptist (Hooker 1987: 59ff.).[3] The specifics of these interpretations will be investigated further in part 2 of this chapter.

Although he does not specify a category for the glory that is found in the transfiguration passage, Ben Witherington III interprets this scene as a "preview of coming attractions," a scene that foreshadows Jesus' future glorious state (2001: 431–32). In terms of the structure of Mark's Gospel, Witherington sees this passage occupying a central revelatory position as one of three apocalyptic stories that serve to anchor Mark's account. "These stories are found at the beginning, middle and end of the account involving Jesus' Baptism, transfiguration and death . . . these three moments are indeed the high revelatory ones in the account offered in support of the thesis statement in 1.1" (2001: 39). Witherington sees these three moments as key events in the gradually revealed identity of Jesus as the glorified Son of God. They thus point toward a future moment when this identity will emerge in its fullness.

Bas M. F. van Iersel also sees the transfiguration story in connection with the baptism scene (1:11) and the crucifixion (15:39). He finds that the transfiguration's effect is much stronger on this broader "macrolevel" as it "not only intensifies and expands the words addressed by the heavenly voice to Jesus alone at the Baptism (1:11), but also prepares for the centurion's confession at the foot of the cross (15:39)." In functioning in this way, the transfiguration also gestures toward a future point of fullness as it "show[s] here in a flash the other side of the picture" (1998: 277).

In agreement with the structural divisions drawn by Witherington and van Iersel, John Paul Heil classifies the type of scene the transfiguration represents as a "pivotal mandatory epiphany." Heil explains that, on the one hand, the climactic "mandate" spoken by God from the descending cloud (9:7) "pivots" the disciples back to the previous teaching of Jesus, and, on the other hand, it "pivots" the disciples forward through the predictions of suffering and death and toward the final coming of Jesus in his heavenly glory (2000: 199). Mary Ann Tolbert expresses similar sentiments when she writes: "Thus the Transfiguration embraces both the opening of Jesus' ministry and its future cosmic culmination" (1989: 204).

A. M. Ramsey sees a similar portrayal of a distant and as yet incomplete glory gradually unfolding during the course of Mark's narrative, but it is a glory that is

---

3. The list of options goes on: the voice from the cloud may be accorded central significance and in this way affirms the developing theme of Jesus' sonship (Witherington 2001: 39); the transfiguration passage is seen as a parallel to Moses' ascent of Mt. Sinai (Chilton 1992: 640); Peter's offer to build tents coincides with the feast of Tabernacles (Riesenfeld 1947: 250, 255) and the sojourn in the wilderness (Ziesler 1970: 267).

nonetheless vividly present in the transfiguration scene: "On the mount of the Transfiguration a veil is withdrawn, and the glory which the disciples are allowed to see is not only the glory of a future event, but the glory of Him who *is* the Son of God" (Ramsey 1949: 119). Following Ramsey, John Anthony McGuckin's reading of the transfiguration narrative also charts the gradual revelation and incremental nuancing of God's glory. McGuckin sees in this scene a depiction of the divine *shekinah*.[4] McGuckin claims that underlying the Markan redaction is a traditional description of the saints enveloped in the radiant *shekinah* of God. Parallel texts can be found in apocalyptic as well as Hellenistic traditions, where radiant garments feature as a description of the spiritual exaltation of the soul (McGuckin 1987: 66).[5] "It is, then, the fundamental concept of the *shekinah* that stands behind Mark's description of the radiance on the mountain and one does not need to look further than this" (McGuckin 1987: 69). Werner Kelber also speaks of the transfiguration scene in terms which serve to emphasize the glory that is revealed rather than the glory still yet to come. Kelber elevates the experience above all others: "The mountain of Transfiguration, however, is an exceptional mountain, for it is the only 'high mountain' (9:2) in the Gospel. Towering above all other peaks of revelation, it designates the Transfiguration as the epiphany of all epiphanies" (Kelber 1983: 78).

C. S. Mann finds in the transfiguration scene a moment that brings the glory of the as-yet-distant resurrection to a moment prior to the passion narratives, so as to provide a heuristic with which to make sense of the suffering still to come. "It is an important early example of theologizing," says Mann, "for it fastens on the passion prediction and provides an interpretation of the death of Jesus as triumph, 'glory'" (1986: 357). By affirming the place of this vision of glorious fullness in the center of Mark's Gospel, Mann not only consolidates its central significance, he also ascribes to it a certain clarifying function.

Although roundly regarded as an enigmatic and difficult text, the transfiguration has nonetheless been granted this clarifying function at numerous times by various commentators, all of whom see this passage operating in a way that reaffirms, elucidates, or makes sense of other sections or themes of Mark's Gospel.[6] For

---

4. The word *shekinah* literally means "that which dwells" (*ISBE*: 7883). It is found in the targums and rabbinic writings but not in the Hebrew Bible. It is often used to refer to "God," and has associations of radiance, glory, and the presence of God. See, for example, Ezek 1:28; 11:23; and Exod 13:21ff.; 33:7–11. In finding this concept of glory in the transfiguration story, McGuckin follows in the footsteps of A. M. Ramsey (1949). Barbara Reid points out that the limitation of viewing this scene purely in terms of the concept of glory in the Hebrew Bible is that it excludes accounts of glory from beyond that source (1993: 21).

5. See below the discussion of Ulansey's (1996) work on the garments of Jesus.

6. George Caird referred to this conflicted experience of working with this text: "The Transfiguration is at once the commentator's paradise and his despair" (quoted in Hooker 1987: 59 from a personal communication). Commentators often begin their studies of the transfiguration narrative by attesting to its interpretive opacity and the difficulty in accounting for its place in Mark. For example, Taylor writes of the transfiguration as follows: "The interpretation of the narrative presents a very difficult

instance, as has already been discussed, the text may function to reaffirm the thesis statement of 1:11 pronounced at the baptism, while at the same time prepare the way for the centurion's comment at the crucifixion (see Martin 1973: 174; van Iersel 1998: 277; Witherington 2001: 39). Other commentators mention the connection between the transfiguration as a way of illustrating and in some way fulfilling the passion prediction that immediately precedes this scene at 8:38.[7] In just such a fashion, Ernest Best views this story as a way for the evangelist to supplement and correct the Christology of Peter's confession (8:29), while at the same time granting divine affirmation and authority to Jesus' recent teaching on his own death and resurrection (8:38; see also Tolbert 1989: 204; Juel 1990: 127; Brooks 1991: 150). Other commentators see in this scene a crucial distinction being made about Jesus' greater status compared with the holy figures of Elijah and Moses (see Best 1983: 206ff.; Hooker 1987: 59ff.).

Robert Gundry's regard for the clarifying function of the transfiguration is reflected in the title for his study of this passage, "Visual and Auditory Evidence That Jesus Is God's Son" (1993: 457). Gundry's matter-of-fact approach to the transfiguration text and his regard for its meaning as a series of unambiguous experiences of the divine relationship coincide with his approach to the Gospel narrative as a whole. Gundry begins his commentary on Mark with a litany of negations. After twenty-five qualifications as to what Mark is not, Gundry sums up by saying, "Mark's meaning lies on the surface. He [Mark] writes a straightforward apology for the Cross" (1993: 1). Such is Gundry's general approach to the Markan text; it is a clear and unhindered reading that demystifies Mark's often-overcomplicated text that can become so tangled in interpretative inquiry it seems like a "riddle wrapped in a mystery inside an enigma" (1). In fact, Gundry indicates that the Markan text is not so much the problem as the "labyrinthian journey through Markan scholarship" (1). Although aware of conflicting traditions that make up its contents, Gundry feels comfortable encompassing the major themes of Mark's Gospel in a walk-through of but a few paragraphs. He sees his major challenge as follows (and in light of Derridean theory, the following statement is telling): "The basic problem in Markan studies is how to fit together these apparently contradictory kinds of material in a way that makes sense of the book as a literary whole" (2). In other words, Gundry seeks an interpretive position that allows him to synthesize conflicting traditions and themes in order to arrive at a coherent and unified reading of Mark. Gundry seeks to do this through a careful and meticulous process of stripping back the interpretive and scholarly encrustations that threaten

---

problem and few will claim that they can give an explanation which completely satisfies them" (1952: 386); Chilton writes: "The account abounds with exegetical difficulties..." (1992: 640); Perry considers the transfiguration story "the strangest by far of all the stories narrating Jesus' public ministry" (1993: 1); van Iersel calls it a "puzzling episode" (1998: 293); Mann describes it as containing "not a few enigmas" (1986: 355).

7. Here Jesus speaks of the Son of Man coming "in the glory of his father with the holy angels."

to waylay the reader with problems and irresolvable conflicts. Gundry's reading looks to the most economic explanations that allow him an uncluttered journey through what is essentially a simple story of "the shameful ways in which the object of Christian faith and subject of Christian proclamation died, and hence for Jesus as the Crucified One" (1).

This general approach to Mark's Gospel appears to inform Gundry's interpretation of the specifics of the transfiguration scene. For Gundry the transfiguration occupies a position of central significance in the Gospel and from this vantage point performs an elucidating role for Mark's broader narrative framework. In locating the transfiguration event at the heart of Mark's Gospel Gundry notes (as Witherington and van Iersel) that there are clear references back to where Jesus' ministry began at the baptism scene, and also a definite sense of looking forward to the passion that is yet to come. Consequently, Gundry sees the transfiguration story functioning in a way that reveals and illuminates the overarching plan of God by removing the scandal of a crucifixion and contextualizing this event in terms of the more expansive unfolding of God's glorious plan.

> Since glory connotes power [v. 6b; cf. 8.38–9.1; 13.26; 2 Pet 1.16–18], the divine glory seen in the transfigured Jesus shows that on this occasion some of those who heard the prediction in 9.1 now see God's rule as having come in power even before the Son of Man's coming in the glory of his Father with the holy angels 8.38. God's rule has become visible in the transfigured Jesus, the glory of whose glistening garments represents the power of that rule (contrast the suffering of the Son of Man—8:31–32a). (Gundry 1993: 459)

Gundry sets this passage firmly within the context of the coming of "God's rule." He sees this coming of God's rule to be authoritatively presented in this moment of startling visual and auditory display, an event whose very brightness serves to emphasize and refer forward to the fullest manifestation of God's future glory. The clarity of vision the transfiguration affords seems to inform Gundry's reading of the entire Gospel.

Whereas Ramsey, McGuckin, and Gundry place particular emphasis on the "presentness" and clarity of the glory that shines through the transfiguration scene, other commentators emphasize the incompleteness of this encounter. To some, "the transformation affords only a brief glimpse of Jesus' heavenly status and destiny" (Juel 1990: 129). The path illuminated by the transfiguration weaves toward a distant but glorious fulfillment; however, to take this path is necessarily to encounter suffering. As James A. Brooks puts it: "He had to suffer, but suffering was not his ultimate destiny. His ultimate destiny was to be glorified. . . . The Transfiguration serves as a preview of the full establishment of the kingdom of God at Jesus' return" (1991: 141). Best observes that this story emphasizes that the only way to glory is the path that takes one through suffering (Best 1986: 206–25). In other words, future glory is seen from a position in the "present" where fullness is yet to be achieved. Moreover, commentators like Best argue that glory will be fully "present" at an end time that can only be reached after completing an ever accumulating and expanding process, but what is more important, a process that has a definite end in sight when the distinction between present lack and future fullness falls away—the arrival of God's glory.

Morna Hooker too promotes a reading that relies on the acceptance of an overarching Gospel structure based on the acceptance of a notion of God's emerging glory. Although Hooker does not see in this scene the coming parousia, she nonetheless adopts a traditional "already-but-not-yet" theological model with which to develop her reading of the transfiguration story.[8] Hooker concentrates specifically on the appearance of Elijah and Moses in v. 4. By identifying Elijah with John the Baptist in light of his function as the forerunner to Jesus, she places the Elijah and Moses question not only at the center of the transfiguration story but at the center of the Gospel narrative. Although focusing on the figures of Elijah and Moses, Hooker's concerns are essentially Christological because she views these figures in terms of what they reveal about Jesus' identity. The transfiguration is then a moment of Christological revelation where Jesus is seen to be participating in God's glory. The understanding of this revelation may not be complete at this point in the Gospel, but it is an important moment in Mark's developing Christology: "Though the Kingdom may be present in the ministry of Jesus, it is not yet fully here.... The Transfiguration is a 'preview' of what is going to happen and, though for Mark the two events go together, it is a preview of the Son of Man in glory, rather than the Kingdom of God coming in power" (1991: 212). Thus, although Hooker focuses on Jesus' identity instead of the nature of God's glory, her investigation can still be said to hold a theological concern and one that orients her reading of the broader Markan text.

The picture of glory that emerges from the transfiguration story is viewed from a number of perspectives. For instance, the glory of the parousia is not necessarily considered the same as the glory of the resurrection. But Hooker is not alone in challenging these types of distinctions. McGuckin, for instance, argues that making distinctions between types of glory is a matter of "idiosyncratic invention." He posits instead a single picture of glory: "In New Testament theology there is no difference between this glory and that with which he shall return at the Parousia to judge the world. There is only one Glory in the creation, as there is only one God, and one judgement" (McGuckin 1987: 67).

For her part, Hooker points out that questions seeking to distinguish between types of glory are not entirely the point:

> Although there has been spirited debate between the theories that the transfiguration points forward to the resurrection on the one hand or the parousia on the other, it is probable that Mark himself would not have understood the controversy. For though

---

8. See Hooker (1987; also 1991: 213–18).

he certainly distinguished between the resurrection and the parousia, both were aspects of the vindication of Jesus, and the transfiguration is a symbol of that vindication. It is doubtful whether he would have wished to emphasise one aspect to the exclusion of the other. If Jesus' identity cannot be understood apart from his suffering, resurrection and final vindication, the scene on the mountain must be understood in relation to all these themes. (1991: 213)

What Hooker sketches is a picture of the transfiguration that necessarily relates, first of all, to a single vision of glory, and, second, to its broader place in the developing thematics of Mark's Gospel.

There is much variety in scholarly opinion over the place and purpose of the Markan transfiguration passage. The common themes to come out of the above discussion, however, include an almost unanimous acceptance of a certain conception of God's glory as presented in the transfiguration scene. Moreover, there is a common search to find the corresponding impact this picture of glory has on the rest of Mark's Gospel. The transfiguration story is taken as an unmistakable moment of revelation, and the clarity of this moment is subsequently used to illuminate various other parts of Mark's theological agenda. Reading the transfiguration narrative, however, appears to involve taking up a particularly metaphysical notion of God's glory. Because of the wider influence this story has on interpreting Mark's Gospel, the contours that shape this theological conception are particularly influential. In the next section, a closer reading of the transfiguration text will go some way toward revealing the metaphysical specifics of this notion of glory and at the same time reveal a text that is larger than this notion can contain.

## Part 2. Reading Mark 9:2–8

### *I. Defining the Transfiguration*

*"And he was transfigured before them" (Mark 9:3)*

A distinction has been made in the way the way the transfiguration passage is interpreted between the transfiguration of Jesus from within and the transfiguration from without. On the one hand, some argue that Jesus himself is transfigured, not merely his garments: "Jesus temporarily exchanged the normal human form that he bore during his earthly life for that glorious form he was believed to possess after his exaltation to heaven" (Nineham 1963: 234).[9] Gundry, on the other hand,

---

9. A. A. Trites expresses a similar understanding and writes that the verb μεταμορφόομαι is suggestive of a change of form involving a change of inmost nature (1994: 34) Brooks echoes this understanding: "In whatever context the Greek or English derivative appears, the reference is to a radical change, to a complete transformation" (1991: 142). Also in agreement is Ramsey: "The word μετεμορφώθη tells of a profound change of form (in contrast with mere appearance), without describing its character" (1949: 114). Baltensweiler maintains that the metamorphosis here is "real" in the sense that

argues that since Mark does not describe any shining of Jesus' face; the transfiguration indeed seems limited to the garments.[10] Thus, for Gundry, the καί that introduces a description of Jesus' garment also introduces a definition of the transfiguration. In order to limit the extent to which Jesus was transformed, Gundry claims that just as the phrase "Robert looks formal, he's wearing a tuxedo" may mean only that Robert is wearing formal attire, not that the exposed parts of this body look formal: "nothing in the text implies that Jesus possesses a glory hidden at other times by clothes and flesh. On the contrary, the divine passive in v. 2 and the emphasis on the glistening of his garments point to a glory bestowed from without" (1993: 477).

Mann draws on the classical Greek sense of στίλβω ("to glisten" or "to shine"), which is used to describe dazzlingly bright or polished surfaces, a comment that would seem to indicate that the brilliance of the transfiguration emanated from a surface, reflected rather than shining from within (1986: 360). Hooker also comments on the reflective quality of στίλβω, noting that in the whole of the New Testament, the word is only used here and so presumably has the sense of a "reflection of heavenly radiance" (1987: 60). Heinrich Baltensweiler, by comparison, sees στίλβω referring to the natural shining of the newly bleached cloth, although he does admit that it gives the impression of being overwhelmed at first glance (1959: 66).

Discussion of Jesus' robes and the related issues of whether the transfiguration was from within or from without, a reflection or an emanation of glory, are further brought into question by David Ulansey in "The Transfiguration, Cosmic Symbolism, and the Transformation of Consciousness in the Gospel of Mark."[11] Ulansey has an original contribution that is worth presenting in full. He takes the spectacle of Jesus' glorified robes to what must be their most "glorious" extreme. Ulansey argues for a triple connection between the tearing of the heavens in the baptism scene (Mark 1:10), the tearing of the temple veil in the crucifixion scene (Mark 15:38), and the glorious vision of Jesus' robes in the transfiguration scene

---

the analogy to being a Greek god rather than a vision would have been familiar to Mark's audience (1959: 63). On the other hand, Markus Öhler reasons that Jesus' appearance is changed first to match the evocation of the heavenly world (1996: 204). Reid sees that the transfiguration has been variously understood "as a subjective, visionary, interior experience, either of Jesus, or of Peter, or of all three of the chosen disciples" (1993: 5). See also J. A. Ziesler: "Jesus is transfigured not merely his clothes" (1970: 265–66). In addition, recall Hughes (1989: 15) quoted above.

10. Agreeing on this point is Witherington, who sees this moment as having nothing to do with the Greek concept of metamorphosis (2001: 263). He differs from Gundry in that he does not exclude the possibility that there was an internal change; he simply notes that any change that did occur was one that was outwardly visible.

11. David Ulansey, "The Transfiguration, Cosmic Symbolism, and the Transformation of Consciousness in the Gospel of Mark" an unpublished paper presented at the 1996 annual meeting of the Society of Biblical Literature. [This paper is currently available at: http://www.well.com/user/davidu/transfiguration2.html].

(Mark 9:3).[12] The baptism and the crucifixion mark the beginning and the end of Jesus' ministry, and Ulansey seeks to strengthen the link between the tearing of the heavens in 1:10 and the tearing of the temple veil, which, because of its description by Josephus as depicting "a panorama of the entire heavens," is also, in a sense, a tearing of the heavens. In this way an inclusion is formed that "brackets off" the extended Gospel unit, giving a sense of structural integrity and closure (Ulansey 1991: 125). The metamorphosis scene fits squarely between these structural brackets with its clear references, first, to the baptism scene, with the voice of God (see 1:11 and 9:7) and, second, to the crucifixion scene, with the darkening cloud (see 9:7 and 15:33).

Ulansey pays particular attention to the way the glorious vision of Jesus' transfigured robes is linked to key moments when the fabric of the heavens is torn in two. He notes that, according to Josephus, the temple veil bore a celestial motif.[13] Following this, he looks to some mythic examples in later antiquity where celestial robes, decorated in much the same way as the temple veil, are worn by powerful deities such as Isis and Mithras. In these stories, celestial robes are often involved in contexts of initiation, boundary crossing, and transformation. Ulansey also finds evidence of cosmic attire within Jewish literature and cites the example of *1 Enoch*, where in chap. 14 "he ascends into the heavens where he enters an extraordinary space described as a cosmic temple made of fire and crystal. There in the center of this sacred space Enoch sees 'the Great Glory' who is wearing a 'gown, which was shining more brightly than the sun, it was whiter than any snow'" (Ulansey 1996).

Ulansey draws a connection between this scene and the vision witnessed at the transfiguration, arguing for some type of "cosmic atmosphere" underlying the details.[14] Ulansey goes on to cite examples from the *Testament of Levi*, the *Apocalypse of Zephaniah*, and *2 Enoch*, which further point to the supernatural and transformative significance of glorified celestial robes.[15]

12. Ulansey's triple formulation comes from an examination in an earlier article of the connection between the tearing of the heavens and the tearing of the temple veil: "The Heavenly Veil Torn: Mark's Cosmic 'Inclusio'" (1991: 123–25).

13. JW 5.5.4 §§ 212–14.

14. David Garland also compares the vision of Jesus' robes with the visions of "a man dressed in linen" in Dan 10:4–11:1 and the Ancient of Days, whose clothing was "white as snow" (Dan 7:9; Garland 1996: 343). The vision of Jesus' shining robes conjures similar images in which the glorification of clothes is an indication, in apocalyptic literature, of the exalted state of heavenly beings (see Reid 1993: 8 and particularly Kee 1972: 143ff.). Witherington cites references to Dan 10:5–8; 7:9; and Rev 1:9–18, as does van Iersel (1998: 294). White clothing is also the garb of martyrs in resurrection (Acts 1:10; Rev 3:4; 4:4; 7:9, 13–14). And there is the question of the "young man" dressed in a white robe who greets the women at the empty tomb (Mark 16:5).

15. In the *Testament of Levi*, seven men in white clothing proceed to dress Levi in wondrous garments to mark his initiation into a celestial priesthood. In the *Apocalypse of Zephaniah*, Zephaniah is surrounded by angelic beings, and he puts on an angelic garment himself as the heavens open to him. Ulansey points out that both Levi and Zephaniah are crossing boundaries (heaven and earth), and are undergoing processes of initiation, (to priesthood, for instance), all of which are features marked by the

A final example used by Ulansey is that of the gnostic *Hymn of the Pearl*, one quarter of which is devoted to the extended discussion and description of a wondrous jewel-encrusted robe. The robe itself is present in the beginning of the story, lost, and then subsequently regained at the story's conclusion. In this story, this robe functions to mark various border crossings of the protagonist, the character of the prince. In this way, Ulansey argues that the tearing of the heavens and the tearing of the temple veil both function to mark similar boundary-crossing moments. The beginning of a special ministry is marked by the rupturing of cosmic boundaries, and, at the conclusion of this ministerial role, tears also mark the movement across the boundary separating life from death.

With the *Hymn of the Pearl*, Ulansey attributes a further, deeper significance to the garment imagery. He points to a passage where the protagonist, the prince, gazes into the garment and sees himself reflected therein.

> On a sudden, as I faced it,
> The garment seemed to me like a mirror of myself. I saw it all in my whole self,
> Moreover I faced my whole self in [facing] it,
> For we were two in distinction
> And yet again one in one likeness. . . .
> (from *Hymn of the Pearl*, quoted by Ulansey 1996)

Ulansey interprets this mirrorlike quality of the garment as a call to look inward, a call to introspection with the promise that a transformed, glorified face will be reflected back. Thus Ulansey concludes that the celestial robe may well symbolize the transformative potential of the psyche.

Although Ulansey does not elaborate further on the connections between the *Hymn of the Pearl* and Jesus' transfigured robes, he is seeing something similar happening on the mountain scene. He appears to be suggesting that the change in Jesus' outer garments also has an interior significance, and thus his interpretation further serves to muddy the distinctions between interior and exterior.

Ulansey's *inclusio*, with the transfiguration at its center, shares much with ways other commentators have structured Mark's Gospel (see discussion of Witherington and van Iersel above). What Ulansey's interpretation makes clear is the common notion of glory that underlies attempts to include the transfiguration passage in such structural schemas. In Ulansey's schema, the notion of glory appears to be

---

donning of celestial robes. In *2 Enoch*, a transformative image can be seen in which, having ascended to heaven, Enoch dons "clothes of glory" and is anointed with oils until he remarks as follows about his own image: "And I gazed at all of myself, and I had become like one of the glorious ones, and there was no observable difference" (*2 Enoch* 22:8–10). Gundry disagrees with these connections, citing a litany of differences between these texts, including the fact that "Enoch passes out of sight into heaven and stays there . . . [whereas] Jesus ascends no higher than a mountain and afterwards descends" (1993: 475).

associated with that of regal splendor and celestial majesty.[16] The robes he describes are decorated with celestial scenes or encrusted with rare jewels and other luxurious embellishments. They are described as shining with a transcendent brightness that surpasses earthly experience. Even the garments that are "plain" in the sense that they are white are awe inspiring and wondrous in their aspect.

Although other commentators do not sketch such a vivid picture of glory as does Ulansey, their conceptions nevertheless share much with the vision of celestial glory described above. Although less "flashy" by contrast, commentators have been shown to nonetheless draw strong links between the vision of the transfiguration and the prospect of the coming parousia, the time when God's glorious plan will reach its magnificent and glorious culmination. The transfiguration is a foretaste of this glorious future; and whether it is an internal or external transformation, it sparkles with brilliant and intense anticipation. Yet the scene will be brighter still when what is promised at the end time, the overwhelming fullness of God's glory, finally arrives.

## II. Mark's Loss of Face

### "and his clothes became dazzling white . . ." (Mark 9:3)

It can often prove difficult for commentators to distinguish between the traditional elements and the Markan additions in the transfiguration text. As a result, there are often gaps and excesses left behind where Mark is seen to have altered the tradition in order to serve his own theological motives. The commentator typically sifts through the text, attempting to differentiate between Mark's intentions and the encrustation of tradition. This sophisticated means of excluding certain features of the text as irrelevant, or at least as invested with less authority, is seen in action most vividly in the discussion of possible parallels between the transfiguration passage and the scene at Sinai.

Much of the controversy over whether there are indeed references to the Sinai archetype rests in the description given in v. 3, where although shining robes appear to be a clear reference to Moses' encounter on the mountain, the glowing face is curiously absent (among those who point to Sinai are Nützel 1973: 161; Lane 1974: 317–18; Chilton 1980: 120; Schweizer 1970: 181–82; Juel 1990: 127; Keenan 1995: 209). Like many critics, Vincent Taylor assumes that this text refers to Moses' epiphany on the mountain in Exodus, where his face is described as glowing: "When Aaron and all the Israelites saw Moses, the skin of his face was shining,

---

16. Here, the interpretation that posits a regal past to the transfiguration story comes to mind. In this interpretation, it is believed that Mark fashioned the present text with its present theological agenda from a preexisting enthronement story. In this interpretation there is the sense that "the transfiguration reveals a kingdom by unveiling the king" (Witherington 2001: 262; see also Riesenfeld 1947: 281–88; Garland 1996: 343–44).

and they were afraid to come near him" (Exod 34:30). But in Mark, the reference to a face is curiously absent. Puzzled by the omission of this detail, when it is included in both Matthew and Luke's accounts (cf. Matt 17:2; Luke 9:29), Taylor goes so far as to posit a possible original Markan text that edits the face back into the description (Taylor 1952: 389).[17]

John Michael Perry attempts to solve the problem by taking his cue from Paul, who in 2 Corinthians explains the difference between the temporary glory, which caused Moses to veil his shining face, and the permanent glory and transforming glory reflected in the unveiled faces of believers.[18] Perry is making the point that the shining face of Moses, which presumably faded in time, represented an impermanent glory, whereas the glory of Jesus pictured in his transfigured robes is permanent (1993: 9–11). Problems with this reading arise as soon as one reaches v. 9 when the scene, along with the vision of glory, ends. Visions of the resurrected Jesus granted to Paul and other apostles may well have provided them with images of the unending glory of the risen Christ. The transfiguration scene, however, is transitory and so is this particular glimpse of glory witnessed by these disciples.[19]

By contrast, McGuckin, who sees in the transfiguration a description of the saints enveloped in the radiant *shekinah* of God, looks to parallel texts in apocalyptic and Hellenistic literature in which descriptions of radiant garments are used to depict the spiritual exaltation of the soul (1987: 69).[20] But rather than attempting to rewrite Mark's text, as Taylor does, McGuckin explains the absence of any reference to a "shining face" as a deliberate editorial decision, whereby Mark sought to remove the Mosaic Christological typology from the original narrative. In other words, to suit the overarching Markan theological agenda, a number of details may have been altered, including the editing out of the face; but the foundations remain unchanged, because clearly the narrative still retains the structural and formal remnants of the Sinai archetype.[21] Furthermore, the description of Jesus' garments has one clear purpose for the evangelist: to reveal the presence of the divine *shekinah* (69). McGuckin severs references to the Sinai narrative in favor of Mark's own theological intentions. In addition, by limiting the scope of reference of this scene, McGuckin is implicitly arguing for less mediation and thereby furthers the cause of finding a meaning that is immediately "present."

---

17. Taylor proposes the following possibility for v. 3: καὶ ἐγένετο στίλβον τὸ πρόσωπον καὶ τὰ ἱμάτια αὐτοῦ λευκὰ λίαν (1952: 389). C. S. Mann also supports the theory that the original text included a mention of Jesus' altered visage (1986: 360).

18. Perry refers to 2 Cor 3:7–18.

19. See also Mann 1986: 360.

20. Compare the appearance in Daniel of the man in shining clothing (Dan 10:5–8; Dan 7:9) and also the description in Rev 1:9–18. White garments are also the garments worn by martyrs; see Rev 3:5, 18; 4:4; 6:11; 7:9, 11 (Witherington 2001: 260). For a discussion of the transfiguration scene as an apocalyptic vision, see Kee 1972.

21. In agreement, Garland writes, "The echoes of Exodus 24 and 34 suggest that a Moses typology undergirds Mark's shaping of the Transfiguration" (1996: 343). See also Lane 1974: 317–18; and Hooker 1987: 60.

McGuckin is not the only commentator seeking to distance Sinai from a reading of this verse. Taking the cause even further, Gundry seeks to dismiss all efforts to find allusions to Exodus 24 and 34. Gundry challenges these supposed allusions, claiming that, at best, they rest on shaky ground. He refers to the missing face, observing that Mark does not describe Jesus' face as shining in the manner of Moses' face. Rather than finding this curious (Taylor 1953: 389; Mann 1986: 360), Gundry regards this as a deliberate and significant omission. He cites a number of other differences from the Exodus parallels, challenging connections drawn between the two texts that rely on using the cloud and the voice, the glistening garments, the building of tabernacles, and the presence of high mountains.[22]

Gundry concludes that regardless of what Matthew and Luke do to conform the transfiguration to the Sinai narrative in Exodus, v. 2 seems not to allude to it, much less grow out of it (1993: 476). Gundry further affirms Mark's own "overarching theological development" over and above other references that would lead one "outside" the text. But historical questions aside, can references to Exodus be altogether excluded? Regardless of the motives of the historical evangelist, if we compare Mark's transfiguration to Matthew's and Luke's versions and then to the Exodus passages cited above, the allusions, altered as they may be, remain. After all, an altered reference is still a reference.

### III. Mark Stutters

*"such as no one on earth could bleach them" (Mark 9:3)*

With a notion of glory informed so strongly by the glitter and sparkle of Jesus' glowing robes, it is not surprising that the next image of v. 3 causes some consternation. In accounting for this curious image of the bleacher, commentators have noticed in the transfiguration text what appears to them to be a certain amount of reticence, reserve, awkwardness, and even, dare we say, inadequacy in the Markan description.[23] Ramsey speaks of Mark's account, compared to Matthew's and Luke's, as possessing "naïve and primitive features" and speaks of the descriptions of Jesus' garments as "quaint" (1949: 112). Kee finds the description "vivid," but despite the radiance of the clothing, he feels that he is left in the dark, and like Ramsey, blames its "naïveté" (1972: 143). McGuckin expresses a similar view, although he does not seem as disappointed. He finds instead what he regards as a

---

22. There are many commentators who note the differences between Exodus 24 and 34 and yet still accept a basic, but qualified, connection based on one more of these images (Chilton 1980: 120–22; Hooker 1987: 60; van Iersel 1998: 294; Trites 1994: 39).

23. This is assuming they deal with this image at all. A number of commentators pass over this part of Mark's description without comment. For example, there is no mention made of the image of bleacher in the following discussions of the Markan transfiguration, although in all cases at least some reference is made to the description of light: Schweizer 1970: 180–83; Hurtado 1983: 144–47; Mann 1986: 360; Tolbert 1989: 204–6; Garland 1996: 343–44.

fairly clear demonstration of the characteristic hand of the evangelist not just in the image of the bleacher but in the description of the robes as well: "The awkwardness of that description [i.e., the shining robes and the image of the bleacher being juxtaposed], with its double superlative 'exceedingly brilliantly white' and the somewhat lame comparison to a bleacher, has all the hallmarks of the evangelist's peculiar style" (1987: 66).[24] For Hooker, the association of glory with light is so self-evident that she sees his hand only in the inadequate attempt to mirror this image with the parochial association of the bleacher: "The dazzling 'whiteness' of Jesus' clothes is presumably a reflection of divine glory, but Mark is out of his depth in trying to describe it, since his experience is limited to what a 'bleacher on earth could achieve'" (1991: 216).[25]

And so, the evangelist is seen to lack the sophistication necessary to account for the glory that shines so vividly in the light of Jesus' robes. Rather than letting the glory, in a sense, speak for itself, Mark offers his own weak and inadequate comparisons that, if anything, diminish the clarity of its glow. One wonders why Mark altered the tradition in the first place. For whatever reason, and however one understands this to have been done, it is becoming clear that Mark has tailored the transfiguration story to suit his own structural needs. The glowing face is omitted, and the scene at Sinai is in this way put at a distance so as to allow Mark to rewrite this scene and incorporate it more readily within his own theological schema. But the images Mark uses are then regarded as gauche and inadequate. Why would Mark forgo the glorious triumph of the Sinai scene in favor of the image of a lowly fuller bleaching his cloth? Mark the author of a masterfully subtle theological treatise is at times "out of his depth," his own alterations "naïve," and his additions "lame" in comparison to the richness of his tradition.

## IV. Elijah Then Moses

### "And there appeared to them Elijah with Moses . . ." (Mark 9:4)

Another case that is considered to be a Markan intervention into the traditional material comes with the appearance of the figures of Elijah and Moses. Interpreters argue for both the central significance of their appearance and at the same time claim this as the most enigmatic moment in the transfiguration story. Often there is mention of the amount of textual "space" these two figures take up: "out of seven verses in the whole, no fewer than three are concerned with Moses and Elijah, who

---

24. McGuckin refers specifically to Goulder 1979: 279–80.

25. McGuckin rejects any parallelism with the eschatological image of the "fuller" and his bleach in Mal 3:2, since if there were a connection, one would expect this to be reflected in Mark's Greek, and there is no similarity here with the LXX version. McGuckin also rejects the theory that the description of Jesus' robes invokes the symbolism of Judaic vestment symbolism. McGuckin argues that were this the case, one would expect such imagery to be carried through to the Passion narrative which, unlike the Gospel of John, is not the case (1987: 68–69).

appear with Jesus" (Mann 1986: 355). Margaret Thrall asserts that "in some sense they [Elijah and Moses] are the figures upon whom the whole story turns" (1969–70: 305). For Hooker, the Elijah/Moses question is central to the narrative and important in what it reveals about the identity and significance of Jesus (1987: 59ff.). But Felix Daniel warns, "No other section of the Transfiguration narrative has presented more of an interpretive challenge than the appearance of these two figures" (1976: 51).

The traditional interpretation of the presence of Elijah with Moses has these two figures representing the Law and the Prophets: through Moses, the Law was given to Israel, and Elijah was the first major prophet in the books known in the Hebrew Scriptures as the former prophets.[26] In more general terms, the appearance of Elijah and Moses has resulted in a wealth of connections to the Hebrew Scriptures.[27] In fact, the figures of Elijah and Moses are looked upon as representative figures from the Hebrew Scriptures "who will participate in the actual consummation of the Kingdom of God" (Thrall 1969–70: 306). Daniel, for instance, provides a number of parallels in an attempt to answer the question of why Elijah and Moses have been singled out: "Both were recipients of revelation at Sinai/Horeb; both ascended to heaven, and both were expected to return at the end of time" (1976: 51).[28] In this and similar ways, the presence of these two Old Testament figures is often seen in eschatological terms, pointing toward the parousia (Taylor 1959: 390; Nineham 1963: 234–35; Witherington 2001: 263). All in all, Elijah and Moses, appearing together as they do here, "were an ultimate summary of the Old Testament economy" (Hughes 1989: 16). However, despite—or possibly because of—the richness of their associations, their particular role within the transfiguration passage and within Mark's Gospel story remains far from clear. What does become clear when looking at these figures is the tendency to interpret

---

26. See, for example, Taylor 1952: 390; Baltensweiler 1959: 76; and Johnson 1960: 155. Although this interpretation no longer dominates, at least not without some qualification, support for it can be made through reference to Mal 4:4–6, where Moses is clearly associated with the law—"Remember the teaching of my servant Moses, the statutes and ordinances that I commanded him at Horeb for all Israel" (Mal 4:4)—and Elijah with prophecy—"Lo, I will send you the prophet Elijah before the great and terrible day of the Lord comes. He will turn the hearts of parents to their children and the hearts of children to their parents, so that I will not come and strike the land with a curse" (Mal 4:5–6).

27. See, for example, Chilton's verse-by-verse "reconstruction of the transfiguration tradition" with his numerous Exodus references (1980: 120–21).

28. Reasons accounting for the presence of these two figures include the following: both figures can be considered suitable companions of Jesus because they both shared the path of suffering on account of their faithfulness (Thrall 1969–70: 306); both these figures traditionally avoided "tasting death" (Chilton 1979: 268–69); both Elijah and Moses were put to death at the hands of the people of God (Mann 1986: 355); Moses and Elijah were prophets associated with the "mountain of revelation" (Juel 1990: 128; Gundry 1993: 459; Perry 1993: 2); both were men of the wilderness (Gundry 1993: 477); both had undergone transformations (Brooks 1991: 142, referring to Exod 34:29–35 and 2 Kgs 2:11); Moses and Elijah are regarded as eschatological figures (Kee 1972: 144–46; Juel 1990: 128; Witherington 2001: 263); and with their appearance in this scene, the narrative points unerringly forward to the coming parousia (Taylor 1952: 390; Ramsey 1949: 103, 110).

them either in terms of a coming fullness (parousia, eschaton), or else as a means of emphasizing the singular quality of this glorious vision of Jesus—something that goes beyond other associations and towards the fullest encounter with God's glory to date.[29] A few examples will help to illustrate this tendency.

Some commentators argue that Moses and Elijah are present so as to provide contrasting figures to Jesus for the purposes of further clarifying his identity. McGuckin suggests that the presence of these two prophets provides a kind of commentary on the vision of Jesus transfigured.[30] When comparing Jesus to the great prophets, McGuckin begins to raise questions about the status of the Old Testament figures with respect to Jesus, as well as to each other. In an effort to answer these questions, McGuckin proceeds to link 9:4 directly with 9:8, the point where the disappearance of the prophets emphasizes the lone remaining figure of Jesus. Jesus is heralded as the "Son of God" by the divine voice (v. 7), which also serves to set him apart not just from prophets in general but from the particular figures of Elijah and Moses. The significance of Elijah and Moses, in McGuckin's explanation, lies in their fame as the two most notable figures not to have "tasted death."[31] Because Jesus' postdeath exaltation will be of a higher order than theirs, the juxtaposition sets Jesus apart as one who is greater. In this way, Mark seeks to establish the uniqueness of Christ's role, the distinctiveness of which sets him apart from even the immortal prophets (McGuckin 1987: 70). McGuckin thereby emphasizes the singularity of Jesus as revealed in this moment, the origins of tradition from which he emerges and supersedes, and finally, in the fulfillment of God's plan to which he is destined.

Like McGuckin, Gundry also views the appearance of Elijah and Moses as a type of commentary on the transfigured Jesus. Gundry regards these two biblical figures as "foils to highlight that [Jesus] alone is God's beloved Son to be heard" (1993: 458). Gundry argues that Elijah's appearance is an eschatological signal to the three disciples. Elijah's role here is that of herald of the day of the Lord. The order of their appearance is important, and Mark mentions Elijah before Moses in

---

29. William Lane writes, "His word and deed transcend all past revelation" (1974: 321).

30. McGuckin calls Elijah and Moses prophets, but there are many more options, as has been noted above (see n. 29 above). Moses' significance here has been attributed variously to his transformed humanity, his role as lawgiver, religious founder, Israel's first deliverer (Garland 1996: 344). The significance of Elijah is understood variously as one translated to heaven on a chariot of fire (Hare 1996: 105), restorer of Israel (Hughes 1989: 16), but overwhelmingly as the decisive figure of the end times (Schweizer 1970: 183; Nützel 1973: 170).

31. The biblical basis for this "tradition" is ambiguous. Even though according to Deut 34:5, Moses is said to have died, the fact that the place of his grave is unknown (Deut 34:6), combined with Exod 34:28 that says "Moses was there with the Lord," has opened the way for speculation (Garland 1996: 344). Besides Elijah (and Moses), Enoch is the only other figure in the Hebrew Bible to have been translated (Gen 5:24 and Sir 44:16; see van Iersel 1998: 295). Supporting the belief that Moses avoided death, Heil refers to an early-first-century document sometimes known as the *Assumption of Moses*. According to this document, Moses did not suffer death at the hand of his people, but "in an extraordinary fashion that strongly suggests his assumption into heaven" (Heil 2000: 109–11).

order to emphasize this eschatological role.[32] Gundry further suggests a possibility to link here between Elijah's not having died and Jesus' prediction concerning some not tasting death.[33] Gundry explains the presence of these two particular Old Testament figures by referring to their shared experience as the only Old Testament figures to have seen a theophany on a mountain.

Hooker makes even more of the order in which the heavenly figures appear and points to Mark's account where Moses is seen to be *with* (σύν) Elijah, and as such plays a secondary role.[34] This order is of special significance for Hooker, who criticizes other interpreters for not accounting for what she considers a highly significant detail: the riddle of placing Elijah first, when Moses was the earlier figure and would always have been the more significant figure in Judaism (1987: 61).[35] She views this detail as a deliberate Markan alteration designed to further refine his developing theological agenda.

Hooker looks for an explanation within the context of Mark's narrative. She asserts that Mark makes use of the tradition of the coming of Elijah, in which Elijah is identified as John the Baptist. In this capacity, Elijah/John the Baptist assumes a role often delineated within the Gospel, that of a messenger pointing the way toward the one who follows, who is greater than he. Hooker links the significance of Elijah in the transfiguration narrative to previous mentions of Elijah—particularly 8:28 where a number of theories are posed as to who Jesus is—and from here forms a link between Elijah and John the Baptist as forerunners of Jesus.

Following on from this, Daniel links v. 4 to other verses in Mark that chart a careful and gradual separation of Jesus from John the Baptiser: the ministries of Jesus and John in 1:14; the resurrection of John in 6:14a, 16, and 8:28; and 9:13a, where Jesus speaks of Elijah as having come. Daniel argues that Mark constructs an implicit identification of Elijah with John the Baptist throughout the Gospel, but culminating in 9:11–13, which in turn hinges on the revelation of 9:4. Daniel argues that to give 9:13a its full weight it must be seen to include 9:4, for it is in this key verse that a clear distinction between Jesus and John is finally made. John is distinguished for his preparatory function and paralleled with Elijah as a witness of

---

32. Van Iersel notes that Elijah and Moses are presented in this same counterintuitive order in Rev 11:5–6 (1998: 295).

33. Mann rejects this argument, questioning the records of such a tempestuous Elijah in the Hebrew Bible and also the reference to Mal 4:5–6, which speaks of an active imposition of peace rather than merely a call (1986: 355).

34. Daniel points out that the phrase Ἠλίας σὺν Μωϋσεῖ is characteristically Markan in style. Not only is their order of presentation unique to Mark, but the use of the word σύν reflects a "Markan technique of adding a second person or group to another prior group or individual" (1976: 56).

35. Van Iersel also notes the order in which they are presented and comments "that the narrator mentions the two men in an order contrary to both the chronology of their appearance and the significance generally accorded them is remarkable . . ." (1998: 295). Kee attributes the order to Elijah's pre-eminence in eschatological expectation (1972: 144; see also Nützel 1973: 171; Hare 1996: 105; Witherington 2001: 263). Chilton accounts for the order by referring to the impending discussion in 9:11–13 (1980: 117–18).

Jesus during the last days. Elijah's precedence over Moses can be understood when the link between John and Elijah is made. It is not surprising, then, that in distinguishing Jesus' identity from John the Baptist, John's own identity is also revealed as that of Elijah. Hooker argues that in providing a glimpse of the glory of Christ to the apostles, the transfiguration pericope also reveals and explains John's true identity as being Elijah (1987: 67).

But what of Moses? The similarities to the Sinai scene are often noted, but how is the appearance of Moses accounted for beyond this? Some commentators see Jesus presented in Mark's Gospel as a type of new Moses. Larry Hurtado writes, "Moses' appearance in the vision of the disciples meant that he was endorsing Jesus as the one he had promised, the one who now bore all the authority of Moses in speaking for God" (1983: 144–45; see also Ziesler 1970: 266). Best points out that although a Moses typology may be possible in the Matthean and Lukan accounts, within the wider context of Mark's gospel there are no themes demonstrating a Moses typology, a "New Exodus," nor is there even a prominent wilderness theme. Hooker also rejects the interpretation that Moses is here to indicate Jesus' place in the succession of great prophets: "The belief that Jesus is a prophet—whether old or new, whether the returning Elijah or a prophet like Moses—even though it springs from a desire to honour Jesus, is mistaken" (1987: 63). Hooker points out that Moses is as much a representative of the prophets as Elijah. Instead, she interprets the presence of Moses as representative of "the Law" in the broadest sense, and "Moses is the obvious figure to represent [not only] the Law, but everything that 'is written'" (1987: 68). Here Hooker is speaking about "the Law" as a generic term for Scripture citations (68). Hooker observes that in a phrase like "Moses and all the prophets," Moses is differentiated from and yet included as one of the prophets, the figure of Moses having a broader religious significance and symbolic value. Thus, Hooker argues that Moses is the obvious figure to represent the broader religious heritage of Judaism. She sums up as follows:

> Elijah—in the person of John the Baptist—is the forerunner of Jesus, and witness to the authenticity of Christian claims about him. Moses, too, the first and greatest of God's prophets, is also a witness to those claims: the things which happen to Jesus—death and Resurrection—are the things which are "written concerning the Son of Man." Moses, like Elijah, appears in the role of Jesus' sponsor. (69)

But Jesus' authority extends beyond the heraldry of Elijah and also the Law of Moses: "Jesus both fulfils the Law and points beyond it. Like Elijah, Moses functions as a predecessor of Jesus, whose role is to witness to the one who is greater than he" (Hooker 1987: 69). Thus the unique position of authority that Jesus occupies as God's son sets him apart from just another figure who continues the chain of prophetic genealogy, and instead he orients the Law toward a new eschatological goal.

72                               *Transfigured*

Yet, despite Hooker's interpretation of the presence of Elijah and Moses, the details of v. 4 continue to vex. Part of the enigmatic quality of this verse is its obvious potential for development in many other parts of Mark's Gospel—an opportunity that, according to McGuckin, does not appear to have been taken up by the evangelist. McGuckin looks to the detail of the two prophets conversing with Jesus and describes this touch in enigmatic terms. The meaning of this detail is ambiguous and yet must have been provocative enough to lead Luke to elaborate and give the content of their discourse. By disclosing the topic of conversation, Luke consolidates the theme of the prophetic destiny of Christ in the Third Gospel (see Trites 1994: 38–39). But this theme of prophetic destiny is not part of Mark's Gospel, especially if we agree with Hooker. Has the unsophisticated, awkward Mark returned? How else would one explain why, when Mark is seen to make the most of every literary nuance, he would include this detail and yet allow it essentially to go to waste?

Gundry notes that Mark's description of the scene seems to imply a certain informality in their exchange of greetings. For Gundry, one would almost be forgiven for thinking that Elijah, Moses, and Jesus are equals. According to Gundry, this suggestion of equality, conveyed by the word συλλαλοῦντες, is introduced solely in order be corrected later on in v. 6.

> [Mark's description of this scene] is a specific introduction into the tradition by the evangelist himself to heighten his subsequent treatment of Peter's suggestion. The whole Transfiguration narrative is Christologically motivated, and the consistent message is that Jesus is by no means an equal to Elijah and Moses but of a wholly different order of importance. (Gundry 1993: 71)[36]

In Gundry's reading, two problematic verses are intimately connected, and conveniently, the connection itself provides the key to both. One could almost say that there is a scholarly attempt here resembling the killing of two birds with one stone. The mysterious appearance of Elijah and Moses serves to explain the involved exchange that now follows immediately after v. 4—Peter's so-called error. Peter's error, at least according to commentators, is precisely that he assumes and takes for granted that all three "prophetic" figures are equals.[37] And so there is some irony to be found in the clamping together of these two ambiguous and problematic verses, which, as will become evident, once joined, serve to further bolster one of the grandest themes of Markan theology.[38]

---

36. Gundry's comments here would meet with support from other commentators, such as Mann, who makes the more general comment: "For varying reasons, all three evangelists were compelled to assert the far-excelling glory of Jesus over against Moses and Elijah, lest in the anxieties of different situations the early Christians be led to evaluate Jesus as no more than the equal of two highly significant Old Testament figures" (Mann 1986: 358).

37. More on Peter's "error" in the next section.

38. Of course, there are other verses used to interpret 9:5. For example, McGuckin links 9:5 with 9:1, where 9:5 is seen as the fulfilment of the prediction of 9:1 (1987: 71).

## V. Peter Misses the Point

*"Then Peter said to Jesus, 'Rabbi, it is good for us to be here; let us make three dwellings, one for you, one for Moses, and one for Elijah'"*
*(Mark 9:5)*

In v. 5, Peter's exclamation and following suggestion appear to be read exclusively as being foolish, misplaced, or at the very least, confused.[39] In light of v. 6, the disciples are described by commentators as being awe-struck, frightened out of their wits, and thus talking nonsense. For instance, McGuckin suggests that Peter's statement is presented by the evangelist to his readers for didactic purposes: "We are supposed to reflect on why the statement is wrong" (1987: 72). Peter's comments and suggestions in v. 5 are a response to the scene just witnessed in vv. 3 and 4. First of all, addressing Jesus, Peter responds on behalf of his fellow disciples saying that it is good (καλόν) that they are there. Following this, he suggests building three tents (καλόν) for Jesus and his heavenly companions. These two elements of Peter's response are roundly rejected by commentators who take v. 6 with its show of fear (ἔκφοβοι) and narrator's aside as demonstrative of his inability to comprehend the scene just witnessed.

Peter breaks the silence even though he is not asked and he is not spoken to (Lohmeyer 1967: 176). Reacting to the scene before him, Peter, speaking for his companions as well as himself, begins by exclaiming how good it is that they are present. B. D. Chilton explains, "What is καλόν about discipleship is explicated in 9.43, 44, 47" (1980: 118). Chilton goes on to say that these latter texts all evoke the need for true discipleship to pay the necessary price of suffering before arriving at the glory of the kingdom. Part of Peter's mistake may therefore be interpreted in the light of Mark 8:32 and 14:28–30 as being the fact that even at this stage he has not got a proper perspective on what is truly "good" about discipleship, that he still has a vision that cannot come to terms with the scandal of the cross.[40]

It is curious to find Jesus addressed as Ῥαββί in such a narrative as this, for Ῥαββί is deemed inappropriate as a title for Jesus in Mark's Gospel (Hooker 1987: 64). But here and in 11:21, such a title is put on the lips of Peter and is taken as an indication that he does not understand Jesus' identity fully. This title is used again in Mark 14:45 on the lips of Judas, who betrays Jesus. Its use in 10:51 is similar, since that pericope also identifies Jesus as the Son of David, a title that Mark also repudiates (12:35–37). Although understood to mean "my great one" or "esteemed

---

39. For example, commentators make the following comments on Peter's response: "wrong. He erred" (Ramsey 1949: 115); "impulsive interjection . . . confused understanding" (Mann 1986: 361); "foolishness" (Tolbert 1989: 205); "lack of understanding" (Brooks 1991: 143); "unthinking response to these sights . . . one can only guess what Peter intended" (Garland 1996: 345); "does not understand the true significance" (Heil 2000: 162); "obviously speaks without really knowing what to say, or even what he is saying" (Witherington: 2001: 264); "What in the world was Peter up to?" (Hughes 1987: 16).

40. Heil finds Peter's comments regarding what is "good" to be a fulfilment of 9:1 (2000: 160).

teacher," Brooks considers the title Ῥαββί, as used by Mark, a less-than-flattering term. Noting that in Matthew's (17:4) and Luke's (9:33) versions Ῥαββί has been upgraded to "Lord" and "Master" respectively, both writers choosing a title of much greater reverence, Brook considers that, by comparison, Mark's term indicates a corresponding lack of respect and thus of understanding on Peter's part (1991: 142; see also Taylor 1952: 391; McGuckin 1987: 72). Daniel notes that the title Ῥαββί as a Christological term, has negative overtones for Mark. After 8:27, the only times it is used by the disciples is in the context of their deteriorating relationship with Jesus. Daniel suggests that the use of the title Ῥαββί can be read as a warning that what follows is contrary to Markan theology (1976: 57). Though Ῥαββί means "my great one," Mark diminishes this connotation by not translating it, as he does other Semitic expressions.

In contrast with other commentators, Gundry notes the scarcity of this title in Mark, but doubts that Peter is, in fact, in error on this count. Gundry regards Peter's use of the title Ῥαββί as in keeping with Mark's played down Christological emphasis and, in this case, the use of the title contributes to the climactic filial declaration in the following verse (1993: 459, 481). Gundry links the "here" (ὧδε) of v. 5 to the "here" (ὧδε) of 9:1 and proposes that the transfiguration is a direct fulfillment of this prediction (see also Heil 2000: 160).

For Daniel, vv. 5 and 6 play a Christological function in that they illustrate a false theological understanding of Jesus' identity as expressed implicitly in Peter's question (1976: 58). Peter wishes to dwell in the presence of Jesus, Elijah, and Moses. But he mistakenly places them on the same level, revealing that his offer has been prompted by an incorrect sense of community (see also Juel 1990: 128; Garland 1996: 345). Peter's mistaken conception of community here is a community without suffering (Nineham 1963: 236; Brooks 1991: 142). These interpretations are further developed when commentators turn to consider Peter's proposal to build three tents (σκηκή) in the second half of v. 5. This component of Peter's "error" has proved particularly difficult to account for by scholars, and it is also the image most closely associated by commentators with Peter's incomprehension.

Eduard Schweizer notes from Peter's comments in v. 5 that he falls back to the more traditional order of Moses before Elijah (1970: 182). Gundry suggests that this reversal serves to emphasize the associations σκηκή draws from the Hebrew Bible, chiefly, the sense of σκηκή as "tabernacle" (1993: 460). Gundry is implying a certain symmetry here: just as naming Elijah first in the previous verse brings to the fore certain associations between Jesus and Elijah, so too Peter's reversal of this order in v. 5, where he names Moses first, brings a certain history and tradition to bear on σκηκή.

The development of these themes in the Hebrew Bible can be seen in the work of H. Riesenfeld, who develops the connections between Peter's mention of σκηνάς and the eschatological significance of the feast of Tabernacles (1947: 146–205; see also Nützel 1973: 127). Just as he believed the feast of Tabernacles retained the ideas of an older enthronement festival, Riesenfeld looks to the historical situation of first-century Judaism as the context in which he believes the Transfiguration story was composed, and sees a depiction of Jesus enthroned as Messiah at a time when nationalistic feeling ran high. Kee describes the apocalyptic quality of the feast of Tabernacles, attributing it to the belief that Yahweh would establish his rule in Jerusalem and that this final victory would coincide with the annual observance of the feast (1972: 147). Ralph Martin also speaks of the apocalyptic dimension associated with the feast of Tabernacles in first-century Judaism, a time when nationalistic sentiment was boiling over. In this context, Peter's suggestion could be interpreted as a call to lead God's people against their enemies—so Elijah—and to freedom—so Moses (Martin 1973: 129–30).

Despite the obvious richness of establishing a link between the feast of Tabernacles and the other perceived eschatological elements of the transfiguration story,[41] Thrall objects to the use of this heuristic for a number of reasons (1967: 264). Among her objections, she notes that there is no evidence that a prior enthronement festival ever existed. Moreover, while the feast of Tabernacles does have an eschatological dimension (see Luke 16:9; 2 Cor 5:4; Rev 21:3), it is more closely associated with the sojourn in the wilderness (Thrall 1970: 264; see also Ziesler 1970: 264).[42]

Hooker also notes, when considering the significance of the σκηνάς, that this term can evoke a whole range of ideas, from the feast of Tabernacles to a reference to the wilderness experience (1987: 64–65). If the reference was to the feast of Tabernacles, Hooker wonders why such a reference has left no other mark on the narrative, nor is their any explanation as to why Peter does not offer to build enough tabernacles for all present. Hooker rejects the notion that Peter suggests the building of tabernacles to house God's glory, as here he was faced with Elijah and Moses, both mere mortals and thus not to be equated with places for the glory of God to dwell.

Hooker opts for a simpler explanation of Peter's suggestion. She suggests that Peter's offer was a show of respect. "Without house or even tent to throw open, how could the disciples show proper respect, except by building some kind of temporary shelter? And indeed, what more appropriate dwelling for these men of the desert than σκηναί?" (1987: 66–67). For Peter, Jesus is included since witness of this transfiguration now places him (mistakenly) in the company of these great Old Testament figures, equally worthy of honor.

---

41. McGuckin doubts the connection to the feast of Tabernacles, but acknowledges that such associations would provide a rich interpretive pool, especially with the mention of "the cloud of Presence," and the theme of the theology of light, so central to this feast (1987: 72).

42. Other commentators do not necessarily see a contradiction here. For example, James Brooks quite happily allows the reference to the feast of Tabernacles to stand beside the wilderness theme: "He [Peter] may have gotten the idea [of erecting three shelters] from the use of booths in the wilderness and at the Feast of Tabernacles" (1991: 142–43). Witherington also sees σκηνάς as equally referring to the feast of Tabernacles and the sojourn in the wilderness and attributes an eschatological dimension to both these understandings (2001: 263–64).

Daniel also argues against interpreting the tabernacles as referring to the feast of Tabernacles. Daniel says that the expression is used by Mark specifically with reference to the idea of the tabernacle as bound to the presence of the disciples, a connection it does not have in Jewish apocalyptic expectations. Daniel considers that v. 5 fulfills a twofold function in Mark's Gospel. Its negative function is to provide an example of the disciples' failure to understand properly both Jesus' identity and pattern of service, not to mention their own. But contrasting with this, it subtly establishes a relationship between the transfiguration narrative and 8:38 and 9:1 by highlighting *what* is not understood properly (1976: 58–59).

For Gundry, a reference to the feast of Tabernacles would imply that Peter's suggestion be understood as a Zealot call to lead God's people into battle—and he notes that this is something Elijah never did. Gundry rejects the claim that the tabernacles mentioned here reflect anything having to do with the festival of Tabernacles proper, because Peter makes no tabernacles for himself and his fellow disciples. Gundry also rejects the notion that the tabernacles are to be equated with eternal tabernacles, such as those in Luke 16:9, for again, Peter would have suggested three additional tabernacles to house himself and his companions (1993: 479).

Gundry's interpretation looks instead to the significance of the tabernacles as an illustration of Peter's mistaken assumption of honoring Elijah, Moses, and Jesus equally, an alternate view that is held by a number of other commentators (1993: 480). Here, the offer to build three tents is a reflection of his faulty understanding of Jesus' identity and destiny. Implicit in Peter's offer is the placement of Jesus on the same level as Moses and Elijah (Heil 2000: 161). McGuckin maintains that it is more likely that Mark intended the significance of the tabernacles as an indication of Peter's mistaken assumption that the heavenly figures before him were equal. Peter erroneously believes that he needs to build the tabernacles in which the heavenly figures will dwell, his presumption being that Jesus will not return down the mountain with him and his companions to live again with mortals. McGuckin sees this as a further indication of the intimate connection between this narrative and the theology of the glorified Christ. He sees Peter's suggestion as an indication of his mistaken assessment of the situation by first assuming that Jesus is equal to his heavenly companions, and that, second, now revealed in all his Father's glory, Jesus' dwelling place is heaven, in the heart of God's glory and not in the realm of mortals.

According to Mann, to identify Jesus with Moses and Elijah is to identify him simply as another eschatological messenger and as a prophet (1986: 360). Such a designation appears only six times in Mark, compared with a higher rate in the other evangelists. Like "rabbi," "prophet" is not considered a suitable title for Jesus. For Mark, a prophet is one who prepares the way for the Messiah, and John the Baptist is the obvious example.[43]

---

43. See also the parable of the vineyard, Mark 12:1–12.

In another approach to the interpretation of Peter's offer to build tents, Peter is seen to be attempting to prolong his experience of Jesus' revealed glory (Taylor 1959: 391; Cranfield 1966: 291; Ernst 1981: 257). Peter makes an effort to provide dwelling places so that he and the other disciples may dwell in the presence of the transfigured Jesus and the heavenly figures. Josef Ernst sees Peter wanting to hold the moment. The glorious reality of the scene seemed so real that he wanted to celebrate an eternal feast of Tabernacles with the heavenly forms (1981: 258). Peter, however, doesn't grasp the way of the Messiah. Peter seeks to prolong the glorious vision, but he doesn't understand that the glory is not complete without suffering (cf. 8:31; Taylor 1952: 391; Hurtado 1983: 146; Juel 1990: 128). Peter's error here consists of his misguided search for the power and glory of the parousia without the necessity of suffering. Peter wrongly concludes that the time of the parousia has arrived (Schweizer 1970: 182). Although Peter correctly interprets 9:2–4 in the light of 8:38 and 9:1, he ignores the teaching of 8:34–37 and thus draws the wrong conclusion, revealing he is still the Peter of 8:32 (Kee 1972: 147–48).

Peter's mistake has been to understand only part of the bigger picture. His comments demonstrate a failure to grasp the grand scheme of things. That said, Peter does not get it *all* wrong; he is just unable, however understandably at this stage, to piece together the various parts of Jesus' message so as to form a whole. It would seem that commentators are determined not to make the same mistake and seem intent on connecting the vision of the transfiguration to Mark's bigger theological picture. This is done by affirming a sense of structure and process and orienting interpretation toward the final goal or end, the "full vision" that Peter is unable to see. Peter does not appreciate that the glory revealed on the mountain can reach its fullness only through death and resurrection, and his true error is his failure to acknowledge the incompleteness that is presented before him.

## VI. Terror of Incrimination

*"He did not know what to say, for they were terrified" (Mark 9:6)*

The understanding implicit in Peter's response to the scene before him is seen to be undermined by what follows in v. 6. A similar pattern occurred in 8:27-33. On this previous occasion, the failure of the disciples—with Peter at their lead—is expressed through a faulty Christological understanding which is quickly corrected. In both cases, faulty assumptions have been made in response to direct revelation (Heil 2000: 159; Heil also points to syntactical similarities, particularly between 8:29 and 9:5). But in v. 6, Peter's error is indicated by the expression of sheer terror (ἔκφοβοι γὰρ ἐγένοντο).[44] The terror expressed by the disciples reveals

---

44. In Mark, fear appears to be a common reaction to God's power at work in Jesus (see 4:41; 5:15, 33; 6:50; 16:8), but the intensive term ἔκφοβοι is only used by Mark here, and is found only once more in the New Testament, in Heb 12:21 (interestingly, with reference to Moses encountering the glory of the Lord on Sinai).

the true significance of what they have just encountered and in doing so, simultaneously reveals the total inadequacy of Peter's casual comment and inappropriate suggestion. Timothy Dwyer, in what he considers an apt parallel to the type of fear depicted here, looks to the appearance of ἔκφοβοι in Greek literature. He notes Aristotle's use of the word: "For when men are frightened their hair stands on end" (quoted by Dwyer 1996: 141). Consequently, in the transfiguration scene, Dwyer finds a moment when "the invasion of the heavenly into the earthly causes a terror in the disciples as to almost make their hair stand on end" (1996: 142). This experience of hackle-raising fear is understood by Dwyer to be an indication of the wonder and amazement that comes as a result of witnessing a "breaking through" of the divine (Dwyer 1996: 143).[45] Hooker agrees, citing a number of verses in Mark that demonstrate that fear is a common reaction to manifestations of God's power at work in Jesus (1987: 66).[46]

Gundry believes that the mention of the disciples' terror keeps the audience of the Gospel from overlooking Peter's mistake. At the same time, it also provides the reason for the error and further serves to bring the other disciples into the situation (1993: 460). Gundry also takes the mention of terror as an emphasis of the disciples' experience of the overpowering glory of God, which they are witnessing as the fulfillment of 9:1 (1993: 460).[47] Mann links the fear of the disciples to the fear of the women fleeing the empty tomb. He sees their terror springing from an inability to comprehend the vision before them, although he acknowledges that the word ἔκφοβος can also refer to religious awe (1986: 360). Daniel, too, interprets the disciples' fear in this way, as a reflection of their lack of theological insight and faith (1976: 60).

Mann establishes a close link between the fear of the disciples and Peter's words in the previous verse.[48] Best notes, however, that there is not necessarily such a tight fit between Peter's previous suggestion and the fear experienced here (1986: 206–26).[49] That said, Best agrees that if fear emerges from the ignorance of the

---

45. Dwyer cites the following examples: 4 Macc 4:10; Dan 10:7; Acts 10:4 (1996: 142).

46. Hooker cites Mark 4:41; 5:15, 33; 6:50; 16:8. See also Nützel 1973: 171.

47. Others who suggest at least a partial fulfillment of 9:1 in the transfiguration scene include: Lane 1974: 312–14; Cranfield 1966: 287–89; and Taylor 1952: 385.

48. Mann goes on to link Peter's confused suggestion not to 9:1 but to the Gethsemane scene (Mark 14:40), where the disciples are unable to say anything to Jesus. In this way, Mann forms a link between the transfiguration and the passion narrative (1986: 360). This linking of the transfiguration and the passion will become especially important in the following chapter. Mann also draws links between the six days of 9:2 and the references to the Sabbath in 15:42 and 16:2; the fear of the disciples in v. 6 and the fear of the women at the empty tomb (16:8). In the latter example he looks at "striking" parallels in Mark's Greek, where "to be here" (ἡμᾶς ὧδε εἶναι, 9:5) can be linked with "he is not here" (οὐκ ἔστιν ὧδε, 16:6; see also Baltensweiler 1959: 113). Mann also places the transfiguration within Mark's general notion of Galilee, linking it with 16:7: "He is going on before you into Galilee; you will see him there."

49. Gundry also exhibits a certain amount of uneasiness between the fear of the disciples in v. 6 and Peter's comments in v. 5 that it is "good" to be there (1993: 480).

disciples, then it is perfectly in keeping with the Markan theme of puzzled discipleship. Considering what they have just witnessed, Witherington is hardly surprised by their fear and speechlessness and sees the disciple's reactions as perfectly in keeping with this Markan theme: "Indeed one gets the sense that they had made no significant progress in their understanding, at least in regard to Jesus' coming suffering, dying, and being raised" (2001: 263–64). Schweizer sees in v. 6 an opportunity for Mark to place "special stress" on the error of Peter's preceding suggestion (1970: 182). Nineham sees in the fear and speechlessness the very reasons behind Peter's response: "Peter's words . . . were an *inappropriate* response to the situation on the part of one blinded by bewilderment and fear" (1963: 236, his emphasis; see also van Iersel 1998: 296).

The fear of the disciples is largely seen as a response to the vision of Jesus transformed and as a way for the evangelist to undermine Peter's previous comments. The vision that sparked the fear and speechlessness of Peter and the disciples is further affirmed in the next verse with the descent of the heavenly cloud and the utterance of the divine mandate.

## VII. Cloudy Commands

*"Then a cloud overshadowed them, and from the cloud there came a voice, 'This is my Son, the Beloved; listen to him!'" (Mark 9:7)*

The appearance of the cloud in v. 7 is seen by some commentators to be set in direct contrast with Peter's offer in v. 5 to build tabernacles. The cloud overshadows the group, removing the figures of Elijah and Moses from view, and singling out Jesus as God's son.[50] This divine movement is seen to bring resolution to the scene, simultaneously dismissing any fear and confusion felt by the disciples, and, with the issuing of the divine mandate, correcting Peter's erroneous evaluation of the vision.

McGuckin looks to the Hebrew Bible for the origins of the imagery. If the cloud signifies the presence of God, then for McGuckin, a whole range of images from the Hebrew Bible are evoked.[51] Other commentators are less concerned about making links to the Hebrew Bible.[52] Gundry points out, when looking at v. 7, that while much of the imagery harks back to the Hebrew Bible, this part of the text is not to be read as a direct allusion to Exodus (1993: 461). For Gundry, the cloud simply signifies God's presence; its overshadowing confirms that Peter's tabernacles were

---

50. In fact, there is no scholarly consensus as to whom precisely the cloud covers: the whole group (Gundry 1993: 460–61); only the three heavenly figures, Jesus, Elijah, and Moses (Öhler 1996: 210–11); the three disciples (Reid 1993: 137); or just Moses and Elijah (Heil 2000: 164).

51. McGuckin cites Exod 16:10; 19:9; 33:1; 40:34–38; Num 9:15–22; 1 Kgs 8:10–11; Isa 4:5; 2 Macc 2:8; and others (1987: 78). Schweizer cites the additional references of Exod 24:28; Ezek 1:4 (1970: 182).

52. See, for example, Mann 1986: 198, 361; Ramsey 1949: 115; Hooker, 1987: 66.

to be honorific rather than just for shelter. For Markus Öhler, the overshadowing cloud represents heaven, *pars pro toto*.[53]

Noting that it was in the form of a cloud that God revealed himself to Israel, Hughes also notes the association of light and luminosity to this cloud: "[A]s Jesus and his inner circle stood in silence in the night air, a luminous cloud appeared and enveloped them" (1989: 18). Brooks also describes the cloud as being "just like the bright, white clothes" of v. 3 (1991: 143). But unlike the cloud of presence from Exod 13:21 and Jesus' brilliant robes, and even more curiously, unlike the cloud from Matthew's account of the transfiguration, the cloud in Mark's story is not described as being bright (see Matt 17:5). One reason for this is put forward by Mann, who says that removing the brightness shows that divine presence is not to be located in the cloud but rests instead on Jesus, and it is from here that God now speaks (1986: 361).

From a close reading of v. 7, Heil limits the cloud to covering only Elijah and Moses. "The voice comes 'from' or 'out of' (ἐκ) the cloud and speaks to the disciples" (2000: 164). The significance of this is that the cloud functions to correct Peter's offer to build three tents (τρεῖς σκηνάς), an offer that mistakenly groups the three figures together in a false sense of equality. Heil notes some irony as the cloud "covers over" or "tents over" (ἐπισκιάζουσα) Moses and Elijah, thus separating them from Jesus. The voice of God is heard, and the irony is maintained as it speaks without any intermediary, neither from hallowed tent nor prophet, affirming the uniqueness of Jesus (Heil 2000: 165–66).

Tolbert finds a "profound irony" in this moment, a moment that also serves to brings the scene to its climax:

> But in a passage where Jesus speaks not at all, where the emphasis is overwhelmingly on vision, the voice from the cloud incongruously commands, "Hear him"... Being divinely required to listen to Jesus when he is not talking but glistening in the whitest of garments turns the whole episode on its head. It is not what it appears to be. The glorious vision of a transformed Jesus with Elijah and Moses that so impresses Peter is undercut by the words from heaven. (1989: 206)

Tolbert finds in this irony a commentary on the true path to glory. The path to glorious fulfillment passes by way of the cross. "Peter is willing to be impressed by seeing a transformed Jesus but unwilling to accept the word he preaches" (1989: 207). The irony of God's commanding voice serves to realign the theological path toward its goal. "The kingdom of God coming in power is not the result of seeing Jesus' shining garments or his communion with Elijah and Moses; it is the result of hearing his words and responding in faith" (207). Kee suggests a more accurate description would be that of a *theoepeia* rather than a *theophany* (1972: 148). Schweizer expresses something similar when he interprets the message of the

---

53. Öhler explains that the cloud descends as though heaven has come down to embrace the three figures. Elijah and Moses are then transported back up to heaven, and Jesus is left as heaven's ambassador on earth (1996: 211, 214).

divine voice as a way for Mark to "call the church away from fanatically longing for the end to come—back to listening—back to the Word" (1970: 182-83).

The voice from the cloud is regarded as the most authoritative testimony to the truth of Jesus' sonship, an identity that has thus far been recognized by spirits of the underworld, humans of the earth, and, more recently, heavenly beings (McGuckin 1987: 79). This ultimate recognition and affirmation of Jesus' true identity and glorious origins by the voice of God mark a turning point in the Gospel narrative. McGuckin sees the voice of God now signaling a new forward momentum, a movement onward, toward the passion narrative.

> From this point onwards in Mark's text, the prophecies of the passion will accelerate our progress into the Passion narrative itself. A similar tradition of a heavenly voice confirming the Messiah's passion is found at Jn. 12:23-30. And further corroboration that we should thus interpret the metamorphosis in terms of such a theology of glory is manifested only through the cross, is provided by the redactive parallels drawn between this episode and the narrative form of the Gethsemane story. (1987: 81)[54]

Heil regards the voice of God as "pivotal" and as such, not only points forward to the crucifixion but also back toward the beginning of Mark's story (2000: 165). The theological path that has led up to this point and that winds its way through the suffering to come began very early on in Mark's Gospel. The voice of God heard here is reminiscent of a voice that has been heard before.[55] When looking at the presence of the cloud and the voice of the Father in v. 7, Chilton regards the heavenly voice as a "deliberate borrowing" from the tradition of the baptismal account in Mark 1:11 (1980: 119; see above for additional scholars in agreement on this point). Schweizer notes the change from second to third person when comparing 1:11 and 9:6 and sees in this a thematic progression whereby "What is transacted there between Father and Son alone is now revealed to the three intimate friends" (1970: 182; see also van Iersel 1998: 296). Seen to be a development of 1:11, what is revealed here is an important new stage in the disciples' "enlightenment" (Juel 1990: 129). By contrast, Goulder (1979: 279-80) and Gundry (1993: 77) view the words spoken by the voice here as the primary account, which has been read back into the baptism narrative. McGuckin sides with the notion of evangelist as theologian, however, and rejects the latter theory for not allowing these traditional images to evolve and be developed as theological themes within the Gospel narrative. "The fact is that both the Baptismal narrative and the Transfiguration are concerned with teaching that Christ's glory is inextricably bound up with the mystery of his sufferings and death" (1987: 77).

---

54. A link to the Gethsemane story was made earlier when discussing v. 6. This link was drawn by Mann, who links Peter's misunderstanding in v. 6 to the disciples' inability to say anything to Jesus in 14:40 (Mann 1986: 360).

55. Although this time, Ernst hears in this voice a clear reprimand directed toward the disciples (1981: 259).

Daniel sees the voice in v. 7 affirming the Christological pattern set out in 8:31–9:1. The disciples are called to abandon their own faulty conceptions and heed Jesus' teachings. Daniel interprets the voice of God as affirming Jesus' singular significance rather than correcting the erroneous disciples. In this way, Daniel sees v. 7 explicitly affirming what has been suggested implicitly in the transfiguration narrative so far: Jesus is the bearer of God's power and glory. Daniel affirms an interpretation of this verse as clearly establishing the transfiguration narrative as functioning proleptically of the parousia (1976: 65). In other words, Daniel poses an interpretation of the Markan story that rearranges things in such a way that the envisioned "end" is set into the "middle."

With the mention of God's voice, the transfiguration passage is most clearly seen to be part of a grand theological arc that traverses the Gospel and extends from the baptism to the crucifixion and beyond. For Gundry, the Father's words help to remove the scandal of the crucifixion by placing the death of Jesus within God's predetermined plan, and known by Jesus as such, the plan is communicated to the disciples, as is the compensatory glory that will follow (1993: 457). Seeing Jesus alone after the cloud lifts emphasizes that it will be in Jesus alone that God's glory has come in power, and it is to him alone that they should pay attention (1993: 461). Gundry points to many grammatical features to support his claim that "the Transfiguration has anticipated the coming glory of the Son of Man, which will also be seen (14.62), and has revealed the power of God's rule that has already arrived" (1993: 462). Boobyer sees the cloud as part of his argument that this scene is a prefigurement of the parousia (1942: 25). McGuckin rejects this notion, which began with Boobyer's account of the cloud symbolizing the "Son of Man's return at the Parousia riding the clouds of heaven" (Boobyer 1942: 84). Here again, we find the view of the transfiguration as a provisional fulfillment of 9:1 (Reid 1993: 25; see above). In rejecting Boobyer's interpretation, McGuckin points out that Mark does not make any mention of clouds in his apocalyptic predictions; moreover, the apocalyptic prediction Boobyer is referring to tells of "clouds" in the plural, and not the singular "cloud" that is described in this passage. The place of God's command is also unclear in this interpretation. Boobyer connects it to the "shout" of the Lord descending at the second coming (1 Thess 4:16). Ramsey finds this unconvincing but nonetheless finds enough evidence elsewhere to see in this scene a foreshadowing of "the glory beyond the passion" (Ramsey 1949: 118).

## VIII. Ending Alone

*"Suddenly when they looked around, they saw no one with them any more, but only Jesus" (Mark 9:8)*

The final verse of the transfiguration text proper is v. 8, which sees the cloud lifting and Jesus alone with the disciples. This event is generally seen as further emphasis of the Father's words in the previous verse with their sole focus on Jesus.

The disciples' looking around and no longer seeing anyone but Jesus alone with themselves gets rid of any possible ambiguity concerning the one declared to be the beloved Son of God, but it also reinforces the point that the disciples should pay attention solely to Jesus because, as they have seen God's rule has come with power in him, not in Moses and Elijah, to whom Mark has attributed no transfiguration. (Gundry 1993: 462)[56]

Baltensweiler finds that Jesus depicted as alone and human reflects this idea that the disciples still cannot comprehend that Jesus is the Messiah and they still view him with their disbelieving (*ungläubigen*) eyes.[57] Some commentators see here a further irony whereby this is not the end of the experience but a culmination (Schweizer 1970: 183; Keenan 1995: 212). The whole vision that has played out before the disciples is distilled in the lone figure of the everyday Jesus—"once more a man among men" (Nineham 1963: 236). Others see in this verse an end and nothing more—a sign that the interlude was just that, a short and limited glimpse of something still to come. (Brooks 1991: 143; Juel 1990: 129) The scene ends abruptly (ἐξάπινα; Ernst 1981: 259; Mann 1986: 361). The preview is over, but the expectation remains and the story recommences so that Jesus' δόξα can continue to unfold (Öhler 1996: 216).

## Conclusion

The majority of commentators base their interpretation of the transfiguration narrative on the overarching theme of God's glory. Although they disagree on exactly how, this theme is seen to be gradually unfolding and increasing in complexity as it threads its way through various stages of the Gospel story. Many commentators interested in the meaning of the transfiguration story find that this enigmatic text plays a distinctive and often pivotal role within this process: "On the mount of Transfiguration a veil is withdrawn, and the glory which the disciples are allowed to see is not only the glory of a future event, but the glory of Him who *is* the Son of God" (Ramsey 1949: 118).

When δόξα is used elsewhere in the New Testament, it is most often associated with the glory of the risen Christ, with a future glory that will be ushered in with the arrival of the parousia (Ramsey 1949: 29–35). At the same time, glory was somehow also present in the experience of believers (1949: 36–45). Certainly δόξα is mentioned in the Lukan transfiguration, and in Matthew's version there are many more signs of its presence. But in Mark's version, the absence of δόξα is another in a series of curious omissions. Certainly for Hooker, the absence in Mark's version is significant. She notes that when Mark does indeed use this word, on rare

---

56. See also Hurtado 1983: 146; Öhler 1996: 216; Heil 2000: 168.
57. Baltensweiler's choice of adjective is of interest here; *ungläubigen* has the sense of an "unbelieving religious infidel" and thus in no uncertain terms continues to disparage Peter for his obtuseness.

occasions, he appears to link it each time with themes of suffering and death (1987: 70).

It would not be difficult to rationalize that δόξα is missing because the fullest glory of the resurrection lies not in the scene witnessed on the mountain but in a future that will come only after suffering and death. Therefore, it would be premature to herald the arrival of the δόξα of Jesus when this scene is interpreted as temporary and limited. Is the promise of the δόξα of Jesus, vividly but all too briefly sketched in the transfiguration, found in its fullness after the death of Jesus? In Matthew's Gospel this is certainly the case (see Matt 28:9, 16–20). In Mark's Gospel, however, it seems that this is not the case at all. Mark's Gospel does not end the way one might expect: there are no dazzling scenes of bright sparkling brilliance; Jesus does not return clothed in power from on high offering promises of enduring presence. After the road through suffering and death has been traversed, could one not expect that the glory witnessed in the transfiguration has now been suitably fleshed out and nuanced enough that a complete vision is possible? Van Iersel expresses these sentiments when he writes of the "narrative gap" found at the empty tomb: "The narrator could easily have filled the gap. He did not, after all, hesitate to represent Jesus as conversing with Elijah and Moses on the mountain (9:2–4), and Jesus, dressed in dazzling white clothes and having a dialogue with these two heavenly figures, would not have been out of place here" (1998: 484). Understandably, commentators seem to feel cheated by the absence of such a vision at the end of the Gospel: "Thus we have a right to expect one final revelatory moment at the end of the Gospel where Jesus' true identity would be made known to the disciples. In short, we would expect the recounting of at least one or two appearances of the risen Jesus to the disciples" (Witherington 2001: 47).

If we take 16:8 as the original ending, Mark's Gospel ends disappointingly with the puzzling darkness of an empty tomb. The transfiguration stands in stark contrast to this scene. As an arguably incomplete vision of God's glory, it nonetheless presents the fullest, clearest, and most intimate picture of glory that the Gospel paints. It is a scene that accords with a specific vision of what this δόξα must be. Its light and sparkle, prophets and clouds, the voice of God, holy terror, tabernacles—all these images coincide with a particular conception of glory. Although the fullest vision that Mark presents, the transfiguration is nonetheless an incomplete vision of this glory, and Peter is seen to be in error believing that the moment has truly arrived. In expecting such a vivid picture of glory, have commentators set themselves up for disappointment? Could it be that there is more to the notion of glory than commentators have "arrived" at here? Is there more to this notion of δόξα than what is expected to be so wonderfully present at a later time? Could commentators in fact also be guilty of committing Peter's error? The missing face, the image of the bleacher, even Peter's so-called error itself, if read differently, could well paint a very different notion of δόξα, one that at the moment remains unseen and unheard, obscured by the splendid glory that so fills this scene.

Derrida's deconstructive exercise looks at the preeminence of notions such as "presence," which, in metaphysical terms, are seen to prefigure all knowledge and meaning. Once he has identified them, he then proceeds to demonstrate how the gaps and fissures within presence, where presence defers and differs from within itself, can in fact be just as convincingly used to disrupt any dominating show of totalization. Derrida reminds us that darkness is a part of light: "The heart of light is black, as has often been noticed" (1978a: 86).

In light of Derrida, is it possible to reread the transfiguration text as not only a celebration of the hallmarks of metaphysics but simultaneously as an evocation of an elusive sense of "otherness"? Jesus, as the *logos,* represents the full presence of the truth in his own being. But is the perceived Markan plot line actually subverted most vividly at this point? This will be the task of the next chapter: to reread the transfiguration narrative with an eye toward these jarring and problematic elements so that an alternate story may unfold, one that takes with it a conception of glory quite beyond its current parameters of light, clarity, fullness, and presence.

## Chapter 4

### REREADING THE MARKAN TRANSFIGURATION

*Introduction*

In the previous chapter, I concluded that within biblical studies a particular image of "glory" has accompanied scholarly interpretations of the Markan transfiguration story. Having gone some way toward delineating the specific metaphysical characteristics of this image, I will be rereading the transfiguration from an alternative perspective, one that does not necessarily superimpose the same glorious template onto this scene. The aim will be to forge a close connection between particular elements of Derridean thought and the images of the Markan transfiguration passage itself.

Throughout this rereading, certain questions will guide the way. These questions are not necessarily so different from those asked by conventional approaches to this text, as we saw, but they are nevertheless fluid enough to allow us to proceed in a very different direction. The statement in v. 2 "and he was transfigured (μετεμορπώθε) before them" (Mark 9:2), sets the rereading (and the questioning) in motion. What exactly does this mean? What is experienced on the mount of the transfiguration, and what is revealed? If something of God's glory is revealed in this scene, and if this glory exceeds the conceptions of conventional scholarship, how can Derrida's work influence the contours of this glory? Moreover, if what is revealed at the transfiguration does indeed impact upon how other parts of Mark's story are read, then how would the Gospel look, and how will it mean, from a more Derridean perspective? How does this story approach a sense of "otherness"?

As a place to begin, the following rereading will focus on those neglected and problematic details of the text that have thus far not played a major part in mainstream readings: details such as Jesus' missing face in v. 3 and Peter's so-called error in v. 5. Added to this are details of the text that have been overlooked, either because they are self-evident and raise no immediate questions (the vision of the sparkling robes; the disciples' fear), or because they are awkward and even embarrassing (the image of the bleacher). These and other similarly neglected and problematic elements will be reread alongside certain key Derridean ideas.

The rereading of the transfiguration passage that is proposed here will be undertaken in two main parts. Each part intersects with a range of Derridean theoretical work at various points, but there will be a more concentrated use of three texts: "White Mythology: Metaphor in the Text of Philosophy" (1974b), *The Post Card* (1987), and *The Gift of Death* (1995).

In part 1, the focus will be Derrida's essay "White Mythology," where he investigates the relationship between metaphorical and philosophical discourse, and argues that the distinctions between these terms are far from clear. Derrida's subsequent formulation of metaphor owes a lot to his reading of Saussurean linguistics, in which he challenges fixed foundations and reformulates signs in terms of their interrelationships. Derrida's discussion of the sun in its unique position somewhere between metaphor and philosophy is of particular relevance to my work here. Along similar lines, I will be reading the spectacle of Jesus' transfigured robes and rereading the motif of light that has had such an overwhelming impact on the vision of glory to emerge from this scene. Continuing this reappraisal of the robes, the problematic and often-overlooked image of the bleacher will be reassessed and its earthy implications explored. Understood as a type of palimpsest, a surface without depth, the robes will call into question notions of inside/outside and assumptions of theological depth. From such a perspective, the very source of glory and the subject of transfiguration can seem like a trick with mirrors. Various other ambiguities will take us from the transfiguration scene to the baptism, and to the crucifixion, as the consequences of an absent face and a cloud that does not shine are further explored.

Part 2 begins with a focus on Derrida's discussion of the experience of the *mysterium tremendum* developed in *The Gift of Death*. Peter's so-called error, his curious offer to build tents, as well as his speechlessness and the disciples' subsequent show of terror (Mark 9:5–6), are reinterpreted in light of the conflicted and paradoxical complexities that inform this most mysterious and terrifying encounter. Rather than erroneous, in these terms, Peter's twofold response is seen to be entirely appropriate. Tents are a most appropriate way to "ground" this experience, and speechlessness and fear are reactions that acknowledge the experience without solving its essential mystery. The motif of fear is taken further with a comparison drawn between the fear of the disciples and the fear of the women at the empty tomb (Mark 16:8). The transfiguration and the scene at the empty tomb are then read alongside *The Post Card*, where Derrida's development of the postal metaphor, with its reformulation of destination, destiny, and the dead-letter office, furthers the link between these two scenes. It is noted that when commentators consider the original ending of Mark's Gospel, even when they accept the oddity and abruptness of this ending, they appear determined to find some sort of closure and fulfillment here, even if it is just a matter of not giving up hope themselves. However, what are the implications of accepting the absence of the tomb as "absence," and accepting the possibility that the "glory" so vividly promised at the transfiguration may never fully arrive?

## Part 1. The Spluttering Sun and the Palimpsest

### *I. Aristotle's Sun*

In "White Mythology," Derrida takes to task some basic philosophical assumptions about the place and function of metaphor within any metaphysical system of thought, but particularly within the logic of philosophy itself. Derrida's reformulation of this relationship between metaphor and philosophy takes into account the possibility that metaphors are oriented by nonmeaning, a condition that is seen to be prior to philosophy. In the course of his discussion, he deals with a number of metaphors, but most relevant to the rereading of Jesus' transfigured robes to follow is his investigation of heliotropic metaphors—and the father of all heliotropic metaphors, the sun itself. Derrida finds that the sun has been used throughout the history of Western philosophy as the ultimate metaphor. In plotting something of the course this history has taken, and in investigating the central significance of this "ultimate metaphor," Derrida first looks to the work of Aristotle and Plato, noting that they both regard the sun as

> the origin, the unique, the irreplaceable (so at least do we represent it to ourselves). There is only one sun in this system. The proper name is in this case the first mover of metaphor, itself non-metaphorical, the first father of all figures of speech. Everything turns on it, everything turns to it. (1974b: 44)

For example, in *The Republic*, Derrida finds Plato, in effect, makes "Truth" and the "Good" both types of "suns":

> Yet of all the organs of sense the eye is the most like the sun? By far the most like. And the power which the eye possesses is a sort of effluence which is dispensed from the sun? Exactly. Then the sun is not sight, but the author of sight who is recognised by sight. True, he said. And this is he whom I call the child of the good, whom the good begat in his own likeness, to be in the visible world, in relation to sight and the things of sight, what the good is in the intellectual world in relation to mind and the things of mind. Will you be a little more explicit? he said. Why, you know, I said, that the eyes, when a person directs them towards objects on which the light of day is no longer shining, but the moon and stars only, see dimly, and are nearly blind; they seem to have no clearness of vision in them? Very true. But when they are directed towards objects on which the sun shines, they see clearly and there is sight in them? Certainly. And the soul is like the eye: when resting upon that on which truth and being shine, the soul perceives and understands and is radiant with intelligence; but when turned towards the twilight of becoming and perishing, then she has opinion only, and goes blinking about, and is first of one opinion and then of another, and seems to have no intelligence? (Plato, *Republic* VI)

For Plato, the "True" and the "Good," modeled as they are after the "sun," become primary sources for the clarity and light that illuminate the rational mind's eye (Derrida 1974b: 43). From this point in philosophy onward, this special regard for the singularity of the sun and the place it occupies as *the* fundamental pivotal point has been a foundational idea in the history of Western metaphysics. Derrida explains that if we were to look for the clearest and most solid example on which to base metaphors, we would not be alone in pointing to the sun, a phenomenon which for many reasons seems to function as the supreme foundational "object." The sun is a unique, concrete, and sensible object of nature. It is a reliable, unshakeable foundation, a natural singularity. While Derrida finds early examples of this central motif of light and its identification with truth, clarity of idea, and origin of thought in the works of Plato and Aristotle, he is also able to trace their continued presence through the work of Descartes, Hegel, Husserl, and others.[1]

Derrida notices that reliance on the sun as *the* foundational referent is not necessarily always accompanied by explicit references to the sun itself. He notes that indirect references can allow the grounding significance of the sun to shine just as brightly. As an example of this, Derrida briefly considers an example from the philosophy of René Descartes. Although in his *Meditations* Descartes does not refer to the sun directly, Derrida observes that Descartes, like Plato, still relies on certain key heliotropes to ground his philosophical system. For example, Descartes finds he is able to move forward again, to move beyond the paralyzing point of his own "hyperbolic doubt," only from within the "natural light" of reason—*lumen naturale*. Noting here that Descartes' argument relies on this notion of *natural* light, Derrida goes further to point out that a connection has been made, one that draws together this light's purity and goodness and the corresponding attributes of an absent God. It soon becomes evident to Derrida that Descartes' God functions as a type of sun whereby "everything becomes clear in this sun, sun of absence and presence, blinding and luminous, dazzling" (Derrida 1974b: 70).

Derrida finds that the impact of the sun on the Western philosophical tradition has been most eloquently described by Hegel:

> The *Sun*—the Light—rises in the East. Light is a simply self-involved existence; but though possessing thus in itself universality, it exists at the same time as an individuality in the Sun. Imagination has often pictured to itself the emotions of a blind man suddenly becoming possessed of sight, beholding the bright glimmering of dawn, the growing light, and the flaming glory of the ascending Sun. The boundless forgetfulness of his individuality in this pure splendor, is his first feeling—utter astonishment. But when the Sun is risen, this astonishment is diminished; objects around are perceived, and from them the individual proceeds to the contemplation of his own inner being, and thereby the advance is made to the perception of the relation between the two. The inactive contemplation is quitted for activity; by the close of the day man has erected a building constructed from his own inner Sun; and when in

---

1. In "White Mythology," Derrida also looks at the work of Fontanier, Bachelard, and Lautréamont (1974b).

90                        *Transfigured*

the evening he contemplates this, he esteems it more highly than the original external Sun. For now he stands in a *conscious relation* to his Spirit, and therefore a free relation. If we hold this image fast in mind, we shall find it symbolizing the course of History, the great Day's work of Spirit. (Derrida 1974b: 71)

Hegel distinguishes here between the sun that rises in the east and the inner sun of thought and contemplation. Derrida elaborates on this distinction between the natural and the conceptual using Aristotle's work on metaphor. For Aristotle, this "natural" dimension to the sun means that it not only orients and grounds philosophical systems from within, as a foundational concept, but it also exceeds these clear and rational philosophical structures.[2] The sun exists simultaneously inside and outside of any philosophical system of thought. Moreover, it is precisely by straddling these realms that the sun maintains some guarantee as to its singularity and clarity of meaning. Rather than being ambiguous in its dual positioning, the natural "fact" of the sun assures that its definition is never in doubt: its twin origins as "*the* sun" and correspondingly, *the truth* of what is meant are assured.[3] In this way the sun represents the Aristotelian ideal where, by virtue of its singularity and its sensibility, it is able to afford a single, identifiable, and controllable meaning. In other words, once metaphors are untangled and deciphered, terms that had been swapped and borrowed can be traced back to their original, natural reality as the sun. This is seen to be especially important for Aristotle, who finds any plurality of meaning, and, at the extreme, any possibility for infinite meaning, a pollution of language—a pollution that pushes language to the point of meaninglessness, and toward its inevitable annihilation.[4]

---

2. This investigation is particularly focused on identifying what is "proper" to the sun, i.e., what is singular and essential, and to what extent this is knowable from the perspective of sensory experience (*Topics*, 5.3.131b22–31).

3. Derrida discusses these notions of centrality and presence, notions that orient and control the play of meaning, in "Structure, Sign and Play in the Discourse of the Human Sciences" (1978b: 278ff.). He speaks of the transcendental signified, an anchoring center point that is paradoxically both inside and outside of the structure. "The center is at the center of the totality, and yet, since the center does not belong to the totality (is not part of the totality), the totality has its center elsewhere. The center is not the center. The concept of centered structure . . . is contradictorily coherent" (1978b: 279). Here we are also close to Derrida's reading of Saussure where the signifier-signified connection is shown to be severed, and free-floating signifiers instead gain meaning from other signifiers. In other words, concepts that go back to the sun are, like signifiers, traceable back to a particular signified. Derrida is arguing that signifiers are not traceable back to anything other than other signifiers in an endless metonymic relationship (Derrida's reading of Saussure and the signifier/signified relationship were introduced in chap. 1).

4. Derrida cites Aristotle's *Poetics* where he explains: "for not to have one meaning is to have no meaning, and if words have no meaning, reasoning with other people, and indeed with oneself, has been annihilated; for it is impossible to think anything if we do not think one thing; but if this *is* possible, one name might be assigned to *this* thing. Let it be assumed then, as was said at the beginning, that the name has a meaning and has one meaning"; Derrida paraphrases Aristotle who makes the same point but in somewhat stronger terms when he says, "At the limit of this 'not-meaning-anything,' a creature is barely animal" (see Derrida 1974b: 49–50).

Contrary to this Aristotelian ideal, Derrida maintains that the apparently solid and grounding presence that the sun provides for metaphor can be revealed to be otherwise. Whereas it is clear that, for Aristotle, the proper place for meaninglessness is firmly and clearly set outside the realm of language, Derrida shows that annihilation, meaninglessness, and absence are all in fact present within this idyllic vision of the sun itself. The sun's place as a supposed foundation is based on our direct sensual perceptions of it, and it is this same sense experience that proves to be at best intermittent. We cannot truly know and rely on the sun in this way, for, according to our senses, the sun is not always present.[5] The sun sets, disappears, becomes invisible, absent altogether from our sense perception. More than this, even when the sun *is* fully present, at the zenith of its midday magnificence, our experience reveals that even then, "one cannot look upon [the sun], on pain of blindness and death" (Derrida 1974b: 43).

The sensible sun limits our knowledge of it, not by how it is *present* to the senses but by the fact that it often *fails* to be present, being hidden or absent. Are we to ground metaphor on such incompleteness, on an elusive unknown that is at best partially present to our sensory perceptions? Or should we instead be taking this phenomenon of partiality as an alternative and possibly more apt description of metaphor? In this way Derrida reevaluates the Aristotelian "truth" of metaphor. He looks at this "truth" not in terms of an exterior, foundational referent that grounds its meaning and significance, but rather in terms of two *interior* observations: Derrida observes that metaphors first of all remain thoroughly connected to other metaphors, and, second, metaphor contains within it the real possibility of not meaning anything—of having no direct and assured connection to *any* specific intelligible referent.

Derrida takes account of and *includes* that which Aristotle *excludes* from his definition of language: the threat of nonmeaning. For Derrida, this "threat" demonstrates how metaphors are able to resist their total reduction to a finite set of distinct and certain underlying meanings. Rather than being destroyed by indeterminacy, metaphors reveal themselves to be sustained by innumerable interconnections to other metaphors, which, in turn reveal their basis to be fluid and ever changing, rather than solid and immovable. The possibility for distinct and reliable meaning is indeed threatened by a web of interconnections linking one metaphor with an infinite number of others in an infinite number of possible contexts.[6] It does indeed, as Aristotle may have feared, introduce disunity, uncertainty, and ambiguity, and

---

5. And, as Derrida explains in "Structure, Sign and Play" (1978b), the rupture within the history of concept of structure occurs when the central presence is revealed never to have been itself, that is, never in fact *fully* present and consequently, "[central presence] has always already been exiled from itself into its own substitute" (280). However, this substitute always assures that full presence is maintained.

6. In such a context, the grounding and orienting force of the transcendental signified is undone and its absence "extends the domain and the play of signification infinitely" (280).

consequently the possibility of undecidable meaning—and possibly meaninglessness itself—into the very heart of metaphor. But an infinite potential for meaning, rather than being annihilating, proves to be a dynamic, enlivening source. This kernel of meaninglessness, which Aristotle seeks to exclude from language, proves to be a source of ongoing metaphorical fecundity, of inexhaustible linguistic fertility. It is like the sun, whose identity is based on an undecidable split between darkness and light, searing presence and elusive absence, its own location somewhere between the boundaries of metaphor, philosophy, and nature. Meaninglessness (or more accurately, as yet undifferentiated potential meaning) thus becomes the place of possibility, the very condition that makes possible metaphor, philosophy, and language itself.

Metaphor is often borrowed and adapted in order to make sense of moments of ambiguity and incomprehensibility that might otherwise elude the grasp of more strictly philosophical formulations. Rather than successfully leading one to a set of assured and intelligible foundations from which a particular meaning could be guaranteed, however, the very nature of metaphor actually assures the uncertainty and equivocation that it was initially employed to overcome. Derrida recognizes this circularity when he says that metaphors contain within themselves the seeds of their own destruction (1974b: 71). Instead of leading one back to the grounding light of an absolute "meaning" or "truth," metaphors reveal instead that there is always an excess of meaning that cannot be accounted for. Meaning cannot be reduced to a single source, and metaphors can lead one back only to their own impossibility. Their "truth" becomes that of laying bare the unlimited potential for yet further meaning. As a means of clarification, metaphor essentially obliterates itself as it "endlessly constructs its own destruction" (Derrida 1974b: 71).

In finding a solution to his "hyperbolic doubt," Descartes is guided not by the light of day but by the light of reason. The path leads him back toward God, who like the sun was at one point visible (to the mind's eye), had disappeared. But even when seemingly gone, the way back to God's rediscovery follows a path that never strays from the clarity of its own light. In other words, the terms may have changed, but the way they are structured remains that same. Derrida reveals that whereas Descartes succeeds in breaking out of one logical circle, he nonetheless inscribes another: the circle of natural light that proceeds from and returns to God (Derrida 1974b: 70). Descartes' attempts to find a place from which to "begin" to reconstruct thought prove to be attempts to get outside of philosophy in order to "get a grip on philosophical metaphor" (Derrida 1974b: 28).

This same sun-drenched path winds its way back to the transfiguration story. Descartes' illuminations resemble the way commonly taken by commentators through the transfiguration story: the light of God's glory, which is revealed in the incomplete vision of Jesus transfigured, guides the viewer toward the fullest vision of glory, the source of divine light, the sun, the Father. It comes as no surprise that, in this case, the heliotrope has found itself aligned with an ultimate "truth" and with the overarching glory of God.[7] Taking Derrida's lead, the sun's apparent inadequacy as a reliable foundation now calls into question the solidity and reliability of what one could reasonably assume to be a full vision of God's glory, either here and now, or to come. What once seemed an unshakable ground upon which to read this passage is now eminently shakable. Considering Derrida's discussion of metaphor one may well ask, Where are the cracks, the fissures, and the sun spots, the blindness and obscuring moments, the eclipses and dark nights of God's glory that simultaneously undergird the miraculous transfiguration vision?[8] If we are to believe Derrida's description of metaphor being based on further metaphor, can we also see God's incomplete show of glory being based on other similar notions of incompleteness?

## II. The Fuller Glory of the Robes

The pure spectacle of Jesus' dazzling white robes is a vision that has become synonymous with the transfiguration scene: "And he was transfigured before them, and his clothes (ἱμάτια) became dazzling white (στίλβοντα λευκὰ λίαν), such as no fuller (γναφεύς) on earth could bleach them" (Mark 9:2–3). The supernatural quality of this event seems obvious. The Markan repetition στίλβοντα λευκά functions as a kind of superlative, and as such succeeds in propelling the scene beyond the limits of the senses and evoking that which lies beyond. Both words forming this repetition carry connotations of brightness, brilliance, and whiteness, all of which contribute to the transcendent, "brighter-than-bright" quality of the garments. It would seem that here the disciples are witnessing a brightness that although recognizable to them as such, is so exceptional, so superlative, that it exceeds its own definitions as "bright" and "white" and "dazzling." Like Aristotle's sun,[9] the vision of Jesus transfigured, although vividly available to the sensory

---

7. While I do not deal at length with the theological question of the glory of God as a heliotrope here, it is enough to see the apparent "naturalness" of such an association.

8. This is not just a question of finding a darkness that corresponds to the light, or an obscurity to clarity, but rather of investigating the complicity between these oppositions. For instance, in *Of Grammatology*, Derrida follows the issues surrounding Leibniz's investigation of the deciphering of Chinese and Egyptian characters in the seventeenth century. The "otherness" of Chinese characters and Egyptian hieroglyphs, differing as they do from the rational speech-based characters of the West, prompted the bestowal of a more mystical identity. And yet in doing so a certain complicity between these terms was recognized. This confrontation between the mystical and rational attributes in writing prompted further questioning as to their complicity generally. Derrida goes on to observe a breaking through of the idea that mysticism is not necessarily that which lies outside the sphere of rationalism, but instead as something that coexists with rationalism. But at the time, "The greatest difficulty was already to conceive, in a manner once historical and systematic, the organized cohabitation, within the same graphic code, of figurative, symbolic, abstract, and phonetic elements" (1974a: 80–81).

9. Referring here to the sun of Aristotle and Plato, discussed above, and in "light" of Derrida's reformulation.

experience of the disciples, refers simultaneously to something quite beyond this experience. As a result, the disciples see a quality of brightness in Jesus' robes that is quite beyond what they could have expected. The superlative brightness of the light affords a correspondingly clear view of glory, not just as evident in the spectacle itself but allowing a vision into a beyond, into a glory that surpasses definition. The motif of light that shines throughout this spectacle and the vision of glory visible within this light appear to be closely connected (Hooker 1987: 60). The sense that they are witnessing something that goes beyond Jesus himself is heightened further by the "divine passive" verbs μετεμορφώθη and ὤφθη (Dwyer 1996: 142). These verbs, combined with the shift from a distinctly active Jesus in the previous verse,[10] show that Jesus is transfigured from without, the glory-filled vision bestowed by a God who intervenes to allow his "exteriority" to break through and be glimpsed as a dazzling, transformative spectacle.[11]

More superlatives follow with the image of the bleacher in v. 3. With this gritty and mundane image following so closely behind, the seemingly otherworldly aspect of the white robes is heightened further still.[12] This reference, which takes one "beyond" the skills that the best bleacher on the earth can offer, would seem to indicate a certain supernatural or otherworldly aspect taken on by these robes. Commentators assume that the imagery used here contributes further to this same sense of what is "exterior."[13]

Although the breaking-in of God's glorious "exteriority" is seen to be celebrated through the imagery used in vv. 2 and 3, the *way* the metamorphosis is described here nonetheless comes under fire from commentators. Not only is the double superlative "exceedingly white"[14] regarded as awkward, but the metaphor of the fuller that follows, although considered an attempt to clarify and further affirm this description, serves only to confuse the scene and reveal the basic inability of Mark to account for what is taking place. Commentators, therefore, speak of

---

10. Nützel notes the contrast between the passive formulation here and the active formulation of the scene just prior, a distinction that serves to emphasize the divine origins of the appearance (1973: 169; see also Baltensweiler 1959: 62).

11. Dwyer explains, "Since christology in Mark is in the context of the breaking-in of the kingdom, ... the Transfiguration again shows how the intervention of God with a focus on Jesus brings wonder in a way consistent with what has been seen up to now in the gospel" (1996: 143).

12. Baltensweiler finds that the earthly and the heavenly are being placed at polar opposites in this scene (1959: 66)

13. Although commentators do not use the term "exterior," there is a sense of God "breaking-through" at various points of the Gospel narrative and particularly in this moment. In light of Derrida's connection of God and the sun and the "exterior" inhabited by the transcendental signified, I would suggest that this "breaking-through" amounts to a similar experience. Dwyer states that "throughout the gospel people reacted with wonder when God intervened through Jesus, and here we see three disciples react with wonder when God intervenes with Jesus" (1996: 142–43). In another example, Nineham regards the fuller image as "a touch meant to put beyond question the whole supernatural, divinely originated character of what happened" (1963: 237).

14. See Porter 1989: 491.

an evangelist who is obviously "out of his depth" (Hooker, 1991: 216) and, as evidence of this, point to the inadequacy and clumsiness of Mark's "somewhat lame comparison to a bleacher" (McGuckin 1987: 66; see also Goulder 1979: 279–80). The question being asked by commentators here is why, when Mark could have made so many rich connections—to the Sinai archetype for instance—did he choose instead to associate the loftiness of this glorious scene with an image of the mundane: the work of a bleacher. The sublime sense of the metaphor of light does not seem to match the connotations that accompany the metaphor of the fuller, which are positively gritty by comparison.[15] That said, I would like to look again at the interaction between these two metaphors. I would like to read the metaphor of the fuller as more than a simple affirmation of the "exteriority" indicated by the Markan repetition. Could it be that the image of the fuller, when out from the intimidating shadow of the transfigured robes, means much more in its own right and actually casts a broad shadow of its own?

The basic work of the fuller is to bleach and clean cloth in order to make it white. In line with this, there is a corresponding sense that the fuller in this way drains fabric of color (see Bratcher and Nida 1961: 274). A garment that may have been colored with all the hues of nature, with the various stains, blotches, and pigments of the earth, can, through the fuller's work, be cleansed of these properties. The fuller uses these same earthy elements in the bleaching process: "The fuller cleansed and prepared the cloth by use of nitrum, fuller's earth, and human and animal urine from the latrines. . . . After the cloth was washed and dried it was often bleached by the fumes of burning sulphur, but this method had no permanent results" (Johnson 1960: 157). What is more, the work of the fuller would involve stepping on the cloth using one's knees and feet until it was suitably bleached (Baltensweiler 1959: 65). Through this process, the accumulated colors wash away and drain from the fabric, and at the same time the visible signs that speak of the origins and history of the cloth are also scrubbed away. As the bleacher works and treats the fabric, the figural as well as literal (true/actual) "ground" is gradually cleansed from view, and the garment takes on a certain "newness," quite apart from its history and origins.

The γναφεύς (fuller) was known not only to bleach and clean but to engage in the carding of cloth. Carding was a restorative procedure which involved using bristles to raise the nap and which resulted in the softening and rejuvenation of the cloth.[16] The bleacher's role here was not to *remake* the garment but rather to restore

---

15. For example, when accounting for the absence of the image of the fuller from Matthew's and Luke's accounts, Sherman E. Johnson implies that a certain earthiness or common-place character to this analogy may have been responsible. He explains that "the meanness [understood in the sense of being base and humble work] of the fuller's trade may have led Matthew and Luke to omit this touch" (1960: 157). Baltensweiler notes that the fuller was from the lowest stratum/walk of life (*Volksschichten*), and as such was in a far from respected profession (1959: 65).

16. Louw-Nida 1988: 48.7.

and rejuvenate it. The warp and woof of the "old" garment remains, but the carding process alters it so that it has an *appearance* of newness.

By removing various tints and scuffs in the bleaching and in the carding process, marks that document a garment's origins and history, the slate is essentially wiped clean. The newly bleached cloth stands apart from its history, ready to receive the new marks and signs of wear that will come to inform its future. These ideas of erasure and reuse are ideas that recall Derrida's use of the palimpsest in "White Mythology." Derrida speaks of Western metaphysics as the driving force behind the creation of a "white mythology," which he defines as a process whereby "metaphysics has erased within itself the fabulous scene that has produced it, the scene that nevertheless remains active and stirring, inscribed in white ink, an invisible design covered over in the palimpsest (Derrida 1974b: 11).

This invisible design swirls beneath the whiteness of Jesus' newly blanched robes as a weave of references and a tangle of possible origins.[17] It would be naive to suggest that the spectacle of Jesus transfigured has no connection at all to a past. As commentators rightly suggest, there are numerous possible references and underlying discourses that accompany the vision of Jesus' changed garments. Mark is suspected by some of covering over a whole collection of references that can be traced from this scene to events such as Sinai, to images of the divine *shekinah* and to other episodes from the Hebrew scriptures (Chilton 1980; Hooker 1987; McGuckin 1987; Gundry 1993). Others see references drawn to corresponding points in New Testament literature, to Revelation or to Paul's letters (Mann 1986; Chilton 1980) or else, and more often, to places within the borders of Mark's own Gospel narrative (Boobyer 1942; Gundry 1993; Dwyer 1996; Witherington 2001). And there are also various instances of such descriptions from extrabiblical sources (Ulansey 1996; Heil 2000).[18] Most, if not all, commentators see in this spectacle some sort of reference to a very particular picture of God's glory.[19] So, often the process of exploring these various trails of meaning involves either selecting some while excluding others or at least ranking them in terms of their probability and their ability to be traced to an origin. Rather than engage in this process of inclusion and exclusion, the palimpsest prompts an appreciation of the warp and woof of the garment. Attention is drawn to the surface of the fabric, to its series of simul-

---

17. The first thing Eduard Schweizer says of the transfiguration passage in his commentary on Mark is that "it is no longer possible to explain the history of the tradition of this passage" (1970: 180). Schweizer is speaking in specific terms about the historical origins of this passage, but this is not all that has been lost. In a similar way, it could be said that a repeated process of interpretive "bleaching" has also rendered lost the literary and theological origins of this story, origins that now coexist in a swirling tangle beneath the newly cleaned surface of the palimpsest.

18. Ulansey mentions the starry robes of Isis and Mithras as well as instances of such imagery in Jewish apocalyptic literature such as *1* and *2 Enoch*, the *Apocalypse of Zephaniah* and the *Testament of Levi* (Ulansey 1996).

19. A more extensive account of these views and of the accompanying conception of glory was given in the previous chapter.

taneous layers, each inseparably merged into the other. The palimpsest asks to be regarded for its own sake, not only in terms of where these various traces may lead. This is not to deny the references that thoroughly encrust the robes but rather to find meaning that is not necessarily formed through a process of selecting and ranking one history or origin over and above a number of others.

This idea of the palimpsest, the document that is wiped clean so as to be used again, is developed further in Derrida's analysis of Freud's "Mystic Writing Pad" (Derrida 1978d: 196–231).[20] The mystic pad is a type of palimpsest. It is a wax slab covered by a sheet of thin translucent paper and then, in turn, by a sheet of celluloid. With a pointed stylus, the pad is "written on," and the writing becomes visible when the light paper adheres to the darker wax surface. It is possible to clear the surface by lifting the two sheets from the wax. Although the inscribed grooves remain in the wax, they are no longer visible through the paper. Over time, the markings on the wax surface increase as layer on layer of markings merge with one another. Soon the wax surface resembles an indecipherable collection of marks or "traces" (Derrida 1978d: 223). The mystic pad was used by Freud to represent the relationship between the conscious and unconscious mind. Derrida adopts this device in order to illustrate the structure of metaphysics:

[T]he *depth* of the Mystic Pad is simultaneously a depth without bottom, an infinite allusion, and a perfectly superficial exteriority: a stratification of surfaces each of whose relation to itself, each of whose interior, is but the implication of another similarly exposed surface. It joins the two empirical certainties by which we are constituted: infinite depth in the implication of meaning, in the unlimited envelopment of the present, and, simultaneously, the particular essence of being, the absolute absence of any foundation. (Derrida 1978d: 224)

Jesus' transfigured garments function as a palimpsest. As such, they function in a similar way to Derrida's understanding of the "truth" of metaphor, whereby metaphor is grounded in its own referentiality. The metaphor of the fuller charts the passage of one metaphor to another, a movement in which preceding meanings are subsumed and covered over, but not eliminated, as space is made for more writing. This means that, rather than referring to a ground which lies "outside"—to a transcendental signified—the garments refer only to their own potential to "mean"

---

20. The link between the "archaic" palimpsest and the more advanced mystic writing pad is made in Derrida 1978d: 228. Derrida's use of the idea of the palimpsest has been used before in biblical interpretation, most recently by Timothy K. Beal (1997). Beal reads Esther as a narrative that writes over itself and in this way is palimpsestlike in character: "Think of the book of Esther as a kind of palimpsest: a story is written, then erased and then a new story is written over the old, erased one" (29). The focus of Beal's reading is on the palimpsest as an example of the impossibility of erasure, and he also explores the qualities of the Derridean supplement with its bearing on the "preface." Beal's reading shows how the movement of the narrative in Esther, as it winds its way back over itself, erasing but not removing what it covers over, is a process that mirrors the movement of the palimpsest.

infinitely, as Derrida phrases it, their own "infinite depth in the implication of meaning" (1978d: 224). In their moment of glorious revelation, the transfigured robes reveal their own resistance to fixed foundations alongside a radical openness to the creativity of future meaning. Cut off in this instant from the limitations of external references, they reveal that the "exteriority" they depict does not lead back to any sun or metaphysical conception of "God" but only to itself and to the ultimate *impossibility* of any such grounds or foundations.

If the glory of God *is* revealed in this moment, it is not a revelation concerning *what* that glory means. The vision of Jesus transfigured is a vision that covers over all that comes before it. By obscuring its own foundations, its own fragmented origins, any notion of a particular meaning is sidestepped, and we are afforded instead a vision of *how* God's glory means. The glory of God is seen not as an origin or foundation but as an openness to meaning, a cleansing of those traces which nonetheless continue to underlie and serve as a reminder of both the impossibility of a singular origin and the infinite possibility for future meaning.

The transformed robes of Jesus, at the moment that they move beyond the possibilities of the fuller's "ground," become in themselves a kind of "groundless ground": they are severed from a recognizable past, even from the possession of the bleacher. Brighter than any bleacher could make them on the earth, they become the infinite possibility of yet-to-be-determined meaning. Innumerable points of reference and connections to previous meanings have been blanched and wrung from a fabric that now shines as though new and unmarked, its possibilities for subsequent meaning untainted.

The bleacher washes and rejuvenates the garment, but does not patch the tears.[21] The traces of what have been left behind continue to linger. The garment's seams are not strengthened in the process of carding. If anything, the stiff bristles (γνάφος) loosen stitches and weaken the overall integrity of the garment. The garment remains whole, only by virtue of the quality of its original construction. But its origins are no longer apparent; they remain only as scattered, fragmentary, and, at best, patchy. There are no doubt many tailors in this garment's secret histories, and it is made of many different types of cloth. Their identities have been erased, washed away with the colors that once differentiated them. They have now been covered over by a homogenous whiteness that merges them into an anonymous, amorphous singularity.

Even the source of the garment itself, the origin of the palimpsest, cannot be traced back to the tailors. Before the tailors were the weavers, the makers of linen, the spinners of wool and flax; before them, the shearers of the flock and the harvesters of the crop, and before that the shepherds grazing the sheep, the raisers of the pastures, and the sowers of the seed with which Jesus' teaching begins in Mark (4:1ff.). This secret narrative can be traced back even further, beyond the sowing

---

21. Compare Mark 2:21 where the patch (ῥάκος) is described as ἀγνάφος, which means "new" and "unshrunken," or in more specific terms "not fulled" or "carded" and therefore not yet treated by the fuller (γναφεύς).

of seeds to the image of the sun casting forth its flame (Derrida 1974b: 43–44).[22] In a sense, the robes become a new sun. As pure surface they are their own foundation. So what the image of the fuller reveals is that when origins are covered over, although traces remain, their disconnected obscurity creates a kind of new "origin," whereby meaning is opened to its fullest potential. The white robes of Jesus transfigured open up the field of meaning to its originary potentiality—origin, not as foundation or ground but as pure undifferentiated potential. At the same time, however, this "origin" is indelibly marked by a weave of traces.

## III. Reflections on/of Glory

What does one see when gazing onto the surface of the newly cleansed palimpsest? As noted in chap. 3, there is a classical Greek use of στίλβω which describes (metal) surfaces that achieve a dazzling brilliance when polished to a reflective sheen (Louw-Nida 1988: 14.47; Taylor 1952; Mann 1986). Although some commentators interpret the transfiguration as indicative of an inner change occurring in Jesus (Ziesler 1970; Evans 1991; Trites 1994), others, more in line with the classical definition, argue that the change is purely exterior in quality (Daniel 1976; Gundry 1993; Witherington 2001). The connection between a surface capable of reflecting light and a glory bestowed from without is seen to be supported both in grammatical terms, by means of the "divine passive" mentioned above, and also through the Markan emphasis on the glistening robes themselves (Hooker 1987; Gundry 1993). The superlative character of the light reflected by robes has led to a correspondingly full account of the glory seen to be at the source of this divine light. If we were to follow Ulansey's lead, for instance, it would appear that God's glory could not be more vividly revealed than at this moment of spectacular metamorphosis.[23] A number of other commentators have suggested links from the transformed robes of Jesus to the wondrous images of apocryphal Jewish and Hellenistic literature and Gnostic parallels (Gundry 1993; Taylor 1952; Mann 1986; Heil 2000; Witherington 2001). Ulansey makes the most of such possible connections, and his account of the "glory" reflected in this moment raises it to particularly lofty and sumptuous heights.[24] Ulansey's work on the transfiguration, work that appears to

---

22. Here, Derrida finds in this image of "solar sowing" and Aristotle's subsequent discussion in his *Poetics* an example of metaphor that has become thoroughly and untraceably unstuck from any origin (1974b: 50).

23. A more exaggerated interpretation than is the "norm" in current scholarship, but still appropriately representative of the general type of approach taken to these images (see discussion of Ulansey's position and his place within scholarship in chap. 3).

24. At one point, he strikes a comparison between the visual splendor of Jesus' garments and the garments of the prince, an extravagant account of which is given in *The Hymn of the Pearl*, a Gnostic hymn dating from late antiquity that devotes one quarter of its length to this description:

My bright embroidered robe, which was decorated with glorious colours;
With gold and with beryls,
And rubies and agates

drive the notion of glory to its grandest and most exquisite extreme, presents a notion of glory that not only reveals itself amidst scenes of high drama and awesome spectacle but also exhibits corresponding characteristics of visual splendor, awesome, almost violent, power, and earthly transcendence.

Ulansey interprets glory in terms of celestial splendor, where light and truth are found in the shimmer of luxuriously bejeweled robes. His discussion of *The Hymn of the Pearl* and the description of the prince's robes found therein lead him to focus on the mirrorlike qualities of these garments and the subsequent parallel with Jesus' transfigured robes. Ulansey concludes that true glory lies not in the splendor and dazzling opulence of these robes but in the believer's own transformed visage that can be seen reflected in their folds and contours. The metamorphosis of the robes results in their ability to reflect. They effectively become a mirror. Consequently, the robes become transparent while remaining opaque, sparkling with a dazzling brightness, yet possessing no light (or darkness) of their own; they allow a far-reaching and well-lit vision of infinite depths, and yet never is it possible to peer beneath their surface. When one probes their reflected depths, searching for the source of transfiguring glory, is an image of the self staring back all that one finds?

Ulansey suggests that the disciples see not simply an image of themselves but something of their own interiority reflected in Jesus' mirrorlike garments:

> By attributing extraordinary beauty and power to the "self" reflected in the mirror-garment, the **Hymn** [*of the Pearl*] ... functions as a call to introspection, a promise of tremendous gifts to be attained by looking within. The dazzling robes of the transfigured Jesus ... can be seen from the perspective revealed by the **Hymn** as a ... summons to an inwardness that results in radical transformation. (Ulansey 1996)

By suggesting this, Ulansey is making an interesting shift that takes one from the mundane exteriority of the garments to the profound interiority of the psyche. This shift is in line with his emphasis on the transfiguration as a moment of border crossing and is in keeping with his discussion of its place in Mark's greater scheme. These ideas of reflection and inner change and their connection with a vision of transformation are also seen to correspond with another closely related passage. The word μεταμορφόομαι is used only three other times in the New Testament, and

> And sardonyxes varied in colour,
> It also was made ready in its home on high,
> And with stones of adamant
> All its seams were fastened;
> And the image of the King of kings
> Was depicted in full all over it,
> And like the sapphire-stone also
> Were its manifold hues. (quoted in Ulansey 1996)

in other instances these themes are even more explicit.[25] In 2 Corinthians, Paul, developing the theology of Moses' epiphany on the mountain, writes, "And all of us, with unveiled faces, seeing the glory of the Lord as though reflected in a mirror, are being transformed into the same image from one degree of glory to another; for this comes from the Lord, the Spirit" (4:18). Paul also speaks of a mirrorlike confrontation and an internal encounter that is transformative for believers.

Aside from the broader structural and theological concerns that these examples raise, the notion of reflected faces, as representations of the disciples' interiority, pose their own challenge to issues of separation and bordering. At the transfiguration, distinctions between inside and outside become blurred. For example, the disciples stare into Jesus' transfigured, mirrorlike garments and see a vision of the outside reflected back, but an outside that is also their own interiority. There is another blurring between inside and outside associated with the question of whether it was a transfiguration of the body or a transfiguration of the clothes: was Jesus himself transfigured, or merely his robes? While this is a point of contention in contemporary scholarship on this passage, it is easy to read this passage from one perspective at the exclusion of the other. In fact, I have already assumed it was Jesus' garments that were transformed in some way and that this change was distinct from that of the body of Jesus.[26] That said, however, it is not so easy to settle on one reading to the total exclusion of the other: some ambiguity nonetheless remains. I am speaking of a certain ambiguity associated with the word ἱμάτια that makes me want to take a second look. Although this word can clearly refer to "robes" or "outer garments," and although this would seem perfectly reasonable given the witness of the disciples, it seems that this same word is used to refer to both exterior garments *and* clothing in general.[27] This means the distinction between outer garments, cloaks and robes, and "undergarments," carries with it its own sense of ambiguity. Jesus' garments were "transfigured," but the specifics remain ambiguous. Are we speaking of a change that occurred solely on the exterior, on the interior, or both?

What appears as a seemingly small point has much larger consequences when one considers how far this muddying of the distinction between inside and outside extends beyond the limits of this passage. As an overarching theme, it can, in fact, be seen to link this place in the narrative with other key moments of the Gospel.

---

25. The word μεταμορφόομαι (to be changed in form, be transformed) appears a total of four times in the New Testament: Mark 9:3; Matt 17:2; Rom 12:2; 2 Cor 3:18.

26. In addition to the "divine passive," the concentration on the garments alone, and the reflective associations of the word στίλβω, some commentators suggests that a previous reference to Jesus' face, a reference that would have tied this story more closely to the Sinai archetype as is the case with Matthew's and Luke's versions, was dropped by Mark (Schweizer 1970: 181; Taylor 1952: 389). This added evidence is then used to give even more weight to the interpretation that it was a transfiguration with respect to the garments Jesus wore rather than his body as such (Gundry 1996: 477).

27. Liddell-Scott 1940: 19777; cf. Matt 5:40; Mark 15:24.

In chap. 3 we saw how there is much textual imagery linking the transfiguration with the baptism and the crucifixion scenes: the voice of God, the presence of the spirit, the tearing of the heavens and the tearing of the veil, the presence of the cloud, the mention of Elijah, and so on. For some commentators, these shared motifs combine to form a triad of apocalyptic moments, moments that reveal Jesus' true identity while also anchoring Mark's Gospel story (Witherington 2001). But the reassurance of having this thematic structure, something that enables one so effectively to encompass the Markan text and provide a meaningful framework within which to contain the transfiguration scene, is disrupted by this same inside/outside ambiguity at a number of points.

In the baptismal scene, the heavens are torn open, and the voice of God is heard as the spirit descends. Nothing seems terribly problematic at first glance, although upon closer inspection it seems that the movement of the spirit can also be read as "stepping down *into* [εἰς] him" (Mark 1:10). Translations of this passage generally take the sense of "descending *on* him" (NRSV) or "descending *upon* him" (KJV). The use of εἰς is thought to be an exaggeration on the part of the evangelist that adds emphasis to this endowment of the spirit.[28] Once again, a small point, but what if this curious preposition's ambiguity were to be read so as to imply that the actual physical boundaries of Jesus were called into question? Or, alternatively, has some sort of physical transformation occurred with the entry of the Spirit into Jesus?

A further and more pertinent ambiguity occurs during the crucifixion scene. The centurion's statement at the foot of the cross has been read as part of the continuum that began with the voice from the heavens at the baptism and which was heard again at the transfiguration.[29] The centurion responds to the sight of Jesus "in this way breath[ing] his last," and he says, "Truly this man was God's son!" (Mark 15:39). This witnessing is accompanied by the previous references to Elijah (Mark 15:35 and 36) and the tearing of the temple veil (Mark 15:38). The ambiguity found here pertains to the question of which temple veil is being referred to: the temple veil covering the entrance to the temple itself or the temple veil concealing the Holy of Holies (Witherington 2001: 399–400).[30] Some have read this scene in historical terms and make the assumption that it is the outer curtain that is torn, because this would be the only one visible to the centurion at the time of his comment (Gundry 1993: 947). Others argue against this on theological grounds. From this perspective, the rending of the outer veil would not really open the way to

---

28. See Gundry 1996: 51.

29. At the baptism, the voice is heard only by Jesus; at the transfiguration, by three privileged disciples; but at the crucifixion, these words appear on the lips of the centurion, a nonbeliever, who is seen to be completing the movement toward the outward dissemination of Jesus' divine sonship, an identity that has been revealed for all people (Painter 1997: 207).

30. Adding to the difficulty in differentiating between the two curtains is the fact that they both share the same name: καταπέτασμα.

God, for God dwells beyond the *inner* veil (see Hooker 1991).[31] It would make sense in terms of the baptism-transfiguration-crucifixion tertiary structure that the outer veil be the one in question, if we are to believe reports that the outer veil depicted the heavens—and thus the heavens are torn once again with the tearing of the veil. However, we are given no further textual clues that this is the case (see Nineham 1963: 430). The Markan text, with its omission of any real description of the veil itself, leaves us without the means of dispelling this ambiguity.[32]

So within these three "anchoring points" (Witherington's term) of Mark's Gospel, the baptism, the crucifixion, and the transfiguration, we can find three moments of ambiguity in which the lines of the inside/outside distinction are blurred. It seems common practice for commentators to attempt to resolve these ambiguities, usually by arguing that they ought to be interpreted one way or the other, their decisions informed by their particular perspectives: historical, narrative, literary, linguistic, and so on. Rather than decide one way or another, however, what would the picture of God's glory look like if these ambiguous moments were left unresolved? In an attempt to provide an answer to this question, I would like to return to the body of Jesus, which I earlier displaced in favor of his robes.

## IV. Erased Face

In parallel accounts of the transfiguration story, there are references to a change in the brightness of Jesus' face in addition to his garments (Luke 9:29; Matt 17:2). In Luke's version, his description makes the merest mention of this,[33] but in Matthew, the evangelist goes so far as to describe Jesus' face as "shining like the sun" (Matt 17:2). Why this reference to the face is missing in Mark's account is even more curious, given the reference in Paul's second letter to the Corinthians (3:18), which shares the key word μεταμορφόομαι, which some believe influenced Mark's account (Johnson 1960; Nineham 1963).

---

31. There are many and various interpretations of the significance of the torn veil, and it is not necessary to go into them at this stage. For thirty-five different interpretations of veil rending, see Geddert 1989: 141–43.

32. It is interesting that at both these moments it is quite a ferocious spirit that descends. In the baptismal scene (1:10), the spirit descends from the torn heavens (εἶδεν σχιζομενους τοὺς οὐρανούς), "into" (εἰς) Jesus, and, as noted above, this preposition almost seems to indicate that the spirit entered him in a way that breached his bodily boundaries. Subsequent to this, the spirit drives Jesus out into the desert: "And the Spirit immediately drove (ἐκβάλλει) him into the wilderness" (Mark 1:12). At the crucifixion, Jesus dies after giving a loud cry and breathing his last (Mark 15:37). The word ἐξέπνευτεν ("he expired") is a cognate of πνεῦμα, and as such also carries the added associations of breath, spirit, and wind. Immediately following this loud cry (φωνὴν μεγάλην) marking the expiration (of the spirit), the temple curtain is torn (ἐσχίσθη) from top to bottom (Mark 15:38), and the beginning of a new political and cultural order is ushered in with the centurion's testimony (Mark 15:39; Witherington 2001: 401).

33. "And while he was praying, the appearance of his face changed" (Luke 9:29).

Commentators have explained this apparent omission in Mark in various ways. One way is to see it as a deliberate change that has been made by the evangelist for reasons of theological emphasis (Gundry 1993; Taylor 1952). By omitting this small detail, itself part of the much larger Sinai archetype,[34] Mark skillfully sidesteps the Sinai reference so that instead of referring to this exterior tradition, the emphasis remains within the scene and comes to rest on Jesus as the embodiment of the divine *shekinah* (see particularly McGuckin 1987: 63–69).

But by removing the face of Jesus, thereby severing the links to preexisting exterior references, the evangelist has actually made this trace stand out among the other traces scrawled over the palimpsest, the traces that constitute the warp and woof of Jesus' transfigured robes. By not being there, by being cut off from a sequence of references, this missing face becomes a trace that offers no certainty as to its existence, let alone its origins. Derrida speaks of this when he differentiates between the trace and the unerasable trace—the trace that is sure to be found—claiming that the assured "presence" of the latter means it remains steeped within metaphysics. Derrida comments on the distinction as follows:

> The trace is the erasure of selfhood, of one's own presence, and is constituted by the threat or anguish of its irremediable disappearance, of the disappearance of its disappearance. An unerasable trace is not a trace, it is a full presence, an immobile and incorruptible substance, a son of God, a sign of parousia and not a seed, that is, a mortal germ. (Derrida 1978d: 230)

The possibility of being erased is disorienting, and it detaches the trace from a trail of references that would otherwise provide an identity and ground from within the limits of metaphysics. But there is always the possibility of a trace losing its origins, the possibility of it being cut off from its history of meaning. This possibility of relinquishing a past, however, simultaneously ensures the possibility of acquiring new meaning and a new future. The missing face, a phantom visage that threatens to vanish without warning, is just such an erasable trace. As part of the body, this is a trace that is not discernible among the innumerable traces scrawled across the palimpsestlike garments. This is a ghost of a trace that will always elude the gaze of the disciples. Gazing into the shining robes, it is not Jesus' face that they see; it is their own, and they are unable to see beyond this.

The missing face of Jesus represents the limitations of meaning and the fragility of coherence. Staring into the robes, the disciples come face to face with the limitations of knowledge and its structures. At the same time, their encounter is haunted by a phantom visage, a spectral mask that allows them to see the inconsistencies and ambiguities, the gaps and fissures, while promising no "outside" to provide a secure foundation, no truth or sun or god that is not already a part of a system breaking down at its very core: the moment when the philosophical system

---

34. Exod 34:29ff. refers to the shining skin of Moses' face.

is called into question and one is confronted by its fundamental limitations, by meaninglessness and absence. The disciples do not bask in the light of Aristotle's sun. The fullness of the sun's presence is not given here; the disciples receive only a trace of its presence: the sun becomes a star. "As soon as we admit that in an analogical relation all the terms are already individually set in a metaphoric relation, the whole begins to function, no longer as a sun but as a star, the pinpoint source of 'truth,' of what is proper, remaining invisible, or swathed in night" (Derrida 1974b: 44-45). In other words, meaning functions not by being grounded on the singularity of the sun but rather as constellations, pinpricks of light made meaningful by the imaginary lines traced between them.

The absence of the shining face in Mark's account, combined with a glory bestowed from without and a concentration on garments alone, could lead to a reading where this metamorphosis has effectively brought about the absence of Jesus himself. What if this curious omission of the "face," a missing "sun" (cf. Matt 17:2) plants an absence that cannot be filled at the center of a scene seemingly dominated by presence? This prospect is intriguing in the light of Derrida's claim: "non presence and otherness are internal to presence" (Derrida 1973: 66). What are the implications of such a lack at the heart of the fully present vision? If the "face" shines like the sun, as Matthew suggests, then the absence of this same face can also be seen as an absence of the sun, and, in this case, the sun is missing from the heart of glory. It may seem strange not to find a sun to ground this vision of glory, a vision that is intimately associated with light. But does this merely mean that the "source" of this light is to be found elsewhere? Maybe this will prove to be the case. If we attempt to follow the traces of the sun, will we be in time to see its rising? Or alternatively, ought one concentrate on the traces that have become cut off from the sun, the pinpricks of light, the stars and the connections between them which in themselves become meaningful as heavenly constellations?

## V. *Cloud of Absence and Presence*

In v. 7 we read that "a cloud overshadowed them, and from the cloud there came a voice, 'This is my son, the beloved; listen to him.'" The cloud (νεφελή) that overshadows them comes with a number of intertexts. In the Hebrew Bible, a cloud is often a symbol of Yahweh's protection and presence.[35] Many commentators explain Mark's reference to the cloud in the same way (Rawlinson 1925; Taylor 1952; Schweizer 1970; McGuckin 1987; Gundry 1993). God's presence at this crucial moment validates (or grounds) the glory to which the disciples are witness. But once again a certain ambiguity can be associated with this image of the divine cloud. The tradition of the cloud in the Hebrew Bible is often accompanied by

---

35. See Exod 16:10; 19:9; 24:15-16; 33:1; 40:34-38; Num 9:15-22; 1 Kgs 8:10-11; Isa 4:5; 2 Macc 2:8.

divine light, but Mark's cloud differs from this tradition, a tradition that appears to be evident in the parallel versions of the transfiguration story. Notably, in Matthew's version, the cloud is described as "bright" (φωτεινός), a description which, like the shining face of Jesus, would appear to strengthen the connections to the Hebrew Bible's theophanic imagery: the divine *shekinah* of Yahweh is made known by the fullness of light emanating from the cloud.[36] This is not seen to be entirely the case in Mark's version. By comparison to Matthew's description of the cloud, along with similar descriptions from the Hebrew Bible, the light is once again missing from Mark's version.

At the same time, in the Hebrew Bible, when Yahweh does reveal himself, he is not always accompanied by awesome pyrotechnic displays of power. In 1 Kings 8, Yahweh's presence is seen to coincide with the *darkness* of the cloud. Solomon attests to this by saying, "The Lord has said that he would dwell in thick darkness" (1 Kgs 8:12), and later, in 1 Kings 19, Yahweh's presence appears to Elijah in "a sound of sheer silence" (19:12). Although Mark does not describe the cloud as the "bright" cloud of Matthew's account, this does not prevent a certain type of presence being found here all the same. It is entirely possible that the darkness of Mark's cloud corresponds to the cloud of the divine *shekinah* that filled the tent in 1 Kgs 8:11. This is what has in fact been done in the case of an apparent parallel at the crucifixion, where a cloud, of sorts, again, is featured: "When it was noon, darkness came over the whole land" (Mark 15:33). The noonday sun is blotted out by this darkness, which some see as signifying the absence of God. There is no voice of God accompanying this cloud, and God is seen to yield to the powers of sin and evil. Others read this moment in terms of God's abiding presence *filling* this moment of darkness: God has not abandoned his son, but remains with him throughout his suffering (cf. Amos 8:9; Witherington 2001: 397).[37]

The blotting out of the sun at the crucifixion scene recalls Derrida's discussion of the sun where he reveals it is only sometimes present to our senses. Unlike Aristotle's sun, which, for philosophy, never sets, Derrida's sun is intermittent and unreliable and as such fails to provide the secure ground for which philosophy yearns. Derrida also draws a link between the heliotrope and the divine in the work of Descartes. If one were to take both the sun and God as functioning in similar

---

36. Note especially Exod 24:15–16 where the glory of the lord is depicted like a "devouring fire" within a mountaintop cloud; similarly Exod 40:34–38, where "the cloud of the Lord was on the tabernacle by day, and the fire was in the cloud by night"; and again in Num 9:15–16: "On the day the tabernacle was set up, the cloud covered the tabernacle, the tent of the covenant; and from evening until morning it was over the tabernacle, having the appearance of fire by night."

37. In fact one commentator (Gundry) goes so far as to see God fully present in this moment, the darkness being just an indication that God has mercifully "dimmed the lights" so that those mocking and jeering as Jesus suffers no longer have him in clear view (1993: 947). In this case, even though Jesus cries in desolation, God is still seen to be an abiding presence that dwells as fully in darkness as in light.

ways, as grounding (transcendental) signifieds, then ambiguity once again surfaces. This time it is an ambiguity associated with presence and absence. The sun, signifying God's presence, is blotted out by darkness at the crucifixion scene as Jesus cries out in abandonment. Mark's cloud, also signifying God's presence, is curiously missing the light of presence that one would expect to find, given the tradition and parallels. In neither scene is God fully present nor fully absent. Like the missing face of Jesus, the glow of presence is strangely missing from the cloud. The cloud may function to indicate a presence, but it simultaneously signifies a mysterious absence.

The cloud of absence and presence proceeds to overshadow those on the mountaintop. Presumably, the cloud obscures the scene, if not throwing it into total darkness altogether, because we are not told how Elijah and Moses depart. A voice from the cloud declares Jesus the son and the beloved and exhorts the disciples to listen to him (v. 7). Finally, when the scene clears, Jesus is seen to be standing alone. The cloud of absence and presence serves to affirm Jesus' qualities as a palimpsest. Jesus is declared God's "son," and the palimpsest becomes the new "sun." The *fils* (threads) of Jesus' robes metamorphose into the *fils* (son). The groundless palimpsest replaces the transcendental signified as the divine cloud obscures the son/sun with its very ambiguity. The voice affirms this, but it is a voice that emerges from the obscurity of the cloud. The dark cloud could not be the source of reflected glory that we see in the transfigured robes, and thus the voice is essentially a voice with no body, a voice with no origin.

Tolbert argues that the voice undermines the whole scene up to this point:

> But in a passage where Jesus speaks not at all, where the emphasis is overwhelmingly on vision, the voice from the cloud incongruously commands, Hear him.... Being divinely required to listen to Jesus when he is not talking but glistening in the whitest of garments turns the whole episode on its head. It is not what it appears to be. The glorious vision of a transformed Jesus with Elijah and Moses that so impresses Peter is undercut by the words from heaven. (1989: 206)

Tolbert ties this ironic twist in with the broader unfolding of Jesus' message and Christological identity. In this irony one could also see a moment when one mode of presence, the clarity of vision, is displaced by another, the immediacy of the spoken word. Presence has been reasserted as "speech" over spectacle, but within this new mode of presence, there remains ambiguity and absence. Where Jesus glows but does not speak, the cloud speaks but does not glow. The cloud becomes an alternate but similarly corrupted origin. Taken together, the dark cloud and the bright robes further evoke the image of Derrida's conflicted sun: darkness and light, twin referents united in their ambiguity, intertwined in their unpredictability as a vision of presence that is at the same time steeped in absence and incongruity.

## Part 2. Peter's Terrifying Insight[38]

### *I. Keeping the* Mysterium Tremendum

In v. 6, Peter and the other disciples react to the scene with fear: "He did not know what to say, for they were terrified" (Mark 9:6). This reaction is seen to be an odd fit in this context, not being easily arrived at from the previous verse (Best 1986: 206–26). In making sense of this reaction, some see it as a remnant of a previous tradition that has been altered by Mark to suit his needs.[39] Others attribute the show of fear as a literary device that prevents the reader from overlooking Peter's "error" (Gundry 1993: 460). There are also a number of interpretations that link this show of fear to the spectacle of God's glory just revealed, a reaction perfectly in keeping with a tradition of encountering the *mysterium tremendum*.

Rudolf Otto investigated this tradition of the "fearful mystery" in *The Idea of the Holy*. Otto looked to the nonrational experience of the "numinous"—of essential "mystery." Otto recognized that *rational* accounts of religious experience tend to dominate, often to the extent of excluding all else (1926: 2). And yet, religious experience appears to go beyond what can be elucidated by rationalistic means: "Religion is not exclusively contained and exhaustively comprised in any series of 'rational' assertions..." (4). Otto sets out to examine these "outer" areas of religious experience that take one away from the rational. He focuses particularly on experiences of the "holy" or "sacred" (4). In these particular, nonrational "moments," one is afforded a primary and pure experience of the "numinous"—an experience not yet rationalized and prior to any schematization. This initial, raw experience is marked by a sense of the eerie, the uncanny, and the dreadful, and in this, its most primitive form, Otto uncovers what he describes as a kind of "daemonic dread": "This crudely naïve and primordial emotional disturbance, and the fantastic images to which it gives rise, are later overborne and ousted by more highly-developed forms of the numinous emotion, with all its mysteriously impelling power" (16).

For Otto, the history of Christianity charts the development of this raw and pure experience of the "numinous" as it becomes increasingly rationalized and is subjected to ever more complex and expansive systemization (1926: 80). But that daemonic, primitive encounter remains, even in the highest forms of the "holy," and is marked by "spasms and convulsions... the strangest excitements... intoxicated frenzy.... It may be the hushed, trembling, and speechless humility of the creature in the presence of... that which is a mystery inexpressible and above all creatures" (13).

---

38. An earlier version of part 2 was published in *Derrida's Bible: Reading a Page of Scripture with a Little Help from Derrida,* ed. Yvonne Sherwood (New York: Palgrave Macmillan, 2004).
39. A similar explanation was given for the "missing face" in the description of Jesus transfigured (see above in part 1).

In focusing on a specific feature of religious experience that escapes the dominant discourse of rationalism, Otto could be seen to be effecting, in his own way, a form of deconstructive reading. He is engaged in an investigation that uncovers repressed features, swept aside by an overlying rationalistic religious discourse. It is not surprising, therefore, to see Derrida taking an interest in Otto's ideas relating to the encounter with the *mysterium tremendum*.

In the *The Gift of Death*, Derrida takes up Otto's insights, while at the same time nuancing this encounter with the *mysterium tremendum* to suit his own purposes.[40] Like Otto, Derrida sees a daemonic seed at the heart of the *mysterium tremendum*, a mystery that he charts as having evolved from the daemonic or orgiastic through the Platonic to find itself now understood in terms of a thoroughly Christian mystery.[41] At the same time, however, Derrida notes (as does Otto) that the most primitive mystery remains hidden within the structure of this sublime Christian encounter with the "wholly other." As deeply buried as it may be, this kernel of the primordial continues to prevent the structure of ordered Christian responsibility from encompassing and owning the entire experience of "mystery." Just as Otto observed that there was something that eluded a rationalistic understanding of religious experience, so, too, Derrida sees something about this encounter with mystery that succeeds in eluding not merely rationalism, but language, thought, and indeed any "economy" that makes shared meaning possible.

Derrida draws from Heidegger's notion of a "being" standing face to face with the singularity of his or her own death: that un-substitutable moment that radically individuates and isolates on the most fundamental level. This confrontation with our own death is a moment that cannot be shared, and yet takes us beyond ourselves. It is also a moment when we do not encounter the "Other" so much as the "otherness" that is our own death—that which is simultaneously the most intimate

---

40. In investigating the experience of the *mysterium tremendum* in *The Gift of Death* (1995), Derrida looks particularly at the heretical writings of Jan Patocka and the question of responsibility, particularly with reference to Abraham's call to sacrifice Isaac in Genesis 22. Curiously, Derrida does not refer to Otto at all, although it seems likely that Otto has had an influence. Derrida takes a different trajectory to Otto, however, and does not end by repositing a metaphysical system. For instance, Otto may challenge rationalism, but his recourse to images of the sublime, to the "void" or to silence and awe to depict the "exterior" or "outside" of rationalism inevitably reposition him within the larger metaphysical system within which he is working. In some ways, Otto substitutes the "being" of God for a sense of absence which can be just as effective a transcendental signified. Consequently, Otto unconsciously represses that which is not only outside rationalism but any economy or system of meaning. For examples of Otto's use of these negatively expressed metaphysical images to posit the "outside" of rationalism, see Otto 1926: 62–73. Derrida attempts to get around this problem of substituting terms by, among other strategies, positing an "outside" that simultaneously remains on the inside of the system—the confrontation with the "otherness" of one's own death (see below for further discussion).

41. Derrida takes up this insight of Patocka: "Patocka speaks of 'incorporation' or 'repression': incorporation in the case of Platonism which retains within itself the orgiastic mystery it subordinates, subjects, and disciplines, but repression in the case of Christianity which retains the Platonic mystery" (1995: 8–9).

and individuating of all experiences. As otherness to what we are, death represents our annihilation and dispersal as beings. Death, however, represents more than just the destruction of the flesh; it is also the chaos of disorder, of engulfing meaninglessness, and of absolute opacity. Derrida speaks about this confrontation with the pure mystery of our own death as an encounter that is radically individuating and that insists on an authentic response. It is also a moment when one becomes aware of the gaze of the "other" which stares from behind its impenetrable secrecy and as such is a radical otherness, the contours of which cannot be known. It is this alarming confrontation with our own death, an encounter of intimate self-knowledge and simultaneously impenetrable mystery, that is identified by Derrida as "the frightening, terrifying mystery, the *mysterium tremendum*" (1995: 28). He observes, "I tremble at what exceeds my seeing and my knowing although it concerns the innermost parts of me, right down to my soul, down to the bone, as we say" (1995: 54).

When confronted with the mystery of our absolute singularity, our first reaction is to respond with fear and trembling. To attempt to communicate this moment would necessarily be to change it because "as soon as one speaks, as soon as one enters the medium of language, one loses that very singularity. Speaking relieves us, Kierkegaard notes, for it 'translates' into the general" (1995: 60).

Just as this experience eludes the grasp of language, it also resists containment within any other shared system of thought, collective agreement, or ethical consensus about what is "right." Such attempts only serve to abandon the individual in favor of the collective and thus abandon the "truth" of the experience: "Far from ensuring responsibility, the generality of ethics incites to irresponsibility. It impels me to speak, to reply, to account for something, and thus to dissolve my singularity in the medium of the concept" (1995: 61). Derrida demonstrates in his discussion of Abraham's near sacrifice of Isaac in Genesis 22 that the only authentic way to respond in the face of such mystery is to respond as an individual in a way that maintains individuality. This is to respond from outside of these systems and collective structures—in effect, not to respond at all, or to respond *irresponsibly*.

> In essence God says to Abraham: I can see right away [*à l'instant*] that you have understood what absolute duty towards the unique means, that it means responding where there is no reason to be asked for or to be given. Abraham is thus at the same time the most moral and the most immoral, the most responsible and the most irresponsible of men, absolutely irresponsible because he is absolutely responsible, absolutely irresponsible in the face of men and his family, and in the face of the ethical, because he responds absolutely to absolute duty, disinterestedly and without hoping for reward, without knowing why yet keeping it secret; answering to God and before God—a relationship which is without relation because God is absolutely transcendent, hidden, and secret. (1995: 72–73)

Derrida goes on to say that if the God of Abraham is completely "other"—"God" being "the figure or name of the wholly other" (1995: 77)—then this God is to be found in all experiences of the wholly other. It is from this point that Derrida introduces the phrase *tout autre est tout autre* (1995: 78). There are two important senses to this tautologous phrase: "In one case God is defined as infinitely other, as wholly other, every bit other. In the other case it is declared that every other one, each of the others, is God inasmuch as he or she is, *like* God, wholly other" (1995: 87).

In other words, "otherness" is "otherness" and does not differ in quality from one instance to another. Consequently, Derrida explains, because individuals are wholly other to each other—"each of us, everyone else, each other is infinitely other in its absolute singularity, inaccessible, solitary, transcendent, nonmanifest, originarily nonpresent to my *ego*" (1995: 78)—then this encounter with what is "wholly other" is also an everyday encounter and occurs in the midst of every human interaction. This encounter with the wholly other lies not just in the space between two people, however. The wholly other is encountered in what is essentially the *mystery* of our own impending death and annihilation. In this case, one engages with an otherness located not on an outside but rather in the interiority of one's own death—a moment that is also incapable of being shared.

By locating a disruptive and subversive heart within all structures of communal interaction, within every "ethical generality" (1995: 78), Derrida uncovers a fundamental aporia: the incommunicable and unknowable other that demands the irresponsible response and inhabits every encounter between every person—interactions that are at the same time governed by structures of generality. In more specific terms, the experience of confronting one's own death, when understood as a secret interiority, cannot be translated using the tools of a system that would allow its meaning to be shared. The process whereby such a secret is translated into a general economy can do nothing but change forever this sense of radical individualism. At the same time, this encounter with the secret mystery that is one's death could be seen, in itself, to be the condition that makes possible one's own sense of individuality or self, and thus facilitates participation in the general economy of meaning. So, in a tremendous paradox, the mystery becomes the condition that fundamentally threatens the cohesion of the self, while at the same time making this *experience* of selfhood possible.

The actual term *mysterium tremendum*, indeed, the very words themselves, are thoroughly informed by this aporia. There are two distinct levels of experience involved here. On one level, as a concept and as language, the term is used to allow this experience to be known and shared collectively. On another, however, the experience itself, as never anything but individual, always eludes the attempts to transcribe it within a shared economy of meaning. In other words, to "name" the encounter with the impenetrable mystery of death is like sharing a secret: "We share with Abraham what cannot be shared, a secret we know nothing about, neither him nor us. To share a secret is not to know or to reveal the secret, it is to share we know not what: nothing that can determined" (Derrida 1995: 80). To share this secret entails trying to provide a structure to, or include within a structure, that which undermines the very possibility of structure itself.

By means of this paradox, Derrida is suggesting that the subversive kernel of the orgiastic remains at work within the *mysterium tremendum*. The most vivid sign of this daemonic kernel is the initial reaction of fear and terror: "For it is a terror that brings us close to the absolute secret, a secret that we share without sharing it" (1995: 79). And fear and trembling are the most appropriate of responses because they are preverbal; they are responses that emerge prior to language as a system of meaning.

## II. Peter's "Error"

Although commentators attempt to account for the fear mentioned in Mark 9:6 in a variety of ways, it seems that it cannot be easily separated from the response Peter gives in the previous verse. There is much scholarly attention given to the possible reasons behind Peter's reaction in vv. 5 and 6. In fact, these verses have received far more attention by critics than has the actual description of Jesus transfigured in v. 3—the meaning of which appears to be quite self-evident by comparison. Traditional readings of Peter's reaction are remarkably uniform in that they quickly dismiss his response as erroneous (hence what has become known as Peter's "error"). It is as though commentators are saying that Peter, in his obtuseness, has missed the point—it seems that *that* much can be taken for granted—and we ought to concentrate on the real task here, which is to reflect on the reason (theological, rhetorical, or otherwise) for this erroneous statement (Gundry 1993: 72).

Peter's comments immediately follow the vision of Jesus transfigured and the appearance of Elijah and Moses, and his response can be seen to be threefold. First, Peter comments on the situation: "Then Peter answered (ἀποκριθαίς) Jesus, 'Rabbi, it is good (καλόν) for us to be here...'" (Mark 9:5). Second, Peter suggests the building of three tabernacles: "Let us make three dwellings (σκηνάς), one for you, one for Moses and one for Elijah" (Mark 9:5). Finally, Peter and the other disciples are revealed to have been dumbfounded and terrified throughout this scene: "He did not know what to answer (ἀποκριθῇ), for they were terrified (ἔκφοβοι)" (Mark 9:6). This *extreme* terror is mentioned in such a way that it informs and infuses the entire encounter.[42] Understood in this way, Peter's prior suggestion, as well as his statement about it being "good" that they are there, are

---

42. Verse 6 is a complex verse syntactically because of the two incidences of the word γάρ. Each instance of this word is seen to qualify what has come before, γάρ functioning as "a mark of cause or reason between events" (Louw-Nida 1988: 89.23). In the first case, the reason Peter said what he did was "because he really did not know what to say" and following on from this, the reason he did not know what to say was "because they were afraid."

both informed by and infused with this terror. Despite this, commentators seem more inclined to minimize the impact of the fear, seeing it, for instance, as a standard rhetorical technique used here, as in other places in Mark's Gospel, to signify a direct response to manifestations of deity, with little other narrative significance.[43] Consequently, apart from noting a certain incongruity, commentators tend to downplay the disparity between Peter's almost cheerful comment and his enigmatic suggestion, on the one side, and the pervasive feeling of extreme terror that informs this encounter, on the other.[44]

Whereas commentators have tended to downplay the terror of the disciples in this scene, the explanation for Peter's second comment on building three tents, by contrast, has provoked a considerable amount of scholarly debate.[45] In many ways, concern over the reason for Peter making his suggestion has overshadowed—or repressed—the other details of this small section, and scholars tend to diagnose the suggestion as a simple symptom of Peter's misunderstanding. The drive behind the numerous interpretations seems to be to reach some sort of fullness in Peter's response: to say that Peter attempts to "sum up" the situation, even if this attempt on Peter's part at full understanding then has to be labeled erroneous or incomplete. Peter's response can then be understood to contribute, rather than detract from, the glorious abundance that purportedly dominates this scene.

The various reasons given by commentators for Peter's suggestion are not unimportant, but maybe there is a different point to be made here: What if Peter's suggestion is necessarily deficient, and if the lack it intimates evokes something of what he and the other disciples have just experienced? Moreover, what if one were to reevaluate the apparent disparity between Peter's suggestion and his subsequent expression of fear alongside Derrida's reworking of the *mysterium tremendum* encounter?

In his suggestion, Peter posits the building of tabernacles or tents, genuine "dwelling places" for the more abstract "presences" that are before him. Perhaps if he constructs these tabernacles he will succeed in encapsulating these presences in such a way that it will be possible to communicate the significance of this encounter to others. The suggestion to build tents can be read as a way of "making a place" for these figures, and also, in a sense, making a place for Peter's interpretation (in v. 5 Peter has already given his own shape to the event by putting Moses before Elijah and rearranging the order in which these figures are introduced in v. 4). If a tent were built for each of these figures, it would be irrelevant

---

43. Other points in the Gospel where fear is expressed in this way are in 4:41; 5:15, 33; 9:32; 10:32; and 16:8. It is interesting to note, however, that the use of the word ἔκφοβοι is used only once in Mark; the slightly less fearful φοβέομαι is the word used in the other instances, even in the case of 16:8 where the women flee the empty tomb.

44. Gundry describes Peter's first comment as "happy" and thus strangely incongruent with the expression of terror that follows (Gundry 1993: 460).

45. See chap. 3.

whether or not what the disciples are encountering actually dwells within these places, because these presences would, in effect, be *replaced* by the tents themselves. The tabernacles would come to represent and in this way assure the "presence" of these heavenly figures and this encounter, long after the event the disciples are experiencing has ended.[46] In this way, the heavenly figures would be able to become part of and participate in a history and a faith in which their ongoing signification would proliferate. Indeed in current scholarship, this is exactly what can be seen to be the case when commentators attempt to account for the presence of Elijah and Moses. These two figures invite a richness of meaning and the search for their significance alone has resulted in a plethora of interpretations—both in relation to this text and beyond.

Peter and the other disciples are witnesses to the appearance of Elijah and Moses and to Jesus' dazzling metamorphosis, but they are also encountering something quite other in the midst of this vision. Their fearful reaction gives us a clue as to the quality of otherness they encounter. By wanting to build tents, Peter is suggesting that the meaning of this event be tied to a ground, inscribed onto the mountaintop. In time, the vision itself may vanish, but it nonetheless is able to endure by being translated, transformed into, and substituted by elements that are meaningful in a traditional, historical, and religious economy. These translated elements maintain their meaning not because they refer back to the vision, but because they are given significance by their new context. In this way, it is possible to share and maintain certain meanings, even if these meanings can no longer capture the encounter with otherness on the mountaintop.

One can't help wondering, however, how reliable a tent really is as a structure for preserving meaning. The term σκηνή may refer to the tabernacle, the dwelling place of the divine *shekinah*, but it simultaneously refers to a nomadic tent that, although a resilient sturdy structure subject to repeated use over the course of many years, is pitched only temporarily before being moved (see Louw-Nida 1988: 7.9). In this way, even though the tent itself endures through time, it is constantly being shifted and moved from "ground" to "ground." In other words, even if the tabernacles were set up for Moses, Elijah, and Jesus, as Peter suggests, their meaning and significance would not necessarily be fixed to the particularity of this foundation of meaning for very long. Like the warp and woof of Jesus' transformed garments, these "houses made of cloth" (Louw-Nida 1988: 7.9) bring together a network of interconnected references, and in so doing become part of the infinite fabric of meaning. This network of meaning functions regardless of the ground on which it is pitched, and as such these tents are not necessarily pegged down to any one particular foundational referent and will not necessarily remain within any one particular interpretive framework. There are no guarantees here for the preservation of a fixed set of meanings. The only guarantee is that these tents, if ever erected, will have the potential for meaning.

---

46. See the various interpretations of the tents in chap. 3, section V.

Peter's translation of the experience into an economy of shared meaning coincides with a demonstration that this event is simultaneously incommunicable. The difficulty in cleanly separating Peter's suggestions from a pervasive fearfulness, the sense that these elements are coalescing while remaining contradictory, is reminiscent of Derrida's conception of the *mysterium tremendum* and the identification of a certain paradox therein. In the encounter with the *mysterium tremendum*, one finds an experience that, while shared and in some sense "known" by a common humanity, is simultaneously an experience of which it is impossible to speak. It is an experience of impenetrable mystery that is radically individuating but which in turn makes possible an individual's participation in an economy of meaning. Each term of this contradictory relation, the shared and the incommunicable, depends upon and makes possible the other but without the possibility of resolution.

The aporetic relation, which forms the very heart of the *mysterium tremendum*, is mirrored in Peter's response to the transfiguration encounter. The symptoms Derrida describes as arising from that incommunicable encounter with one's own death compares well with the quality of fear that runs through the transfiguration. At the same time, the extent to which the experience of such an incommunicable interior mystery is shared is indicated by Peter's suggestion to build tabernacles. With the inclusion of Peter's enigmatic reaction, incompatibilities are brought together and form an impasse that resists resolution as the terms are linked tighter still. Moreover, in accordance with this Derridean reading and with specific reference to the empty tomb, Peter's fearful trembling can be read as a demonstration of a certain responsibility (precisely in his unresponsiveness) to the "truth" of this encounter. This is because, in his speechlessness, Peter stops short of attempting to articulate the inexpressible: the secret remains a secret. In Peter's enigmatic response and fear-filled reaction, these incompatibilities are brought together. They tell different stories: first, of an impenetrable opacity that shares the heart of a scene that seems to brim so vividly with presences; and, second, of the impossibility of a desire to share what cannot be shared.

In accounting for Peter's error, commentators pardon his obtuseness, claiming it is "right" for him to misunderstand the significance of this encounter. His true error lies in his failure to acknowledge that only after the path of suffering and death have been trod can one truly appreciate the fullest vision of God's saving glory. And so turning from here to the end of Mark's drama, one feels justified in cultivating a certain expectation that this most complete vision of glory will have arrived to be witnessed with fullest understanding. What one finds instead, however, much to the consternation of commentators, is that expectations are dashed, and one is left to deal with the darkness, absence, fear, and failure of an empty tomb.

### III. End of Fear

If we take 16:8 as the original ending, Mark essentially ends his story on a note of fear: "So they went out and fled from the tomb, for the terror and amazement had seized them and they said nothing to anyone, for they were afraid" (NRSV). More recent interpretation has attempted to come to terms with this jarring ending by incorporating it into Mark's broader theological message. Interpretations have ranged widely, with some seeing in this scene a final irony,[47] others finding a total appropriateness here in keeping with Mark's broader Gospel themes,[48] and still others finding here a reassuring parallel for an oppressed readership.[49] The fear of the women fleeing the tomb is itself tied in with these explanations, either as a sign that what they have just experienced within the empty tomb is "beyond" words,[50] or in association with the promise of 16:7.[51] Not finding satisfactory closure in the narrative itself, another common interpretation seeks to resolve this abruptness by placing the responsibility for closure with the reader.[52]

47. "Here is Mark's final irony. In the rest of the story, Jesus has commanded men and women to say nothing about the truth they have glimpsed, and they have frequently disobeyed. Now that the time has at last come to report what has happened, the women are silent!" (Hooker 1991: 387). Danove calls the ending a "tender trap" that impels the reader to take up where the story left off: "Thus in the final analysis the story indeed fails. However, the failure of the story reveals the true success of the plot through which the model of discipleship is generated and through which the real reader recognizes the basis for coherence of the story world. The failed story becomes a parable for the real reader" (1993: 221).

48. "Contrary to general opinion 'for they were afraid' is the phrase most appropriate to the conclusion of the Gospel" (Lane 1974: 592; see also Juel 1994: 110).

49. Mann explains that the evangelist "wrote a community overtaken by fear, a community which needed the reassurance that even those who were the first to hear of the vindication of Jesus in the Resurrection had been terrified" (1986: 670). And whether or not they were oppressed, this readership was at the very least "expectant" of the arrival of a future fullness: "Those who seek, in the resurrection, closure for the story of Jesus and a program for the mission of the church should turn to another Gospel. The significance of Mark 16:1-8 lies instead in its understanding of the basic life-stance of a Christian: expectancy" (Williamson 1983: 286).

50. "Their fearful silence eloquently enough proclaims the truth that the first word and the last word of the good news is not anything men and women can think or say or do... abrupt though it is, [Mark's ending] could hardly have declared more effectively that God's Word is mightier than man's words" (Anderson 1976: 358); "The threefold reaction of the women [terror, flight, speechlessness] dramatically represents the proper human response to the incredibly powerful activity of God" (Hare 1996: 226).

51. "Verse 8 alone—the failure of the women—is not the closure after all. It is vv. 7 and 8—the failure of the women juxtaposed with the promise that is able to overcome it" (Lincoln 1989: 295-96). Juel also finds a hopeful rather than disappointing open-endedness: "Jesus has promised an end. That end is not yet, but the story gives good reasons to remain hopeful even in the face of disappointment" (1994: 116). Hope also wins out for Garland, who sums up as follows: "The message of Jesus' resurrection transforms a hopeless end into an endless hope" (1996: 625).

52. "This unfinished story puts the ball in the reader's court. It puts us to work; we must decide how the story should come out" (Williamson 1983: 286); "The failed story becomes a parable for the real reader. However, unlike the parables of the story world which frequently conceal, this parable reveals (4:22) the manner in which the story of the real reader similarly may fail. The model of discipleship provides an integrative perspective through which the real reader can avoid the failure of his own story by fulfilling the requirements for complete action. Thus, the interpreter of the Gospel narrative becomes a project for the real reader" (Danove 1993: 221); "The ideal readers are called to finish the story, to

On a number of occasions, commentators make reference to the transfiguration passage when commenting on the scene at the empty tomb.[53] C. S. Mann is one such interpreter, and he draws strong links between the transfiguration and the empty tomb (1986: 356).[54] Mann comments on the similar wording ὧδε εἶναι in 9:5 and οὐκ ἔστιν ὧδε in 16:6 as well as the linking γάρ phrases: "He did not know what to say for they were terrified" (9:6); and "and they said nothing to anyone, for they were afraid" (16:8). Mann attributes these links to an effort on the evangelist's part to "emphasize that the Resurrection explains the occurrence on the mountain" (1986: 356). In other words, Mann is looking to reedit the missing "glory" back into this scene.[55]

In one of the more sustained reflections on the scene at the empty tomb, J. Lee Magness closely links the transfiguration story to Mark's suspended ending. In making sense of the ending, Magness treats it as a "suspended" ending, thus attributing intention and meaning: "We will focus on and attempt to delineate an ending which is not there, not the absent, not the omitted, not the lost ending, but the suspended ending of Mark" (1986: 14). Magness argues that the anticipation of Jesus' resurrection which fills the transfiguration scene is so graphic a foreshadowing that "the readers expect and in their expectation read a risen Jesus, appearing and present to his disciples, inaugurating a ministry of missionary proclamation among his fearful followers" (1986: 113). But even someone such as Magness, who purports to take the ending of Mark on its own terms, as incomplete and abrupt, does not deal with the absence at this endpoint as an actual

---

proclaim what happened. The readers alone have remained faithful to the last and are now left with the choice to flee with the women or to proclaim boldly in spite of fear and death" (Rhoads, Dewey, Michie 1999: 143; see also Hooker 1991: 392; Brooks 1991: 275; Keenan 1995: 397; Garland 1996: 618).

53. The connections made are chiefly between the young man wearing white in the tomb and Jesus' white robes in the transfiguration and the fear of the women at the tomb and the fear of the disciples on the mountain. See, for example, Lane 1974: 587–90; Hooker 1991: 384; Gundry 1993: 991. That said, the actual *emptiness* of the tomb is not seen to refer far beyond itself, let alone to the transfiguration scene. Lane comments, "The emptiness of the tomb itself provides no factual value in itself. It simply raises the question, What happened to the body?" (1974: 588).

54. Andrew T. Lincoln also links the empty tomb to the transfiguration, where the transfiguration stands as a prominent guarantee of the promise of glory despite the failure of the disciples (1989: 294; see also Danove 1996: 391–92). Garland writes, "They [the readers] know that the news has been proclaimed. Readers can deduce this from the text. How else could the report of the Transfiguration, witnessed only by Peter, James, and John, have been made known? Jesus commanded them not to tell what happened '*until [he] had risen from the dead*'" (1996: 622).

55. Mann actually makes the comment that the word for "glory" is characteristically used by Mark of the *parousia* (cf. 8:38; 10:37; 13:26). In this way, by finding the absence of this word problematic in this passage, Mann is in keeping with the majority of scholarship who also find the omission at least curious and thus demonstrate their desire to posit presence at this moment of glorious revelation. It is interesting that, when discussing Paul's instructions in Phil 2:12, Derrida notes that Paul's instructions are that the disciples seek salvation not in the presence (*parousia*) but rather the absence (*apousia*) of the master (1995: 56–57).

"absence."[56] Instead, by viewing 16:8 as a suspended ending, Magness, nevertheless, fills this passage in with "presences" and finds in this jarring moment a strong sense of narrative closure and resolution.

Magness achieves this by interpreting 16:8 as a synecdoche, this scene essentially stands in for an absent fullness that is filled in by the reader. The reader is called to find presence in the absence of the empty tomb and the rupture of 16:8. In light of this readerly obligation, it is not surprising to find Magness making claims that "absence is the most permanent form of presence" and "literary absences do not necessarily produce theological absences" (122). In the end, he can claim that in the face of absence and narrative rupture, "Mark" (with co-operation from the reader) is able nonetheless to achieve "bone fide narrative closure in its very openness" (119). By finding closure and presence in the empty tomb, Magness creates what is yet another alternative ending to Mark's Gospel, an ending that essentially covers over the absence with a fresh set of presences. And so, even when absence is more immediately evident than it is in the transfiguration scene, and it is hard to think of a place in Mark where it features as prominently as it does at the empty tomb, it is quickly substituted with a set of absent presences. Magness links the transfiguration scene and the empty tomb on the basis of presence (παρουσία), but what if a link were to be formed based instead upon the "absence" (ἀπουσία) found at the heart of both these scenes?

## IV. Tomb without End

On the basis of commentators' readings of the empty tomb, one would be forgiven for thinking that, despite the premature ending, the messages and meanings of Mark's Gospel nonetheless arrive and are present to the reader. In deftly finding these presences in a moment of gaping absence, the meaning of the Gospel is finally able to be drawn to a close. Just as the transfiguration is a scene that exceeds the parameters of presence and fullness, could it be that the empty tomb can be read for more than closure and resolution? Rather than finding closure of one sort or another in the empty tomb, is it possible to preserve a scandalous sense of incompleteness? What if this abrupt ending is read not in terms of a yearned-for fullness

---

56. Magness refers to "the insights of modern literary theory," which provide "eyes for openness and minds for the meaning" (1986: 113). Also pertinent here is Crossan's article "A Form for Absence: The Markan Creation of Gospel" (1978). Here Crossan argues that the absence of the empty tomb was a polemic opposing a theology of the abiding presence of the risen Jesus. To accept the absence in the empty tomb is to accept the absence of Jesus (cf. 14:7) until his future return in glory. To compensate for the difficulties of 16:8, Crossan lengthens the duration of the absence whereby it is filled not by a resurrection appearance as might be expected but by the coming of the "very imminent" parousia. "Death and resurrection mean, for Mark, death and departure, death and absence pending the parousia" (Crossan 1978: 51). Although arguing for a "message of non-message" and an abiding absence, Crossan nonetheless conjures an absence that becomes more present than presence: "Indeed, [absence] may well be the deepest and most permanent form of presence" (53).

but as a moment when previous expectations and possibilities are lost or abandoned? By ending the story mid-sentence and fleeing before the fullest vision of glory arrives, is it possible to read in Mark's Gospel a radical openness that subverts not only the closure of the story but the coherence of the self?

The women's reaction at the empty tomb, a reaction of fear and terror that causes them to flee, provides a clue that they, like the disciples in the transfiguration (9:6), are reacting to an encounter with the *mysterium tremendum*. They, too, tremble in the face of an annihilating death. In this encounter, they are confronted by a vision of absence that dwells at the heart of presence: the singularity of their own death that pervades their sense of life. On one level, the failure of both the male and female disciples to *communicate* "the meaning" of the death and resurrection of Jesus by either "getting it wrong" (as in the transfiguration, 9:5) or simply fleeing the scene (16:8) is indeed a failure and a scandal. Once at the empty tomb, there is no longer any possibility of communicating this goal to which the Gospel ostensibly moves. At the moment of this abrupt ending, the goal of seeing God's glory fulfilled in and through Jesus is possible only by locating new endings that lie beyond the scope of the Gospel story.

If we resist the urge to go "beyond" the empty tomb to less scandalous endings, resist moving from absence to presence, is tragedy our only alternative? In *The Post Card* (1987), Derrida challenges these criteria for success or failure as they relate to the transmission and destination of meanings. Derrida does this by taking a closer look at the structure of the postal service. Rather than marking the efficiency of a system where meaning reaches its intended destination, for Derrida, the flag flying above the mail box marks instead a point of closure. The arrival of the letter at its intended destination marks its end, its journey finished and its purpose fulfilled. But at the same time, the possibility of the letter not reaching its intended destination has also had to be considered in the development of the postal service, and indeed has been dealt with formally through the establishment of the "dead-letter office." The existence of the "dead-letter office" signifies for Derrida the formal acknowledgment that

> a letter can always not arrive at its destination. . . . Not that the letter never arrives at its destination, but it belongs to the structure of the letter to be capable, always, of not arriving. And without this threat . . . the circuit of the letter would not even have begun. But with this threat, the circuit can always not finish. (1987: 444)

The most vivid example of the fragmented letter that never arrives at its destination can be seen in the first half of *The Post Card*, a two-hundred-fifty-page love letter, a partially burnt preface to a book not yet written—a composition consisting of a series of fragments, the surviving remnants of a succession of post cards, open letters to an unnamed lover.[57] In addition to representing less than half the

---

57. Like *Glas* (1986a), *The Post Card* is written in two columns, and the text being accompanied by a picture of a post card depicting the cover of *Prognostica Socratis basilici*, a thirteenth-century

original correspondence, fragmentation can be seen in a number of other ways. The post cards themselves are incomplete: they are fragmentary in that lines are missing or have been destroyed, seemingly at random. In addition, even though they are dated, not even their order can be taken for granted.[58] In his preface, Derrida gives a hint as to the logic of what follows: "You might consider them, if you really wish to, as the remainders of a recently destroyed correspondence. Destroyed by fire or by that which figuratively takes its place, more certain of leaving nothing out of the reach of what I like to call the tongue of fire, not even the cinders if cinders there are" (1987: 3).

Derrida's deconstruction of the letter and his newly formulated postal metaphor pervades every section of *The Post Card*. He shifts the focus toward the implications of the dead-letter office, and what could easily have been considered a paradigm for the logocentric era, the letter, reveals the end of this same era: "The post is but a little message, fold (*pli*), or just as well. A relay in order to mark that there is never anything but relays" (1987: 191–92). In "Envois" Derrida is much of the time in the process of demonstrating this idea of relay without destination. In the later chapters he states more conventionally, and in more philosophical terms, this central motif as he plays with issues of destination, arrival, sending, death, and life within the psychoanalytic work of Freud and Lacan. In the chapter entitled "La facteur de la vérité," Derrida reads a Lacanian seminar dealing with Poe's story *The Purloined Letter*. Even the title of this chapter deserves comment in terms of the postal metaphor Derrida is constantly elaborating: the word *facteur,* from the chapter title "La facteur de la vérité," can mean both postman and factor and thus as the postman/factor of truth raises the question of the delivery of truth in psychoanalysis (1987: 413 n. 1). Questioning Lacan's search for psychoanalytic "truth" in this particular story, Derrida reveals instead that

> *The Purloined Letter* operates as a text which evades every assignable destination, and produces, or rather induces by deducing itself, this unassignableness at the precise moment when it narrates the arrival of a letter. It feigns meaning to say something, and letting one think that "a letter always arrives at its destination," authentic,

---

fortune-telling book discovered in the Bodleian library. This curious picture of Plato and Socrates folds out so as to sit parallel to the text. The postal principle links together many and various ideas during the course of *The Post Card* in complex interrelationships. Unpacking these ideas and their implications for biblical studies would be a mammoth task and beyond the scope of this thesis. For a summary of some of these key themes and a particular interest in the links between Derrida and the communications revolution, see Ulmer 1981. For another approach to the scene at the empty tomb from the perspective of *The Post Card*, see the chapter entitled "Jesus' Postcards" in Moore 1992: 38–47.

58. The lines that are missing are always indicated by fifty-four blank spaces, which make it unclear if what is missing is as little as a single comma or as much as numerous pages of text. Chronology is thrown into question on pages 204–7 where there are nine entries in which the date of composition is put as "between 9 and 19 July 1979." Moreover, some cards are grouped together under one month, such as "March 1979." In this case, the order of these entries is also called into question and the reader cannot necessarily take for granted the sequence that they are printed in "Envois."

intact, and undivided, at the moment when and in the place where the feint, written before the letter, by itself separates from itself. In order to take another jump to the side. (1987: 493)

Lacan attempts to find the "truth" of *The Purloined Letter*, and this represents to Derrida an effort to arrive at a conclusive destination. Derrida explains that "At the moment when the Seminar . . . finds the letter where it is found . . . the deciphering of the enigma is anchored in truth. The sense of the tale, the meaning of the purloined letter . . . is uncovered. The deciphering . . . uncovered via a meaning (the truth), as a hermeneutic process, itself arrives at its destination" (1987: 444). But what Derrida demonstrates is that "the meaning" of *The Purloined Letter* overflows any attempt to deduce its ultimate meaning. One way Derrida shows that the story in this way eludes the grasp of the seminar's attempt to pin down its "truth" is through its membership in a kind of trilogy which includes two other works by Poe: *The Murders in the Rue Morgue* and *The Mystery of Marie Roget*. The interconnections that exist between these stories exceed the approach taken by the seminar to the text and are omitted in their discussions. When redrawn, these interconnections essentially disrupt the interpretive framing which has been constructed by the seminar and which essentially makes their conclusions about "truth" possible (1987: 458–59).

The letter, which is no longer tied to a singular destination, maintains a "life" of unlimited potential destinations, a potentiality that is otherwise lost in the death of arrival. Derrida shows that, because the possibility of a "letter" not arriving is part of its structure, a "letter" is always from the beginning divided, torn into pieces, and never truly arrives in its entirety. And the opposite is exactly what Lacan's seminar sought to do with their analysis of Poe's *The Purloined Letter*. According to Derrida, it sought to suppress the fragmented quality of the letter, replacing it with an idealized solid and singular letter that would arrive in one piece: "If it were divisible, it could always be lost en route. To protect against this possible loss the statement about the 'materiality of the signifier,' that is, about the signifier's indivisible singularity, is constructed. *This 'materiality,' deduced from an indivisibility found nowhere, in fact corresponds to an idealization.* Only the identity of a letter resists destructive division" (1987: 464). There is always some element of the letter—and writing[59]—that fails to complete the journey, an element

---

59. In a translator's footnote, Allan Bass explains this connection between the letter and writing: "'*La structure* restante *de la lettre.* . . .' For Derrida, writing is always that which is an excess remainder, *un reste*. Further, in French, mail delivered to a post-office box is called *poste restante*, making the dead-letter office the ultimate *poste restante*, literally, 'remaining mail.' Thus, Derrida is saying that Lacan's notion that the nondelivered letter, *la lettre en souffrance*, always arrives at its destination overlooks the structural possibility that a letter can always *remain* in the dead-letter office, and that without this possibility of deviation and remaining—the entire postal system—there would be no delivery of letters to any address at all" (1987: 443 n. 17).

that essentially remains in the dead-letter office. This remainder always exceeds the frames of reference used to guide meaning to a destination. And so, the dead-letter office at once signals the disconnection of the letter from teleological determination—and the comfort of a meaningful beginning and end—and opens up a plurality of possible meanings.

At the empty tomb, the address has been given, and the reader expects the arrival of this particularly glorious "letter" at the site of the tomb, but what one finds instead is that the letter has gone astray and the tomb is empty. The letter is either lost, or, at the very least, the expected destination has been changed: "He is going ahead of you to Galilee" (16:7). The letter remains on its journey, still in the process of being sent; and at the end of the text the letter has not arrived, even though the promise of its arrival is maintained. In this way, the message of Mark, like the structure of the letter, will always be partially located in the dead-letter office. The message, like the letter, is fractured and will never fully arrive at any one destination.

Aligning the empty tomb with Derrida's post office metaphor becomes easier in the light of James Williams's discussion of Mark 16:1–8, which he entitles "Envoi." Williams doesn't mention Derrida or *The Post Card*, and seems to be referring instead to the message of the young man "sending" the disciples to Galilee. Although Williams sees the closure of Mark's story as the responsibility of the reader, he does hint at a deeper meaning to this passage which comes close to the postal metaphor:

> In a deeper sense . . . Jesus remains in control of the ball. No ending proposed by our decisions can contain him, any more than the tomb with its great stone could. Always he goes before us; always he beckons forward to a new appearance in the Galilee of the nations, in the Galilee of our daily lives. We never know where and when we shall see him; we only know we cannot escape him. (1985: 286)

A Derridean reading would reformulate this interpretation, substituting the "him" of Jesus with the confrontation with the *mysterium tremendum*. The coherent "him" that is Jesus is brought into question in the same way that the postal system is brought into question by the dead-letter office. In the transfiguration scene, despite the lights and spectacle, one finds that it is much more difficult to delineate a body for Jesus than it first appears, and at the empty tomb, another encounter with the *mysterium tremendum*, the body of Jesus, seems to be missing altogether.

The reaction of fear at the end of Mark's Gospel signals an awareness not just of the *mysterium tremendum*, but at the same time, of the effect of the dead-letter office. In the same way that the disciples see that which undermines their coherence in their confrontation with death and annihilation, the reaction of the women demonstrates their sudden awareness of the dead-letter office. Their expression of fear holds within it the awareness of that which undermines meaning without going beyond meaning and in this sense avoids mapping out an "exteriority." For, by delineating a "beyond," one would effectively be sketching the parameters of a "transcendental signified." This fear, however, avoids this by being read as an affirmation of the power and catalyzing effect of that which exceeds a metaphysics of presence—while not actually going "beyond" metaphysics at all.

This suggests ways of reading the disciples, the women, and their collective fear as more than symptoms of misunderstanding or foils to aid the arrival of the "letter." By *not* grasping the theological message as traditionally charted through the Gospel, but by displaying a profound terror instead, the disciples maintain their authenticity before that blank potentiality that remains undefined by a conclusion, by closure and end. By fleeing in fear and by not delivering their message, the women appreciate the absence of Jesus' body and the significance of his and their own "deaths." This encounter is both a fundamental threat to coherence and, at the same time, the condition that makes possible not only gospel theology in general but the structures of language and thought and identity.

In what seems a curious exchange, when the women enter the tomb, Jesus is gone, but in his place they find a "young man" (νεανίσκος). The white robes worn by a young man in the empty tomb have often been connected to those of Jesus at the transfiguration.[60] As on the mountain, the robes are described as brilliantly white (λευκός, 16:7). Paralleling the disciples, it is as though, upon entering the empty tomb, the women enter the cloud that descends at the transfiguration scene (9:7). It is as if they have found, in this cloud that blocks out the sun, the shining white robes, more splendid than ever. The body of Jesus is absent, however, and the young man explains that Jesus' presence is not to be found here; the time when they will see him is yet to come (16:7). But it is not at this future time in Galilee that Mark ends his story; it is with "ἐφοβοῦντο γάρ" (16:8).

Mark ends his Gospel with fear, and with "for" (γάρ). As a conjunction, γάρ is an intermediary word, a link, however remote or tenuous, between two ideas or events (Louw-Nida 1988: 89.23). As such, the Gospel "ends" with an intermediary term, with a sending, an *envoi*. By all accounts a curious ending, and yet if the dead-letter office reveals the postal service to be "a relay to mark there is never anything but relays" (Derrida 1987: 192), then the fear of ending with γάρ is as much about avoiding an end, about resisting arrival, as it is about ending with a nonending. Jesus' absent body will not "arrive," in the sense of being present at a destination. But, by the light of the transfiguration, the empty tomb is revealed to be an eternal *différance*, a resistance to meaning whereby the body of Jesus becomes but a trace. It emerges at various points (as robes worn by the young man in the tomb; in Galilee) but is never yet truly, fully present.

It is the interruption of this subverting potentiality that evokes the fear of the women, and they flee rather than take the risk that they, themselves, will provide

---

60. See Taylor 1952: 606; Gundry 1993: 991; Hooker 1991: 384; and Lane 1974: 587—all who make a link here with Jesus' robes at the transfiguration and, along with Anderson (1976: 355), comment on the presence of robes here as a general indication of the splendor of God's glory.

a destination for the body of Jesus. In their scandalous flight from the tomb, the women affirm the "truth" of their fear, whereby the realization takes one essentially beyond the voice, beyond meaning, and toward the disruption of the coherent self. To speak, to attempt to give voice to this "divine insight" which accompanied both these encounters, would be to limit and reduce it. The fear shared by the disciples and the women is a fear of an unspeakable, ungraspable subversion, an infinite lack in both subject and spectacle. The fear is a response to that which enables the emergence of any system of meaning while at the same time posing a fundamental threat to it. This is the impassable paradox that inhabits the *mysterium tremendum*, the rupturing vision of Jesus transfigured and the horror of a tomb without end.

## Conclusion

The question that I have attempted to answer in this chapter pertains to Mark's statement "And he was transfigured before them" (Mark 9:2). What can this mean in light of Derrida's thought? Did Jesus' transfiguration also involve a change on the disciples' part? Was the encounter something from without, or something from within? In the first part of this chapter, I likened the transfigured Jesus to the qualities of the palimpsest, a reinscribable surface without depth. Through a discussion of the sun, which was revealed to be inadequate as a ground to philosophy, Derrida's "truth" of metaphor, as grounded on an infinite series of interconnections, emerged. Points of ambiguity located in the distinctions between surface and depth, inside and outside, led to a discussion of the mirroring qualities of Jesus' dazzling robes. In turn, other ambiguities led to an investigation of a certain absence that was seen to inhabit the vision of glory vividly present in this scene. At the end of part 1, I concluded that there is a vision of glory in this scene that is based on fragmentation and ambiguity, grounded on the palimpsest, cut off from a past and opened toward a future. This vision of glory shares more with a notion of textuality, as Derrida conceives of it, than with other more pervasive conceptual, metaphysical terms.

In the second part of this chapter, I continued to develop the notion of glory as a fragmented, incoherent idea whose indeterminacy was essential to its potentiality. Through an investigation of Peter's error in light of Derrida's discussion of the *mysterium tremendum* and the postal metaphor, this picture of glory as undetermined deferral becomes an encounter with something both intimate and interior, while at the same time being radically and unknowably other. The empty tomb proved to be a contrasting facet of this encounter. Whereas the transfiguration is dominated by light and spectacle, the empty tomb baffles with absence and blighted hope. The two scenes come together to present a vision of glory that is fundamentally threatening, while at the same time being vitally life giving and brimming with pure potential for further meaning and creativity. In this paradoxical notion of glory, the transfiguration scene can be reread and the metaphysical idea of glory reimagined.

Although Derridean theory leads one away from many of the conclusions of contemporary biblical criticism on the transfiguration, in the end, this reading has still maintained some basic traditional parameters. For instance, I still assume that God's glory is being revealed in some way in this passage. I am also adopting notions of structure and coherence, which although influenced by Derridean ideas of "play," nevertheless frame my reading of this passage and its place within Mark's broader work. There are also the inevitable blind spots and repressed elements to consider, whereby certain images have been omitted or pushed to the margins. However, it has not been my intention to offer an exhaustive and "full" account of this passage, accounting for and incorporating every detail into an interpretive whole. This reading has differed from other readings of the Markan transfiguration scene in that I have been interested in exploring and teasing out certain elements in the text, as well as in the textual commentaries, that will allow for a different conception of glory to emerge: a conception informed by the encounter with "otherness." This exploration has led me to reread in what can be described as a distinctly allegorical style, although allegory of a philosophical rather than traditionally theological character. Such an approach can be seen as one implication of following Derrida's lead, and more will be said about allegory in the next chapter.

In the next chapter, I intend to explore a number of implications arising from a rereading that sets about reconceiving the glory of the transfiguration in a literary mode. To do this I will be taking the notion of transfiguration beyond the Markan scene and beyond Derrida in order to develop further the more literary sense of the term. During the course of this exploration, the work of Maurice Blanchot will be introduced, along with poetry by Edward Blodgett and Jacques Brault. Subsequently, I will look to the intersection between literary theory and theology and tease out the impact of such a meeting for the work of biblical scholarship.

## Chapter 5

## NEW FIGURATIONS: IMPLICATIONS AND FUTURE DIRECTIONS

### *Introduction*

In the last chapter I reread the Markan transfiguration story from the perspective of Derridean theory. Though it was clear (from my review of the scholarship in chap. 3) that there exists a tradition of reading this story from a perspective favoring metaphysics of presence, I chose instead to reread the transfiguration story in a way that favored incongruity, absence, and lacking. These neglected elements, when read alongside Derridean ideas, resulted in an unconventional, alternative reading of this story, one that has led to a very different conception of what is revealed in this encounter. In this final chapter, I will attempt to sketch briefly some implications that such a rereading brings as well as indicate where a continuation of this project might go.

I began the previous chapter with two questions: What does the transfiguration mean? What is revealed in this encounter? I share these questions with contemporary approaches in biblical studies to the transfiguration story, but in my attempt to answer them, Derridean theory has provided an alternative perspective. I will consider further the implications of engaging with these questions from a literary-critical perspective. Moreover, I will extend the field of view, so as to include something of literary theory beyond Derrida, as well as literature that goes beyond the biblical canon. The purpose here is to locate the transfiguration beyond the Markan text, beyond the biblical corpus, and beyond Derrida in order to explore further this notion of "otherness." Continuing on a literary trajectory, I will look to literary theorist Maurice Blanchot, who finds a particular type of transfiguring moment within poetic discourse. After briefly elucidating his notion of metamorphosis as a particularly "sacred" moment, I will turn to a poem that to some extent demonstrates the type of literary encounter with otherness of which Blanchot speaks. This poem is connected to the transfiguration by name and by theme, although the type of transfiguration depicted is not necessarily consonant with what would be expected from a traditional reading of the Markan vision. Finally, I turn to questions and issues more theological in nature and consider how these might accompany a distinctly literary sense of the "sacred" and a corresponding sense of "transfiguration" when placed alongside the Markan text. All in all, the original question of what is revealed in the transfiguration story is shown to have literary, religious, and theological responses.

The mode of my rereading of the transfiguration story in the last chapter could be described in allegorical terms and so, having dealt with something of the peculiarities of poetic language, I spend some time exploring the appropriateness of "allegoresis." Allegory, understood in a certain way, becomes a way of dealing with the ambiguous and undecidable character of poetic language. Much of Derrida's and Blanchot's readings of sacred texts takes the form of allegoresis. Following their example, this mode of reading reads for language rather than for God, and in such a way that it preserves *différance* and opens toward an encounter with a literary notion of the "sacred."

What complications accompany a literary approach to a sacred text and what is the relationship between literary theory and theological discourse? In gauging the ramifications of this rather complex issue, I will look to the work of poet and literary critic Kevin Hart. When Hart's work questions the relationship between theological discourse and the literary-theoretical approach, it leads not only from the poetic text back to the biblical text but also from wider considerations of literary theory back to Derrida. The question that ends this chapter stems from the terms of this relationship between theology and literary theory: If the literary-theoretical approach I have utilized is indeed open to theological development, what would this vision look like? How different would it be from the conception of glory that is seen to emerge from traditional approaches of biblical studies to this text?

A response to these questions can be found in Richard Kearney's *The God Who May Be*. In this book, Kearney uses the broader transfiguration tradition as one source for his hermeneutic reconstruction of a God who stands apart from "being." I look particularly at the way this "traditional" version of the transfiguration story shapes Kearney's reading and influences the extent to which he arrives at a postmetaphysical conception of the divine. Finally, this chapter returns to Hart, who, in conversation with George Aichele, addresses the limitations and transformations of the biblical canon in the process of theological inquiry.

Admittedly this trajectory promises to hurtle past complex and well-documented issues, and I should say from the outset that I will not be able to deal with these at great length or in great depth. For instance, both the first and second parts of this chapter introduce major issues (e.g., poetics, Blanchot's thoughts on literature and death, the question of theology in sacred and secular approaches to texts, the adoption of Derridean theory within the fields of theology and hermeneutics). My intention here is to indicate the beginnings and the trajectory for further work. It will be enough to open up certain consequences of the rereading begun in the previous chapter to broader textual and theoretical vistas.

## Part 1. Transfiguring Transfiguration

For Blanchot, the poet is the speaker of the "sacred." He explains:

> The Sacred is the day: not the day as it contrasts with the night, or the light as it shines from above. . . . It is the day, but anterior to the day, and always anterior to itself; it is a before-day, a clarity before clarity to which we are closest when we grasp the dawning, the distance infinitely remote from the daybreak, which is also what is most intimate to us, more interior than all interiority. (Blanchot 1995: 121)

Blanchot speaks here of the paradox of experiencing that which cannot be experienced, a "before" experience. It is a moment that lies beyond the bounds of comprehension, before the dawning light of reason illuminates it and renders it intelligible. It is an "experience" that precedes any mode of comprehension or structure of understanding.

For Blanchot, this encounter with the "sacred" is mediated through literary language, particularly by means of poetic discourse. Poetry marks the emergence within language of a certain opacity whereby language exhibits the qualities of an indecipherable object more than those of an intelligible medium of clarity.[1]

> My hope lies in the materiality of language, in the fact that words are things, too, are a kind of nature. . . . A name ceases to be the ephemeral passing of nonexistence and becomes a concrete ball, a solid mass of existence; language, abandoning the sense, the meaning which was all it wanted to be, tries to become senseless. Everything physical takes precedence: rhythm, weight, mass, shape, and then the paper on which one writes, the trail of ink, the book. (Blanchot 1995: 327)

This is the moment when one experiences the impossibility of meaning. It is this point that comprehensibility is exceeded and one encounters that which cannot be known: the "sacred." At this sacred moment, one is confronted with an unbreachable impasse where meaning cannot be determined and language stands only for itself. The word no longer gestures toward a meaning; it no longer functions as a transparent mediator; it exists only as an indecipherability positioned always beyond any such utility.

In exploring this sense of the sacred in poetic language, Blanchot expresses an interest in the poems of Czech poet R. M. Rilke. Although a poet of the modern era, Rilke's poetry shared much with the symbolist movement of late nineteenth-

---

1. Blanchot's work on Rilke is linked to his wider notions of otherness and its associations with literature and death, notions he has developed at length over a career spanning more than sixty years. It is not my intention to account for these complex and enigmatic ideas at this point. Although elements of Blanchot's thought will be introduced, they must remain undeveloped at this point because I wish to limit my interest in Blanchot to his reading of Rilke and specifically the notion of transformation and transfiguration which will be briefly outlined below.

century Romanticism. As such he sought to express something of the dark and mysterious inner life through the power of language. To this end, Rilke saw the poet occupying a very specific and privileged cultural role. Blanchot appears to agree with these sentiments and reads the work of Rilke, along with Mallarmé, Kafka, Hölderlein, and others, as exemplars of this particular sacred quality of poetic language.

Rilke chooses his own language to speak about these abysslike depths and shrouded mysteries, but although their terminology differs, Rilke's "invisible" and Blanchot's "sacred" appear to share much. Blanchot goes on to explore the connection Rilke makes between the "invisible" and a notion of "true death." Like the "invisible," and the "sacred," "true death" cannot be known. In the same sense that the sacred is a radical exteriority, always eluding the structures of meaning, true death gleans no meaning from the dichotomy between life and death. Just as the sacred is encountered in poetic language when one strays from the bounds of intelligibility, Rilke's true death represents a point that goes beyond one's own self-knowledge and self-conception. Blanchot is interested in the ability of Rilke's poetry to engage with this sense of the invisible as well as with a sense of one's own true death, but engaging in such a way that one avoids investing them with "visibility" or with "life."

Blanchot finds that Rilke's poetic dealings with notions of true death and the invisible are somewhat different in character when compared with other symbolist poets who deal with notions of otherness and negativity. Blanchot draws a particular comparison between Rilke and Mallarmé (1982: 158–59). Although he uses Mallarmé's notions of poetic language to develop other dimensions of his thought, Blanchot notes that, by comparison to Rilke, Mallarmé sees the moment of absence, the moment of pure negation, as a moment of clarity. For Mallarmé, the moment of negation is a moment of purity when, for an instant, everything falls back into nothingness. At this moment, the total absence becomes a kind of pure presence: when everything disappears, disappearance shines like the sun.[2] In other words, negation for Mallarmé is so intense that its very emptiness evokes a certain form and feeling.

This giving of form to nothingness is at odds with Rilke's approach. Rilke avoids the distinctions between presence and absence by linking the invisible with a sense of true death. In this way he shows how a radical exteriority is simultaneously a radical interiority. In exploring this melding of the inside and the outside, Blanchot speaks first of the poetic process. The poet who begins to write encounters this possibility of the sacred and is confronted by what Blanchot calls an "essential solitude." Here, he is describing a sense of isolation that is encountered through the experience of writing in the poetic mode: "To write is to withdraw language from the world that declares itself, the clear light of day that develops

---

2. "This is pure clarity apparent, the unique point where light is darkness shining, and it is day by night" (Blanchot 1982: 158–59).

through tasks undertaken through action and time" (1982: 26). This is not the same as the poet withdrawing to a romanticized "place" from which to write. Instead, the unintelligible side of literature, the sacredness of poetic language, is found to be always external to all categories that would render it meaningful. The poet is left exposed to a radical exteriority. In order to be faithful to this exteriority, the poet must respond, but with care. This exteriority is not simply an outside to a corresponding inside, but a sense of being beyond such dichotomies—but "beyond" in such a way that one avoids extending the bounds of meaning so as to create yet another option. Encountering this "space" of literature, one encounters a gap, an elision with no dimensions and no duration. It is at this impossible point of essential solitude (essential because it cannot be engaged with in any way and so is necessarily isolated) that the poet finds that all subjectivity and objectivity have melted away; only formless existence remains. Inside and outside, exterior and interior, in fact no categories of meaning are of any use at this point, for the possibility of understanding must be relinquished in order to be "true" to the encounter. When confronting the sacred in the essential solitude of poetic language, the poet is left without the comfort of meaning, the orientation of time or place and without the refuge of subjectivity.

Blanchot observes how Rilke, as a poet, responds to just such a sacred encounter. First, he notes Rilke's commitment toward this encounter. Rilke claims that poets are "the bees of the invisible": "We are the bees of the invisible. We ardently suck the honey of the invisible in order to accumulate it in the great golden hive of the Invisible" (Blanchot 1982: 140). In this statement, Rilke allocates to the poet the role of cultural seer, a gifted person equipped with the linguistic and creative skills with which to plumb these depths of existence and express the profound and ever-shrouded mysteries found therein. He looks toward an invisible space longed for outside of ourselves and finds that this is something that is at the same time most intimate to us—our personal confrontation with our own true death. That said, and in contrast to Mallarmé, he avoids delineating the character of this personal true death. Rilke looks to the point where within oneself, one belongs to the outside. This is the point where true death and invisibility meet and as such, the point where one is no longer oneself. He understands that to face true death one must jeopardize oneself entirely and, in the end, perish. In seeking true death, one is, in effect, forced to die outside of death. In other words, the search for real death inevitably leads away from what we make of death and away from what we know of ourselves.

Blanchot goes on to explore the limitations that make Rilke's encounter with the invisible impossible to live. He notes that Rilke sees a conflict between the self-awareness necessary for consciousness and the absolute openness of nature. The gaze of the conscious subject allows one to create meaning through the use of representation, but the particularity of representation as a face-to-face encounter (i.e., the fact that it focuses our attention onto particular things and thus at the same time away from other things) limits one's ability to engage with the absolute totality that is totally other: "When we look in front of us, we do not see what is behind. When we are here, it is on the condition that we renounce elsewhere. The limit restrains us, contains us, thrusts us back toward what we are, turns us back toward ourselves, away from the other, makes of us averted beings" (1982: 133–34). The condition of consciousness, the only way one can be self-aware, is from within this face-to-face relation to representation: "Such is the human condition: to be able to relate only to things that turn us away from other things and, graver still, to be present to ourselves in everything and in this presence not to meet anything except head-on, separate from it by this vis-à-vis and separate from ourselves by this interposition of ourselves" (1982: 135).

We gaze out into the world and are limited by a field of view. We may gaze inward, but even there we are confronted by limitations. We see not our depths but the various representations of these depths. What we do find is that the inside mirrors the outside. The poetic search for the unlimited openness within the subject is simultaneously the search for the vastness of nature which always exceeds representation: "If the poet goes further and further inward, it is not in order to emerge in God, but in order to emerge outside and to be faithful to the earth, to the plenitude and the superabundance of earthly existence when it springs forth outside all limits, in its excessive force that surpasses all calculation" (1982: 138).

The search for an "outside" to human experience and the effort to bring the fruits of this search to visibility represent for Blanchot the impossible quest.[3] But rather than abandoning all that can be known and languishing in a despairing desire for the impossible, Blanchot reformulates the quest as one of becoming as fully conscious as possible of our existence.

> Man is linked to things, he is in the midst of them and if he renounces his realizing and representing activity, if he apparently withdraws into himself, it is not in order to dismiss everything which isn't he, the humble and outworn realities, but rather to take these with him, to make them participate in his interiorisation where they lose their use value, their falsified nature, and lose also their narrow boundaries in order to penetrate into their true profundity. Thus does this conversion appear as an immense task of transmutation, in which things, all things, are transformed and interiorised by becoming interior in us and by becoming interior to themselves. This transformation of the visible into the invisible and the invisible always more invisible takes place where the fact of being unrevealed does not express a simple privation but access to the other side which is not turned toward us nor do we shed light upon it. (1982: 140)

Bringing the sacred into the field of representation may well be an impossibility for Blanchot, but it is also far from the point. What is deemed more important

---

3. Blanchot continues on this theoretical trajectory with his rereading of the Orpheus myth and Orpheus's hopeless quest to bring Eurydice, in the fullness of her death, back into the light of day (1982: 171ff.).

is the transforming, transfiguring process whereby representations of "things" are internalized and, by becoming disconnected from their exterior referent, are made to encompass a far greater range of potential possibilities. For Blanchot, this process of internalization is the process through which ordinary language becomes poetry. This is a distinctly literary notion of transfiguration. Poetry and literature are forms of language within which one can recognize these qualities of the sacred to which we are denied access. In the sense of creative multivalence and linguistic density, in going beyond the utility of the everyday and in this way creating a space for the inaccessible, for essential solitude, poetic language is language transfigured. "In the world things are transformed into objects in order to be grasped, utilized, made more certain in the distant rigor of their limits and the affirmation of a homogenous and divisible space. But in imaginary space things are transformed into that which cannot be grasped" (1982: 141).

In this transfiguration, meaning dies, but in its death, language continues to live. The poem accrues a density and solidity so that in the words it uses, meaning ceases to be thin and transparent, its meaning readily apparent. The poem is flooded, crammed, and covered with meanings, and as such words become disconnected from everyday references and cease to function as simple mediators. This superabundance makes poetic language overly meaning*ful*. However, by always exceeding the conditions of comprehensibility, the very limitations of the face-to-face relation, poetic language also becomes meaning*less*. Blanchot calls this meaningless and obscure state of language that underlies any text the "work" buried in the book. It is this space of densest meaninglessness that Blanchot speaks of as being transfiguring:

> In a poem, one of his last, Rilke says that interior space "translates things." It makes them pass from one language to another, from the foreign, exterior of language into a language which is altogether interior and which is even the interior of language, where language names in silence and by silence, and makes of the name a silent reality. "*Space (which) exceeds us and translates things*" is thus the transfigurer, the translator par excellence. (1982: 141; *his emphasis*)

The essential solitude of the poem mirrors the same quality of solitude in the self. What is revealed here is that our own true death is the part of ourselves that lies outside our self-knowledge and, as such, is only manifest as a dispersal of consciousness and a dissolving of subjectivity. To encounter this sacredness, this invisibility, is immediately to lose oneself completely because it is never possible to actually "live" the encounter. Yet to take this risk and abandon all that is known, to look to the opacity of language, to delve into the death of representation is to be involved in a transfiguring movement. According to Blanchot, this is the privilege of consciousness and the task of the poet. It is the poet's role to return the word to its origin, to its invisibility. And so we return to Rilke's bees, which "ardently suck the honey of the visible in order to accumulate it in the great golden hive of the

Invisible" (Blanchot 1982: 140, quoted above). The poet busily gathers words and images from the field of representation only to transfigure them, to effect a metamorphosis within the essential solitude of the poem. "And our vocation, to establish things and ourselves in this space, is, not to disappear, but to perpetuate: to save things, yet, to make them invisible, but in order that they be reborn in their invisibility" (1982: 145).

Blanchot sees in Rilke a response to the sacred that effects a type of transfiguration. Blanchot is not delineating a kind of transfiguration that would resemble those proposed by the biblical critics discussed in chap. 2. In a distinctly antimetaphysical conception, Blanchot's formulation challenges distinctions of inside and outside, of presence and absence, dichotomies that dissolve as the poetic word is translated toward its original meaninglessness.

In order to explore further Blanchot's regard for the transfiguring qualities of poetic language, I will now turn to an example. In the poem I have selected, I will look in particular to two dimensions of Blanchot's work. First, I will look to this sense of the sacred, the experience beyond experience that Blanchot finds within poetic language. Second, I will explore the response to such an encounter—the fusion of interior with exterior, of nature with subjectivity, the transfiguring consequences of such a sacred moment.

The poem selected has an oblique connection to both the transfiguration story and to the notion of transfiguration as a kind of transformational moment. I am going to read this poem as a type of allegory of the Markan transfiguration story and, in doing so, follow the terms of Blanchot's discussion of the sacred encounter. I will be looking for that impossible experience that belies a reading of the transfiguration spectacle as a miraculous vision of fullness. Along the way I will also be revisiting certain elements of my Derridean rereading from the previous chapter.

Entitled *Transfiguration* (1998), the poem is a collaborative effort between E. D. Blodgett and fellow Canadian poet Jacques Brault. The sense of "transfiguration" here is of the movement of images carried from one poet to the other and back again, a *trans-figura*. Of particular interest is how the themes to emerge from this *trans-figuring* collaboration help one edge closer toward the sacred, an encounter with the impossible moment of profound invisibility.

## Part 2. Poetic Comment

### 1. Transfiguration: The One-Legged Pas de Deux

Blodgett and Brault's *Transfiguration* is a collaborative composition loosely based on the form of the Japanese *renga*. Despite the title, there is no direct biblical allusion, and, as I mentioned above, the title appears to relate more to the *trans-figuring* movement of images carried from one poet to the other and back again. Traditionally, the composition of a *renga* involves the collaborative creation of a number of stanzas. Lines of prose are penned by the first poet, and then a response to these lines is given by the second poet. Each stanza generally has a theme—traditionally this theme is the seasons, a convention that appears to have been upheld in Blodgett and Brault's version. The final product encompasses a series of scenes linked by a progression of words and images but without plot or narrative. Although highly structured, it is difficult, if not impossible, to determine all the conventions Blodgett and Brault have used as guiding principles in the composition of *Transfiguration*. All we do know is that no single predominating rule was followed. Brault comments to this effect in his *liminaire*: "We didn't know where we were going and we didn't follow one pre-established rule."[4] Blodgett likewise confesses in his prefatory note that the process has resulted in the poem taking on a life of its own, neither poet capable of completely determining its course nor its contours (1998: 8).

*Transfiguration* is written in two languages, French and English. Each poet has been translated by the other, a process creating a poem that exists not only between two poets but somewhere between their two languages. Commenting on the process of composition, Blodgett explains in his prefatory note that the *renga* that follows is like a poem invented for one-legged dancers: "As one of us would leap into the air, the leap was made in the faith that the other would complete the leap. Both depend on the other for their *pas de deux* to be completed" (1998: 8).

As each poet writes a letter to the other and each responds in turn, the correspondence is in some ways reminiscent in its form of Derrida's prefatory "love letter" from *The Post Card* (1987).[5] Although they may not be lovers in the sense that Derrida portrays, they are indeed lovers of the dance, the one-legged dance, where each contributes his own limping step that, when combined, becomes an elegant pas de deux. In *The Post Card*, Derrida reads a double sense into the French term *pas*. He brings out both the sense of *pas* as a "step" and also as the most common word for negation. He thus illustrates, with particular reference to Freud's work, a step that goes nowhere.[6] In terms of Blodgett and Brault's poetic *pas de deux*, on the one hand there is a sense of a dance step meant for two, but at the same time a sense of being "not of two." In other words, there is something that is quite apart from the one-legged dance undertaken by Blodgett and Brault, something

---

4. *Nous ne savions pas où nous allions et nous n'avions à suivre aucune règle préétablie* (Blodgett and Brault 1998: 9).

5. Here I am referring particularly to Derrida's extended preface "Envois," which is presented as one side of a correspondence to an unknown lover (Derrida 1987: 1–256). There are some obvious differences, however; the main one is that in *Transfiguration* one is presented with not one but two sides of a correspondence. One finds, however, that some of the same issues raised in "Envois" through Derrida's postal metaphor apply in this case. For instance, the loss involved as the "message" is translated prevents it from fully reaching its intended destination. Conjured in this way is a kind of "dead-letter office," where the poem goes beyond either poet and their respective intentions for meaning.

6. See Derrida's punning on the word "legs"/"legacy" and also *demarche*, with the corresponding implications for the dance and the *pas de deux* in *The Post Card* (1987; see notes on pp. 293–94 plus entry on "legs" in "L Before K," p. xxiii).

that is not limited to their poetic to-ing and fro-ing, something quite beyond either of them.

> Each dancer must surrender to the other to create the figure that the dance not the dancers requires. And so we have chosen to call this renga "transfiguration" to suggest how each dancer, while remaining himself, is drawn into the figure that possesses both dancers that becomes one dancer, whom they did not imagine. Only the poem that they participate in is capable of imagining it. This is the dance that our imagination became, unknown to ourselves as me and you, but something other and more complete. (Blodgett and Brault 1998: 8)

As in "Envois," narrative coherence does not appear to be a major concern in *Transfiguration*. The absence of formal punctuation means it is often unclear where one idea begins and another ends, and sometimes it seems as though words or sections of text are missing altogether. Consequently, a sense of incompleteness pervades *Transfiguration*. It is a poem that occurs on the margin between two poets, in the space between two languages, where it is both contained by and is constantly exceeding their creative efforts. By each deferring to the other, Blodgett and Brault attempt to relinquish ownership of the poem. At the same time, they affirm the tendency of words to go beyond both authorial intentions and control. As such, they are acknowledging the ability of the text to take on new meanings and go beyond any original context or set of boundaries. Similarly, they demonstrate an appreciation for language to stand apart from intention, free to take on further meanings as it will. By relinquishing authority over the poem, they in effect send (*envois*) their message to "no fixed address." The message is left without a destination and thus remains a celebration of its future possibilities.[7]

Part of this freeing up of the poem to undetermined possible meanings and destinations involves disconnecting language from transparent utility. In this way, *Transfiguration* can be seen to be an affirmation of Blanchot's sense of the sacredness of poetic language whereby language is saturated with meaning and translated back to its invisibility. The poem, by not being limited to the poet's vision, becomes to a certain extent opaque and approximates Blanchot's sense of words as objects. It is as though Blodgett and Brault are attempting to cultivate that sacred dimension of writing by encouraging their words to exceed intention. This excess is further embellished with the continual translation of imagery from one language to another.[8] This play in the space between two languages, where a poem is written twice and only once, brings the role of translation to the fore. The poem is translated from one poet to another and from one language to another. In the losses

---

7. From the perspective of Derrida's postal metaphor, such a letter, lost to its destination, finds a home in "the office of living letters," formerly "the dead-letter office." This metaphor has already been discussed in chap. 4 with particular reference to Mark's empty tomb.

8. Brault calls it *entretraduits librement,* or "liberal inter-translation," and gives the process the sense of a kind of intricate combination or interweaving (Blodgett and Brault 1998: 9).

and additions that saturate this process, there is a sense of moving from the visible to the invisible. In acknowledging the complexity of this inter-interpretive movement, Brault speaks of the resulting poem as resounding with the voice of otherness and, at this point, heralding a type of transfiguration: "And so we have written in strange familiarity thanks to a friendship that has not given an excuse to erase our differences. If the poetry is also the voice of the other in itself, then this little book constitutes perhaps and in many respects a Transfiguration" (1998: 9).[9]

*Transfiguration* can be read as a poem that, through vivid word-painting, conjures a picture of nature as in some way sacred, that is, existing quite apart from what we "know" of nature, in its own essential solitude, outside of thought and without witness. To achieve this effect, one notices the use of a number of poetic devices. Of particular note is the way images are turned in on themselves either through the use of paradox, contradiction, or unlikely associations. Three consecutive stanzas of *Transfiguration* will further elaborate the preceding discussion.

*Transfiguration*

winter is a paleography

imperatives dissolve
time forgets

a sparrow sits on the fence

if it sang its song
would never reach the ground

scattered clouds of breath
alphabet in ruins

*l'hiver est une paléographie*

*toute urgence disparaît*
*le temps oublie*

*un moineau se tient sur une clôture*

*s'il chantait son chant*
*jamais n'atteindrait le sol*

---

9. *Ainsi avons-nous écrit en étrange familiarité, grâce à une amitié qui ne s'est pas donné d'alibi en cherchant à gommer nos différences. Si la poésie est aussi la voix de l'autre en soi-même, alors ce petit livre constitue peut-être, et à maints égards, une Transfiguration.*

> *vapeurs d'haleine qui se dispersent*
> *alphabet en ruines*

..................................................................

*écriture parcheminée sur le ciel*
*ardoise*
> *des essaims d'oiseaux charbon*
*redonnent au temps d'avant le temps*
> *son mutisme*
> *son néant*

> wrinkled writing across the sky
> slate-grey
> > swarms of charcoal birds
> return to time before time
> > its muteness
> > its nothing

..................................................................

silence settles on the lakes

it is not stars that fall
but afterthoughts of stars floating
flowers their roots long

ago within the sky

> *le silence s'établit sur les lacs*

> *ce ne sont pas des étoiles qui tombent*
> *mais des arriére-pensées d'étoiles fleurs*
> *flottantes leurs racines depuis*

> *long temps au sein du ciel*
> > (from *Transfiguration* 1998: 48–50)

Winter is a "paleography"/*paléographie*, a study of ancient writings and ancient manuscripts. In what way is this to be understood? This quality of winter appears to be explained and elaborated by a number of images that follow. In setting the scene we read that "imperatives dissolve" and then "time forgets"/*le temps oublie*. Authority, urgency, all sense of emergency (*urgence*) disappear (*disparaît*) as time forgets and opens to oblivion (*oublie*). This is the context of the study, the analysis of the ancient texts of winter. A sparrow sits on a fence, and the French *clôture* gives the added sense of it being more like a cloister wall.[10] The sparrow is silent, but even in the event that it sang, its song would never even barely touch from a distance (*n'atteindrait*) the ground. The sparrow need not sing, there is no urgency to its "text"; it is a song that barely exists. The song is lost like a pen that never touches paper. This song that is not sung becomes mere scattered clouds of breath, *vapeurs d'haleine qui se dispersent*. Winter is an insouciant "paleography" and cares not that the song fails to find its way to the ear of the earth where it could take root and be inscribed there in its fullness. Instead we receive hints that there is no one left to hear and no one who can sing in response. No one is here to witness this scene. Breath disperses on the breeze, and all that remains are the crumbling fragments of an "alphabet in ruins." Being described in this scene is a moment that comes before experience and before language—a moment that goes as unknown to time and demands of any kind as the unsung song of an anonymous bird perched amidst the ruins of an abandoned monastery.

Across the sky, one finds writing, wrinkled, shriveled, and parchmentlike (*écriture parcheminée sur le ciel*/"wrinkled writing across the sky"). The ancient texts of winter are not found among the ruins of the earth but are scrawled across the stony, slate-grey sky. The sky is a writing slab covered with wrinkled words. Unreadable, charcoal-like crows "swarm" about (like bees?), illegible smudges spread across a slate-grey sky hinting at nothing. Just as the unsung sparrow's song escaped the ear, these black marks make no sense to the eye, but in their obscuring and erratic flapping they follow by road (from *parcheminée* to *par chemin*) toward a "time before time." This "time before time" has the sense of "oblivion" (*le temps oublie*). It is an experience that exceeds the conditions needed for experience. In the English, there is a sense of "returning" to this point, as though it has a certain familiarity of a place known and longed for, but in the French there is more the sense of "giving back" or even "beginning again" (*redonner*), as though another chance is being given to participate in something that remains unknown. It is a "time" when speech fails (muteness), and it is an encounter with unknowing (*néant*).

Another wintry pallet covers the waters of the lakes: "silence settles on the lakes"/*le silence s'établit sur les lacs*. It is not the crows that lead the way to the "sacred"; this time the path of destiny is left to the stars. Scattered on the silent waters are the floating "afterthoughts of stars." Not the stars themselves, but the palest reflections, glistening dots of light, like flowers floating. But they flow and waver, lacking resolve as they surrender to the whim of the water and wind. They appear as scattered flowers, enjoying the connection bestowed by alliteration, but remain separated by the poet's whim, the translation further confounding their

---

10. In addition to the sense of *clôture,* this monastic setting is further evoked by the association of *moineau* (sparrow) with *moine* (monk).

## New Figurations

relation by syntactical variation (floating, flowers/*fleurs, flottantes*).[11] The starflowers long ago had their origins in the sky. But now they are stars no more. With "their roots long" one can trace their history back a great distance, but their origins are not found by uncovering the earth. Like the sparrow's song that never touches the ground and like the *écriture parcheminée sur le ciel,* the ancient wintry text is found in the sky, but this time, the sky as it is reflected in the waters.

And yet, eventually, spring emerges:

>         spring is not the sun
>         reborn it is
>         language that invisible
>
>         explodes across the air
>
>         its herald single crows
>         that fall miraculous
>         from uninvented alphabets

*le printemps n'est pas le soleil*
*qui renaît c'est*
*le language invisiblement qui*

*explose au long de l'espace*

*ses corbeaux un à un messagers*
*qui tombent miraculeux*
*d'alphabets incréés*

(from *Transfiguration* 1998: 60)

This stanza announces the appearance of spring emerging from a winter that has departed from memory. The poet makes a curious distinction between the season of spring and the sun. As we saw in chap. 4, the sun has long been a founding metaphor for philosophy, a natural phenomenon whose experiential and intellectual singularity has been used to stabilize the flux of meaning.[12] The sun represents clarity and visibility, reliable meaning and foundational presence. But it is made clear that "spring is not the sun"/*le printemps n'est pas le soleil*. The season

---

11. Here I am referring particularly to the alliteration of the words, the fact that their meanings are reasonably transparent and yet there is a difference in word order demanded by English and French, and also the further division that has been made by the placement of words on separate lines of the poem.

12. I introduced this understanding of the sun as the ultimate heliotrope in my discussion of "White Mythology" (1974b) in chap. 4.

of spring has associations of its own. It conjures up a sense of fertility, of rapid change, rebirth, and future fruitfulness. But if the spring is not the sun, then there is also a sense that the spring is at least partly shrouded from view; there is something here that eludes our gaze and escapes our understanding. There is a part of spring that goes beyond experience into a forgotten realm where associations and attributions are left behind. Spring is not identical to the sun. We cannot know the spring in the same way, and it doesn't present itself to be known in its clarity and fullness. The spring is not simply the sun rising again in another form (*renaît*). This spring simply "is" ("it is"/*c'est*). It is a spring without a history; it is a beginning with no meaning and no identity. It is an opaque word, the object that precedes understanding; it is the language of the invisible at the threshold of meaning, the moment when the seasons shift. This spring is a moment of lost language at the instant of its own undoing. But it is not the languid and careless paleography of winter; it is on the verge of energetically bursting forth. This invisible creativity and rejuvenation, language of the "sacred," "explodes across the air." The explosion is far reaching, as it stretches across space and time (*explose au long du l'espace*), but it remains invisible and silent. It is not the sun. The only signs of this invisible drama are the heralding succession of single crows that fall, miraculously, one by one from places as yet unknown: "its herald single crows that fall miraculously from uninvented alphabets"/*ses corbeaux un à un messagers qui tombent miraculeux d'alphabets incréés*. These miraculous crows fall, flow, droop (*tombent*), translated from alphabets not yet known. Before invention, these letters form words that explode across the air, but even after we are alerted to their message, they remain uncreated (*incréés*), unspoken, and invisible.

The crows that fall—are they dead, falling (*tombent*) to their tomb (*tombe*)?—are the only signs of an invisible spring. It is only by means of a miracle that the entry of the sacred is marked: "Single crows that fall miraculous." The transfiguration described here is an explosion that occurs within language, an event that mirrors not the ever-present sun but the bursting forth of an invisible spring in all its fecundity and freshness. The transfiguration described here marks this impossible movement between the invisible and the visible, a movement that is dramatic and far reaching, but not marked by the light and splendor of the sun. In a single falling crow, an unknown moment of explosiveness is revealed to be a moment of transition and translation, and a moment of transformation. Thus echoes the resounding voice of otherness that heralds the moment of transfiguration, a transfiguration quite different from the splendor-filled vision of Jesus transformed. Instead, it is a sense of transfiguration that extends its reach beyond the sun toward the sacredness of an invisible language.

## *II. Vision of Bees*

Sometimes, messengers are needed to make such a journey. Blodgett and Brault frequently use the image of bees in *Transfiguration*, as if they are aware that poets and readers require this mediation.[13] Bees, in fact, mark the poem's boundaries, the formal beginning and end, perhaps as an indicator of the beginning and end of the visible and invisible within the poem itself. In this way, and in light of Rilke's regard for bees, one could take their presence as a statement of the ongoing poetic task of translating the visible to the invisible. Blodgett and Brault have gathered together natural images from the fields of representation, and, in the construction of the poem, these images have taken on a certain invisibility. What has been found in these two poetic excerpts is a sense of transfiguration that occurs away from the sunlit places, aside from the glowing, fully present vision of light, and far removed from any memory of dawn. This encounter with an invisible transfiguring movement involves a confrontation with a certain sacredness. The encounter is always exterior to experience, but at the same time it is more intimate than the most interior part of the self.

Speaking of one's relationship to this sense of sacredness, Blanchot expands on Rilke's image of the bee, extending its scope to include more than just the realm of the poet. He elaborates while rereading the biblical motif of Noah and the ark:

> Every man is called upon to take up again the mission of Noah. He must become the intimate and pure ark of all things, the refuge in which they take shelter, where they are not content to be kept as they are, as they imagine themselves to be—narrow, outworn, so many traps for life—but are transformed, lose their form, lose themselves to enter themselves, untouched, intact, in the pure point of the undetermined. Yes, every man is Noah, but on closer inspection he is Noah in a strange way, and his mission consists less in saving everything from the flood than, on the contrary, in plunging all things into a deeper flood where they disappear prematurely and radically. That, in fact, is what the human vocation amounts to. If it is necessary that everything visible become invisible, if this metamorphosis is accomplished perfectly of itself, for everything is perishable, for, says Rilke in the same letter [see quotes on poet/bee above], "the perishable is everywhere engulfed in a deep being." What have we then to do, we who are the least durable, the most prompt to disappear? What have we to offer in this task of salvation? Precisely that: our promptness at disappearing, our aptitude for perishing, our fragility, our exhaustion, our gift for death. (Blanchot 1982: 140)

Blanchot thus comments that it is not just the poetic task but the very condition of being human that one be impossibly quested to find a way back to the sacred—to find that "space which exceeds us and translates things" (1982: 141). But more than this, in this "gift for death," this ability to take meaning beyond its meaningfulness, the subject possesses some small part of what is necessary for this transfiguring journey on which all is lost and yet reborn at the same time. It is here that the word is returned to its origin in the dark waters of unknowing that flood the spaces of literature.

---

13. See Blodgett and Brault 1998: 10, 30, 52, 85.

If we take our discussion of this poetic transfiguration back to the Markan text, our question emerges once again: What is encountered at the transfiguration scene? The answer to this question in part has involved extending the notion of transfiguration beyond the sun's domain. The transfiguration is also an event that is encountered in the outer fields of experience, indeed in the unexperienceable. However, in developing this notion of an "other" transfiguration, what has been the subsequent impact on those theological conceptions so clearly evident in traditional approaches to this text? If the questions I am asking are not dissimilar to those raised in traditional readings—what does the transfiguration mean and what is encountered—then ought not there also be certain theological implications that accompany this literary rereading?

Even though I have been following a literary, and arguably by association, secular trajectory, it seems that theological concerns cannot be altogether excluded. Looking to the passages selected, for instance, one finds that in the French text of *Transfiguration* there appear to be a number of intrusions of a more conventional or expected sense of sacredness. I have already noted the associations drawn from *moine* (from *moineau*) and *clôture,* but there is also a certain sacred aspect to that of *corbeaux*, which, it seems, can refer to "priest" as well as to "crow." More pointed is the sense of *le ciel* as "the sky" or "the heavens." In my reading, *le ciel* has played a particular role as the metaphorical locus for the sacred. Accompanying this literary association of *le ciel* is the colloquial sense as "deity" or "God." A similar meeting of the literary and the religious can be found in the word *écriture*. The parchmentlike *écriture* is scrawled across *le ciel* (*écriture parcheminée sur le ciel*). As a text, it provides the sacred *ciel* with a connection to language and to writing. But where *le ciel* is understood to mean "deity," *écriture* takes on a corresponding sense of religiosity by invoking a particular reference to the "scriptural text." Such a connection prompts an investigation of the relationship between theology and literary theory. This will be the subject of the remaining section of this chapter.

## Part 3. Reading the Sacred Text

Blanchot's straying into the biblical canon with his analysis of the Noah story is reminiscent of Derrida's use of biblical texts to develop his own theoretical interests.[14] But as has become apparent in the above readings, there is more than a passing resemblance between these two thinkers. Derrida has drawn from the writings of Blanchot at numerous times during his career. While this is not an investigation of the extent to which Blanchot has influenced Derrida's thought, one theme

---

14. I discussed Derrida's interpretation of the Babel narrative in chap. 1 and in chap. 3 briefly looked at Derrida's reading of the sacrifice of Isaac in the *Gift of Death* (1995). Blanchot has also made use of the story of the raising of Lazarus (1982: 194–96).

emerges here that bears consideration.[15] When looking at their readings of certain "literary" texts, there appears to be a certain allegorical character common to both Blanchot's and Derrida's approaches, particularly in their dealings with sacred texts. Rather than reading for God or the divine, however, the particular allegorical hermeneutic (allegoresis) used by Blanchot and Derrida involves reading for language. Here, allegory is regarded for its ability to reveal the conditions for language to be language. In this sense, reading allegorically means reading the word as word and reveals the material qualities of textuality to be endlessly referential and internally conflicted. The result of reading in this way is that the experience of a language so conceived is laid out bare.[16] Although allegory has a long and distinguished history within theological modes of reading, this literary sense of allegoresis, of employing an allegorical hermeneutic, coincides with the reception of allegory within literary studies in more recent times.

According to Gregory Ulmer, there are two sides to this literary-critical work on allegory. The first instance is the concentration on allegory as a point of impasse where the literal and figural both stand as valid options. This sense of allegory, where one encounters an undecidable aporia, corresponds with de Man's work on irony and the "pun," and consequently engages the enduring question of the relationship between literature and philosophy.[17] Although demonstrating a keen interest in the literature-versus-philosophy debate, Derrida's interest in allegory leads to the second use of this mode of reading, one that regards the ambiguities that are

---

15. Charting Blanchot's presence in Derrida's thought would be a much larger project than I have time for here; suffice it to say that it is an ongoing and evolving influence. Derrida engaged with Blanchot in an early essay, "La Parole soufflée" (1978c). Later, in speaking of his fascination for the writings of Blanchot, Derrida explains: "It is true that Blanchot has been very decisive for me. . . . I thought I had introjected, interiorized, assimilated Blanchot's contribution and had brought it to bear in my work . . . and then rather recently, a few years ago, I read what I had never managed to read in a way which was at bottom—how shall I say?—an experience. I began to read and reread certain of Blanchot's *récits* and to discover certain of these texts that I thought I had read but which I had not really succeeded in reading before . . . my relation to Blanchot's texts has been transformed and I feel far more overwhelmed by that text than I though I was at a given moment, for example at the time of 'La Parole soufflée'" (Derrida et al. 1988: 78).

16. I will not be going further into the complexities of allegory and its bearing on Derridean thought although the implications here, and on my work in the previous chapter, are many and far reaching. In addition to de Man's work on allegory (*Allegories of Reading* [1979] and *Blindness and Insight* [1983]), see the references cited by Ulmer 1985 that explore this literary-theoretical regard for allegory. These include Craig Owens, "The Allegorical Impulse: Toward a Theory of Post-Modernism," *October* 12 (1980): 59–80; and Maureen Quilligan, *The Language of Allegory: Defining the Genre* (Ithaca, N.Y.: Cornell University Press, 1979). For an extended discussion of allegory and its place in both de Man's and Derrida's thought, see Hart 2000: 155–62.

17. In *Applied Grammatology* (1985: 88–89), Ulmer speaks of de Man's practice of allegorical reading and the importance of allegory as a mode of reading that embraces undecidability, that is, the ambiguity of the literal versus the figurative and the point at which the boundaries between philosophy and literature blur. Hart also develops this debate in *Trespass of the Sign* (2000: 150–62). Within biblical studies, Stephen Moore's work, in which he engages deconstruction with certain New Testament texts, is the best example of this first approach. See particularly his reading of Luke's Gospel (Moore 1992).

sought in allegoresis as markers indicating the work of *différance*. This being the case, allegoresis is given enormous scope because it has the potential to engage with the conditions that underlie the creation of all meaning.[18] Derrida, in his adoption of allegoresis, avoids the reinscription of certain metaphysical modes of thought that are remnants of a theological past. In particular, Derrida challenges the need to allegorize in a way that fashions classic narrative. Instead, he allows for a mode of reading that, as Ulmer states, "liberate[s] the allegorical narrative from its onto-theological ideology" (Ulmer 1985: 90). In further explaining this point, Hart looks to the comparison between Philo's account of allegoresis and the challenge raised by Derrida's adoption of this mode of reading: "Allegoresis, Philo tells us, is a 'wise Master-builder' concerned to establish a tower wherein the truth may abide forever, outside the ravages of time and the slippages of textual meaning. But if allegoresis is grounded in allegory . . . the tower—like the tower of Babel—nonetheless remains subject to that which it seeks to transcend" (Hart 2000: 156).

But although a Derridean allegorical hermeneutic poses a challenge to its theological past, the question of a religious and sacred nature need not be eliminated altogether. In chap. 1, I introduced Derrida's reading of the Babel narrative, a reading that ends with a discussion of the text as sacred. Investigating the truth of language, Derrida located the most sacred (and this is a literary sense of sacredness much like that developed by Blanchot) moment of the text in the unknowable moment where it is still yet to be translated. For Derrida, the untranslatable name "Babel" comes closest to this moment when the text insists on being translated, and at the same time foils any attempt.[19] According to Derrida's reading, this is what is named in the Babel story: "the law imposed by the name of God who in one stroke commands and forbids you to translate by showing and hiding from you the limit" (2002b: 32). This is the point at which pure transferability becomes impos-

---

18. Hart gives the sense of this extraordinary scope by defining "meaning as the allegory of a text" (2000: 155–56), a formulation that includes deconstructive readings within these dimensions: "A deconstructive reading of a text, despite what it does to previous readings, will always be an allegory of the text and, as such, be subject to a deconstruction to the second degree" (2000: 158). This experience of language encountered through allegoresis is not unlike what is encountered in different guises elsewhere in Derrida's writings. There are a number of essays where, by employing certain key terms—*pharmakon*, supplement, *différance*—Derrida demonstrates these qualities of textuality and preconditions of meaning. As I have discussed in my introduction to Derridean thought in chap. 1 (where I dealt particularly with Derrida's neologism *différance*), these terms demonstrate those qualities of language that lead one to experiences of displacement and referentiality in spite of assurances of transparency and self-identity.

19. As discussed in chap. 1, Derrida is here pointing to the dual meaning of Babel as proper noun—name given by God—and common noun, meaning "confusion." These meanings cannot both be simultaneously translated into a corresponding term. In *The Ear of the Other*, Derrida points to an attempt in a recent translation to account for both these meanings: "So what he does is to write: 'Bavel, Confusion,' capitalizing Confusion. In the language of the original text, there is only one word, whereas the translation has recourse to two words. But the translator realizes that without the capital letter, he loses the effect of the proper name. He thus arrives at this same manner of compromise, which, naturally, is insufficient, but which has been forced on him by God's deconstruction" (Derrida et al. 1998: 104).

sible, the moment when ideal translation is revealed as a false promise. Because Derrida locates the sacred moment of the text at a point that is always prior to the movement of translation, it could be said to be positioned at a point of absolute beginning. Derrida's location of the sacred at the point of absolute beginning is in some ways a contrast to Blanchot's sense of sacredness. Blanchot's sacred is encountered through a transfiguring movement from the intelligible to an absolute opacity. Blanchot's movement into the sacred is also a movement into true death, and, as such, into absolute end. Although at opposite ends, Derrida and Blanchot appear to be on a continuum: just as Derrida's sacred both allows and resists translation into the intelligible, Blanchot's movement into the sacred from the intelligible is similarly contradictory in that it is possible to achieve but impossible to know.

Both Blanchot and Derrida indicate that an encounter with the sacred is in some way possible and is influenced by the way that language is approached and attended to. While the sacred remains radically unknowable, what *is* discernable here is the implication poetic and sacred moments have for the choices one makes when approaching and reading texts. Allegoresis is one example where the question of approach or the discernment of an appropriate mode of reading has been answered to the extent that it considers the conditions that influence a reader's experience of language. In other words, the reader's relation to the text and to meaning is affected by the reading structures (traditional or otherwise) one adopts. In the next section, the link between the literary and the theological is explored further in order to consider more closely two distinct notions of transfiguration: the literary and the theological.

## Part 4. Sacred Literature, Sacred Scripture

When discussing this search for the sacred, both Blanchot and Derrida speak of a particular kind of writing. I have limited my reading of Blanchot's interests to poetic discourse; but Blanchot, like Derrida, would extend the scope of this encounter to fall within a broader literary type. In discussing the quality of this literary encounter, both Blanchot and Derrida are keen to say something of the relationship between text and subjectivity. From their respective theoretical inquiries it becomes clear that both these thinkers are approaching sacred texts, and coming to a sense of the sacred, from a literary rather than a theological perspective.[20] In the first part of this chapter, I raised the question of what is revealed in the transfiguration story. Going from Blanchot and Rilke and their work on a kind of poetic transfiguration to a recognition of theological considerations within the poetry of

---

20. This is not the place to elaborate further on the relationship between two complex and interrelated theories of sacred writing. For a discussion by Derrida about what makes a text "sacred," see Derrida et al. 1998: 98–110. For Blanchot's development of his notion of the "sacred," see his essay "The 'Sacred' Speech of Hölderlin" (1995: 111–31).

Blodgett and Brault, I have expanded the question of what is revealed in the type of transfiguration being explored here to include a theological dimension—questions such as the following: What does it mean to bring the work of Blanchot and Derrida to bear on a text that has been and is regarded with a very different sense of sacredness? What are the theological consequences of reading what is generally regarded as a theologically informed text from a literary perspective? If from what we have seen so far in this chapter, a transfiguration is a moment when one is brought to the limit, to the point when language is encountered as sacred? What are the implications of viewing the Markan transfiguration in this way?

Hart notes that this taking of the Bible as a "text" aside from its religious and devotional associations has been a prominent tendency within the Western application of deconstruction, in which deconstruction has become synonymous with atheism in the minds of many literary critics (2000: 43). Hart cites as the most prominent example of this Gayatri Spivak's influential translator's preface to Derrida's *Of Grammatology*. Here, with a certain sternness of tone, Spivak reiterates, "Let me add yet once again that this terrifying and exhilarating vertigo is not 'mystical' or 'theological'" (Derrida 1974a: lxxviii). Hart, however, disagrees and reveals Derrida's influences to be founded on a far broader pallet than Spivak acknowledges. Spivak sees Derrida following Nietzsche, Freud, and Heidegger. Hart extends this scope of influence to include (but not be limited to) such writers as Isaac Luria, Emmanuel Levinas, and Edmond Jabès, all of whom draw from a distinctly religious (Jewish) tradition. Hart charges Spivak with totalizing Derrida's work, first, by limiting his influences in this way and, second, by claiming a distinctly secular identity for *écriture*.

Following Spivak, the trend in literary theory has been to read "text" or "writing" as the usual translation of Derrida's use of the French *écriture*. Hart suggests that alignment of *écriture* in this way, with writing and textuality, has meant a subsequent aligning of Derrida's writings—and this includes deconstruction as well—with secularism. Hart observes, however, that there is another sense of this word in the French that has been largely overlooked. This usual translation of *écriture* to mean "text" and "writing" has in practice excluded another meaning of this word: *écriture* as "scripture." To limit the meaning of *écriture* to "writing" and "text" is to make certain elements of Derrida's work puzzling until, as Hart explains, the alternate sense of *écriture* as "scripture" is restored.[21]

---

21. In *Trespass of the Sign* (2000), Hart provides examples of this overlooked regard for *écriture* as "scripture" in Derrida's writing. First of all, Hart notes "how Derrida defines Judaism as 'the birth and passion of *écriture*' and that it is 'The Jew who elects *écriture* which elects the Jew'" (Hart 2000: 50). Hart goes on to cite some otherwise "puzzling" examples from Derrida's writing that can be explained from this extended sense of *écriture*: "'The Jew is but the suffering allegory' and 'The Jew is split, and split first of all between two dimensions of the letter: allegory and literality.'... The point of 'allegory' is most keenly registered here if one recognises that the means whereby Jewish scripture was linked with its 'other'—Greek metaphysics—was through the operations of the allegorical hermeneutic" (2000: 50–51).

Consequently, deconstruction need not be by definition atheistic, although the sense with which theology and mysticism are conceived may well be scrutinized by a deconstructive approach. That said, it seems that scriptural writing and religious themes are congenial enough to Derridean thought so that one need not fear betraying literary principles by doing an overtly theological reading or simply engaging with nonliterary elements. The point to be made here is that approaching a sacred text from a literary perspective need not rule out the faith-oriented questions that may accompany that particular text.

This wider question, as well as the more specific implications of reading a sacred text using a literary methodology, has been presented briefly but rigorously by Hart in his essay "The Poetics of the Negative" (1991). Hart begins this essay by questioning the relationship between literature and literary criticism, and it is not long before he finds that the scope of this question needs to be broadened so as to acknowledge the peculiar position occupied by the Bible as an example of sacred literature. For Hart asserts that to read the Bible *as* literature is immediately to reduce it. The Bible is experienced as a social, political, and historical document that is invested with a particular institutionalized authority, factors that a more particularly "literary" study cannot adequately take into account. There is no doubt that the Bible *is* literature, but its significance goes beyond this distinction (Hart 1991: 330).

Hart then turns his eye toward the literary critics themselves. He observes that certain schools of literary theory in fact display many of the hallmarks of negative theology, and then goes on to argue that there is more than just a casual likeness between literary theory and negative theology.[22] He demonstrates that contemporary literary theory actually deals with what would be termed from another perspective certain key theological issues. Hart is particularly interested in the place of negative theology within literary theory. He observes the similarity (but he is careful not to imply a shared identity) between literary theorists and negative theologians:

> As the negative theologian longs for the god beyond Being, that is, who is beyond all philosophical determinations of Being, so the literary theorist searches for a literature and a critical vocabulary that escape or thwart philosophical categories. And so, whether one has a regard for philosophy even while placing it at risk . . . or whether one utterly rejects the vocabulary of philosophy in the context of criticism . . . one can see how literary theorists can, at a pinch, be taken for negative theologians. (1991: 287)[23]

---

22. There is, of course, a large area of scholarship devoted to the encounter between Derrida's thought and theology as well as the development of the relationship between literary theory and theology generally (see, e.g., Taylor 1984; Ward 1997; Caputo and Scanlon 1999).

23. Hart continues this inquiry, asking the more specific question about the relationship between negative theology, philosophy, and deconstruction in *Trespass of the Sign* (2000).

By "negative theology," Hart is speaking of that mode of theological enquiry that, rather than attempting to gather knowledge of God in his effects (i.e., *positive* theology), gains "knowledge" of God by denying the adequacy of these concepts and images and in doing so questions the very capacity of language itself to speak of the divine. "The one [positive theology] assumes a movement from presence to representation, the other [negative theology] a movement from representations to presence (or, perhaps more accurately, to that which is otherwise to presence)" (2000: 190). One could easily argue, for instance, that Blanchot nears the borders of negative theology with his poetic language of negation and his continual turning away from representation. And Derrida, too, exhibits a definite fascination with theological issues. This is apparent not only in his interest in the *mysterium tremendum* and the story of Abraham's sacrifice of Isaac (1995), which themselves belie an interest in the features of negative theology, but also in other more theologically aligned writings that I have not dealt with directly in this book.[24] The theological reception of literary theory or even the uses of theology within literary theory will not be put forward for consideration here. Taking this trajectory would be to open a vast horizon of scholarship and would take this book in a very different direction. At this point I would like to limit the field of view so as to provide a more immediate implication—a question that is beginning to sound familiar: How can theological concerns be part of a literary reading and where can theological concerns figure when secular and sacred distinctions are challenged?

In order to explore further this theological question that shadows the application of critical theoretical modes of analysis to biblical texts (specifically Derrida's), once again we put the focus on Derrida's reading of the Babel story. Hart finds a reading that he suggests condenses "much of what interests him [Derrida] under the rubric of 'deconstruction'" (Hart 1991: 312).[25] He notes that Derrida's reading of this biblical, sacred, text has much in common with his reading of Joyce's *Finnegans Wake*, a literary text that Derrida would also speak of in terms of sacredness (Hart 1991: 315).[26] Hart finds that Derrida's analysis demonstrates that *Finnegans Wake* is as much a part of the tower of Babel as the tower is of the

---

24. See particularly "Of an Apocalyptic Tone Recently Adopted in Philosophy" (Detweiler 1982: 63–96) and "How to Avoid Speaking" (excerpt in Ward 1997: 167–90) for Derrida's thoughts on negative theology; see also the recently published collection of essays *Acts of Religion* (2002a) for his thoughts on theological and religious issues. What could possibly be Derrida's final thoughts on these issues can be found in the fascinating dialogue "Epoche and Faith: An Interview with Jacques Derrida," published in *Derrida and Religion: Other Testaments* (Sherwood and Hart 2005: 27–50).

25. Derrida speaks of his Babel reading in similar terms: "The deconstruction of the Tower of Babel, moreover, gives a good idea of what deconstruction is: an unfinished edifice whose half-contemplated structures are visible letting one guess at the scaffolding behind them" (Derrida et al. 1988: 102).

26. The question of what determines a text as "sacred" in the theological sense as well as the literary sense is of course a complex question and will not be taken up here. Hart points to the work of Benjamin and Ricoeur as well as to Derrida's own attempts to tackle the question (see Hart 1991: 313–12). What one finds with Derrida's account is something that comes very close to Blanchot's notion of the "essential solitude" whereby language is experienced in its capacity as opaque object.

wake.[27] For instance, Hart demonstrates in Derrida's work a complex interweaving of secular literature and sacred text. In another example he likens Derrida's modes of reading to those of rabbis of the *Midrash Rabbah* and the *Zohar*. These rabbinic modes of reading, by affirming the "inexhaustible fullness of God's work," further "sacralize the text" (Hart 1991: 317).[28] Moreover, with techniques that at times seem closely aligned to this rabbinic strategy, Derrida appeals to a mode of negativity—*la différance*—that ceaselessly generates meaning. It is in this excess that one sees the link between the sacred text, poetry, and a certain type of literature—literature such as *Finnegans Wake*. Drawing ever-closer associations with what appeared at first incompatible textual forms governed by incompatible interpretive traditions, Hart concludes this section by observing that the bond between literature and scripture has something to do with singularity and with the subsequent inability to be translated. What happens in the sacred text is an event that cannot be translated without loss.

> Reading Hölderlin, Heidegger thought that poetry teaches us, in this dark time, to see the unknown god as unknown. Poetry points us, by a negative way, toward the holy. Derrida, too, thinks that literature has an irreducible secrecy; it "unveils a secret only to confirm that there is a secret, withdrawing, protected from hermeneutic exhaustion." This is not a consequence of hermeticism but of the irreducible idiom that makes a text literary. No interpretation, however agile, thorough and cogent, can formalize a text without remainder. If Genesis or Finnegans Wake is literary it is because of an idiom, a singularity, in the text, not by virtue of any special teaching contained there. And the same would be true if we decided to call either or both those texts "sacred." For Derrida, "literary" and "sacred" are two ways of ascribing originality. Literary and sacred writings alike function as proper names; on the one hand they resist translation, clinging to their singularity, while on the other hand, they allow themselves to be transformed and deformed, "Babel" becoming "balal" or—amazingly enough—Genesis becoming Finnegans Wake. (Hart 1991: 318)

## I. Unbinding the Text?

In *The Trespass of the Sign* (2000) Hart develops the association and supposed similarity between negative theology and deconstruction. He concludes that it would be inaccurate to claim that negative theology *is* deconstruction, but instead claims negative theology is *a* deconstruction. The qualification of negative theol-

---

27. Derrida is also quite aware of the presence of Babel in the Wake: "A Babelian motif runs from one end of Finnegans Wake to the other" (Derrida et al. 1988: 98).

28. It is interesting that, in a footnote, Hart points out that Derrida denies any direct knowledge of rabbinic interpretation (1991: 108, 338). Nonetheless, Derrida's self-conscious example of "modern midrash," "Shiboleth," appears alongside a piece by Edmond Jabès in a collection entitled *Midrash and Literature* (Budik and Hartman 1986). Sherwood summarizes Derrida's apparent influence from being "among the Rabbis" in *The Prostitute and the Prophet* (1996: 194–99).

ogy as something not to be identified with deconstruction and which is itself subject to deconstruction raises its own questions as to the participation of theology in literary theory. If deconstruction can so effectively reveal the metaphysical scaffolding propping up the theological tradition, how can theology become a legitimate part of reading in this way? And if it is possible to read deconstructively *and* theologically, what type of theology are we speaking of? Driven by similar questions, Hart explores the possibility of theology after Derrida:

> What consequences does this argument have for theology? Derrida points out that difference does not annul positive and negative theologies but rather renders them possible as discourses. At the first this might seem like small consolation for a theologian. After all, what is the point of a theology without God? Yet to show that God does not abide in the immediacy and simplicity of a present moment is not to deny God. It is to demonstrate that God is conceived metaphysically within theology, even within negative theologies. To be sure, a negative theology may partially deconstruct the metaphysics that shapes the God of a positive theology. But to the extent it conceives approaching the God beyond being without recourse to language, this negative theology will itself call for deconstruction. To turn to another point. The theologian should remember that Derrida nowhere rejects the notion of presence. He argues that presence cannot present itself; the possibility of inscription is a necessary one, and one that ensures the possibility of division. There may be a God, and this God may be pure self-presence; but He cannot be intuited or revealed in the present. (Hart 1997: 164–65)

A recent work that explores the possibility of a theology undertaken in the way Hart sketches can be found in Richard Kearney's *The God Who May Be* (2001). In this work, Kearney explores the possibility of a God not aligned solely with notions of being and presence, terms that have so thoroughly defined the tradition up to this point. Of particular interest is the fact that Kearney uses a number of scriptural sources with which to flesh out his "postmetaphysical" picture, including the scene of Moses at the burning bush and the Song of Songs, but most relevant to this discussion, the transfiguration.

Kearney reads the transfiguration as a moment when the *person* of Jesus is metamorphosed into the *persona* of Christ (39). By *persona*, Kearney is introducing a phenomenological component of individual identity whereby "each person embodies a *persona*. *Persona* is that eschatological aura of 'possibility' which eludes but informs a person's actual presence here and now" (10). For Kearney, the *persona* represents an incidence of "otherness" in the individual and, as such, preserves a sense of infinite possibility. In its elusiveness to consciousness, the *persona* always situates itself "beyond" and thus prevents a person being objectified or reduced in time and space (10). In his reading of the transfiguration, Kearney finds a revelation of the *persona par excellence* in the transfigured face of Jesus. As Kearney puts it, the transfigured Christ is "not all there" (47). As a manifestation of *persona*, the transfigured Christ cannot be reduced to an actual personal presence. When we encounter the *persona* here, and elsewhere, we encounter an irreducible instance of God's transforming power within the limited materiality of our existence. Consequently, this opens up a surplus of meaning on Mount Tabor, and we are left with a site of infinite possibility for God's action in the world. Kearney uses the transfiguration passage as a way of developing one part of his broader conception of a God "who may be," in particular *how* this god is revealed to us. What interests me even more, however, is exactly *how* this text is read by Kearney.

Kearney makes a caveat early on in his reading of the transfiguration. He describes his approach as "a phenomenological-hermeneutic retrieval rather than that of theological exegesis per se" (39). For this reason his reading tends to be based on the established tradition associated with this story—a kind of composite of Matthew's, Mark's, and Luke's versions, but also the version retold by Paul in 2 Corinthians 3. As I noted earlier (see chap. 3), this same well-established tradition is used by biblical scholars to iron out difficulties in Mark's version. It provides a general template to which the details of any particular text ought to correspond. For instance, as in traditional readings of the transfiguration, Kearney emphasizes such motifs as the face of Jesus, the voice of God, and the presence of dazzling light (39–44). Moreover, other details have similarly been neglected. Take, for example, Mark's use of the metaphor of the bleacher. In chap. 3, I described how the bleachers used phosphates and nitrates for their work, and the most ready source of these compounds was animal waste, chiefly urine and excrement. Consequently, Mark compares Jesus' transfigured visage to work that carries with it, at the very least, a whiff of unpleasantness. In Kearney's discussion of the imagery of Jesus' metamorphosis, he affirms a tradition of associating light with divine glory. He begins by citing Matthew's version of the transfiguration as a key reference illustrating this association. He goes on to quote from the tradition of commentary on this story but adds to this passages from Melville's *Moby Dick*. These passages provide yet another layer of commentary on the quality of whiteness witnessed in the transfiguration scene. Kearney uses *Moby Dick* to show that whiteness represents a point of ambivalence as both absence and fullness of color and, as such, the point between belief and nonbelief (41). Restricted to sight and to a question of faith, Kearney's notion of the divine light is far removed from the senses assaulted by Mark's more vivid imagery: the stench of urine, of ammonia and phosphates, eyes watering in the acrid vapors, gagging, wincing, and revulsion heightened with the added weight of ritual impurity looming large—in short, an experience not quite as palatable to heady philosophical conceptions of the divine.

Kearney upholds a tradition of reading the transfiguration that emphasizes certain qualities over others. In the example of the bleacher these are more specifically certain modes of embodiment over others: sight, sound, light, clarity, intellect, understanding vs. dirt, ignorance, impurity, smell, bodily functions, and so on. This very traditional division appropriated by Kearney seems curiously at odds with his explanation of the relationship between person and *persona*. The *persona* is a reflection of the inner flux of the impossible becoming of God. But in describing this encounter with otherness, Kearney is careful not to split the embodied from the eternal dimension of human experience, in which the physical body is seen as distinct from the other. Instead, he describes a constant exchange or relation between the two and in this way seeks to prevent a clear break, indeed opposition, between them. This effort is undermined, however, by his use of the tradition of the transfiguration, which, as has been shown, is steeped in similar kinds of binary distinctions.

By appropriating the transfiguration tradition, Kearney situates his notion of God within a number of canonical and doctrinal parameters. While he readily challenges the philosophical/theological frameworks traditionally employed in hermeneutics, he implicitly reaffirms the doctrinal frames of reference inherited from the same Christian "tradition." In the end, Kearney provides an eminently recognizable God, but one who has been positioned differently so as to avoid "being." Kearney's is a God molded and fashioned more by the tradition of the transfiguration and less by the specifics of one or more of the texts that presumably ground and inform this tradition.

And so, Kearney demonstrates a fidelity to a recognizable set of devotional and traditional structures. These structures remain intact despite the challenge to the conventional theological/philosophical repertoire typically employed when thinking "God." Kearney, however, is not alone in challenging one set of canonical texts (philosophical/theological) while championing others (doctrinal, traditional, even the canon of English literature with his use of *Moby Dick* as an exemplar).

In a certain way, Hart is doing the same. Hart promotes the possibility of reading *écriture* as "scripture," but at the same time, he also promotes particular parameters within which the possibilities of interpretation are confined (the limits of doctrine, the Catholic tradition, certain established devotional and intellectual boundaries, and so on). Hart demonstrates at once a critical openness to the play of language, while at the same time asserting limits to the play of meaning by means of traditional canonical structures. There is always the possibility that reading texts such as the transfiguration can lead interpretation to places not only outside the structures of traditional metaphysical conceptions but also outside the traditional canonical structures. Just as *écriture* can't exclude "scripture" as one possible association, the meaning generated by the scriptures cannot be entirely controlled by the authority of the canon.

Hart's position becomes clear when he engages in a vivid conversation with George Aichele. In this fascinating *renga*-like conversation published in the recent *Derrida and Religion* (Sherwood and Hart 2005), these two scholars respond to issues of forgiveness, canonicity, and the distinction between exegesis/eisegesis while focusing on the story of the adulterous woman in the Gospel of John (8:1–11). What is apparent from this dialogue is that when it comes to the broader consequences of Derridean theory for interpreting the biblical text, they represent two starkly contrasting visions. As is the nature of the *renga*, however, it is the tension in the space between that is most compelling.

Aichele is at odds with Hart in a number of ways, but chief among these is the issue of the authority of the biblical canon and the challenges to its well-established influence on, indeed control of, interpretation. This is not only a matter of distinguishing what is clearly inside from what is outside the canon. Aichele argues that even within the canon there have always been problematic passages, jarring elements, and ambiguities that resist what must be a clear, singular, and Absolute Truth (2001: 20–21).

Aichele finds these examples in abundance and in fact cites the entire Gospel of Mark as a prime example (2001: 194–200). Mark's language is poetic in character, its story open ended; it is composed of obscure and conflicting imagery, all of which resist canonical control. One way of controlling the "wild connotations" of Mark, observes Aichele, is to situate it between Matthew and Luke so that the "wild" version is book-ended by more reliable accounts. Another method might involve abstracting and absorbing Mark's story into a traditional version where a certain reading is preserved—and the prominence of Matthew's, Luke's, and Paul's versions of the transfiguration, at the expense of the details found in Mark, is a smaller-scale example of this. The canon, however, is not always able to explain itself sufficiently through these means. Sometimes more is needed to control meanings that threaten to disrupt the status quo. In this case, Aichele explains, control typically requires the cultivation of extracanonical commentary. He describes commentary as a process that serves to affirm and perpetuate the ideology of the canon from the outside; the use of the transfiguration tradition as a lens or template for interpretation, such as that practiced by Kearney, would be an example of this. The power and governance of the canon assure that the messy work of the bleacher need never offend.

Elsewhere, Aichele has much more to say about the history, development, and, in his view, eventual demise of the canon. In the conversation with Hart, however, their attention is focused on the limits of canon and what is arguably an "orphan" text in the Gospel of John. Aichele and Hart's discussion intensifies when they consider the extent to which the biblical canon retains and ensures power over contemporary interpretation. Hart sees that at least implicit authority is still given to this collection of sacred texts within Western (specifically U.S.) culture. Aichele argues that in contemporary North America such influence is at best losing ground. The biblical canon fails because it can no longer function authoritatively for all. The authority of the canon and its ability to control interpretation and meaning are being steadily eroded away within a large and diverse hypertextual society.[29] He prefers to look to postcanonical possibilities for these texts (indeed, he describes himself as a "postcanonical theologian").

Aichele finds a provocative example of the loss of canonical authority in the details of John's text. He notes Jesus' unknown writing in the sand that is part of

---

29. Incidentally, Hart and Aichele's conversation was originally a trans-Pacific e-mail correspondence; not quite hypertextual but still firmly within the realm of cyberspace.

the scene in question, and this action emerges as an evocative and ironic image—writing that while written by Jesus himself is unable to be included in the canon by virtue of its indecipherability. However, despite offering a pointed challenge to Hart's reluctance to relinquish canonical authority, one wonders if it is possible to do away with the structures and limits of canonicity altogether. Is such a goal altruistic, considering the way Christianity and the ideology of Christianity have shaped and continue to shape Western society and culture?

As with any text, the tradition itself has always had excesses and surpluses that resist being harnessed and homogenized—Jesus' writing in the sand being a particularly illustrative example of this for Aichele, but of course there are also examples to be found in Mark's transfiguration. Ironically, at the end of their dialogue, Hart offers an example that at once confirms and exceeds both their claims. In doubting the possibility that a clear line can be drawn between canonical and non-canonical readings, Hart ends with the following story:

> A few years ago when one of my favorite Australian writers, Helen Garner, wrote a book about feminism and forgiveness, based on a specific incident in a university college only minutes from where I used to live, she called it *The First Stone*. The book caused quite a furor, and it was willfully misunderstood in all sorts of ways, though I cannot recall anyone not catching the allusion in the title. I have no doubt that one of the vanishing points of that brave book was precisely the story that has intrigued us today, the story we now look for in the fourth gospel. (Sherwood and Hart 2005: 259–60).

In Hart's example the limits of canonicity are sorely tested. On one hand, the canon can be seen to be exerting authority over a moral and social issue (namely, a case of sexual harassment). On the other hand, it is manifest in a way that escapes traditional interpretive uses of this text (the fact that this was not a specifically religious issue and that presumably the text from John's Gospel was not itself read in any traditional way alongside the events as they unfolded). In addition, Garner's story is a fictionalization of the events in question, and thus we now have an intertextual reading of John's Gospel story (if not a type of secular commentary). While this relation affirms the cultural authority of this text, clearly the institutional authority governing its dissemination and tradition of interpretation is no longer functioning in traditional ways. So, Hart cites an example that exceeds the traditional authority of the canon but demonstrates to Aichele that the authority of the fragmented canon nonetheless functions outside of more traditional totalizing structures.

Given the criticism leveled at Kearney's palatable God without "being," it is also relevant that the case retold in Garner's book involves sexuality and inappropriate uses of power in such an embodied context. As such, this is the only place in their dialogue where "fleshiness" and corporeality are featured. Despite the fact that this dimension of John's story is so prominent, it receives little attention within Hart's and Aichele's more theoretical musings.

Hart's example demonstrates both the end (of a certain type of canonical authority) and the perpetuation of the canon within Western culture (the authority of the canon continues to influence but in far more diverse and fragmented ways than were traditionally recognized). But, of course, a number of questions remain. How does one deal with the challenge of canonical authority, particularly when one is deliberately seeking to rethink such parameters? Indeed, when is it appropriate to challenge the authority of tradition and canonicity, both of which can be a rich source of inspiration and often keep us from "reinventing the wheel"? Can Garner's book contribute to "theology" (moral or otherwise), considering its place outside tradition parameters? If it is not theology, at what point have we wandered far enough from the tradition that our musings no longer resemble the musings of faith? Indeed, is it even possible to speak of inside/outside distinctions when texts such as the Markan transfiguration can lead one in starkly different and unexpected directions than traditionally anticipated? As Aichele suggests, we ought also to consider the influence of a hypertextual world in which contexts are positioned in radically different ways. There may well be a need to shake up the traditional limits of the Christian canon and certainly scrutinize the use of a "canon within a canon" but, of course, before this work is even started, one is faced with a host of additional questions, such as, How is this to be done? By whom? And to what end?

## *Conclusion*

The course of this chapter can be plotted beneath two overarching questions: What is the transfiguration? and What is revealed in this encounter? These questions were identified in chap. 3 as integral to more traditional approaches to the Markan text and indicative of certain theological frames of reference that lie behind these approaches. These questions were then carried over into a Derridean rereading in chap. 3, where I attempted to interpret the transfiguration in ways that eluded certain presuppositions that traditional approaches have brought to bear on the Markan text. I discovered, in plumbing the depths of the obscurities, gaps, and fissures of the text, that revealed there is an unexpected encounter with the sacred. This encounter with a marginal and fragmentary sense of "otherness" was one that, to a certain extent, sidestepped the metaphysical, and in the process revealed, by not revealing, something of the alienating and fragmentary conditions of language, of meaning, and, by extension, of self-experience. This revelation prompted the investigation of the work of Blanchot and his theorizing of the sacred moment in literature. The results of this investigation revealed a distinctly poetic sense of transfiguration. This notion of a literary transfiguration was further developed in dialogue with the poetic that itself had thematic connections to the transfiguration.

I discovered in the process of these readings that while some of the questions asked remain familiar to traditional approaches to the Markan text, the way these questions have been phrased and attended to has resulted in considerable divergence. A literary/poetic sense of transfiguration, a sense that seeks to respond to a particular notion of otherness, was developed in favor of the metaphysical vision of glory that was seen in chap. 3 to be underlying traditional approaches to this passage. Joining these questions about the meaning of the transfiguration were additional questions that sought to account for employing a "secular" reading strategy with a text that has had particularly vivid theological consequences. With this in mind, in the last part of this chapter, I limited my scope, focusing on the point of encounter between literary theory and theology. Following a brief return to Derrida's treatment of the Babel story, I pursued Hart's discussions of the sacred sense of *écriture* as well as the relationship between negative theology and aspects of Derrida's thought. What emerged from this was the realization that theological conceptions need not be excluded in a Derridean approach to interpretation. Moreover, my rereading of the transfiguration passage demonstrates the possibility of an encounter between those theological conceptions of the divine and a more literary sense of sacredness. This relationship, however, is conditioned by the recognition that where Derrida's work is utilized, the way forward must be marked by a certain amount of theological reformulation.

In a brief introduction to an excerpt from Derrida's "How to Avoid Speaking," an essay in which Derrida engages some of the complexities of negative theology from a literary (rather than theological) perspective, Hart writes about the implications of Derridean thought to theology: "Perhaps Derrida's most important legacy for theology is not his reading of negative theology, fascinating though it is, but the thought that theology must be maintained or recast in a 'negative form'" (Hart 1997: 165). Just as biblical ways of reading have influenced Derridean theory, with the appearance of allegory and Midrash, so too literary notions of writing and the limits of philosophy have pervaded biblical studies so that theological frames of reference have been considerably broadened.

The impact of Derridean theory on biblical studies and the corresponding demand to reevaluate a theological element that has a history within both these discourses has special relevance to the transfiguration story, a story that proposes to reveal something of the nature of the divine. Works such as Kearney's *The God Who May Be* go some way toward incorporating such theoretical influences into the work of theology. However, they remain bound by canonical limits that prevent the more problematic elements from being dealt with. In fact, canonicity could be a major issue when it comes to meeting Derrida's challenge to the history of metaphysics and the notion of God that emerges from this tradition. Aichele introduces an ideological reading of canonicity that reveals what may be for some a nonnegotiable limit in theological discourse after Derrida. Questions emerge from the conversation between Aichele and Hart which demonstrate that, given our contemporary cultural and technological context, the way forward is far from clear. The canon may well continue to function, albeit in markedly different ways, and may continue to shape interpretation and meaning despite its disconnection from its traditional locus of authority.

In returning to the questions that began this chapter, it becomes apparent that not only is the question of *what* is revealed in need of reformulation, but it seems of equal significance to now ask *how* this revelation occurs. We also need to consider how the outcome of these questions not only affects one's theological formulations of the divine but how they simultaneously affect the way the text is read and, in turn, one's self-understanding.

CONCLUSION

I began this book by observing that the Markan transfiguration is a text that, despite its apparent clarity, plays host to a number of problematic and obscuring elements. I introduced Derridean theory, with its attention to the structures of metaphysics and its focus on textuality, as a way of accounting for these problematic textual moments. It was from this alternative perspective that I then reread Mark's version of the transfiguration story.

In chap. 1, I introduced Derridean theory and noted certain features of its application in biblical studies. I presented Derrida's own reading of the tower of Babel story as a key example and then briefly explored his reception within the fields of literary criticism and philosophy. Then, in chap. 2, I pursued Derrida's reception within biblical studies to greater depth and observed that applications of Derridean theory within this field of research, although largely deconstructive in character, reveal a certain attentiveness to the implications of this theoretical approach. A number of critics whom I discussed demonstrated an awareness of the impact on both traditional scholarly methods and the demands of a notion of "otherness." I concluded chap. 2 by looking at an example of the incorporation of Derridean theory within an overall approach to biblical interpretation (Francis Landy's work). While I don't write in the style of Landy, his example is significant in that he demonstrates a particular mode of reading that would influence my own allegorically informed rereading to follow.

Chapter 3 was a survey of traditional scholarship in biblical studies on the Markan transfiguration. Here, it became apparent that underlying approaches to this text was a certain conception of God's glory, a glory that was synonymous with light, presence, and fullness. Critics tend to see the glory revealed in the transfiguration as a central clarifying point in Mark's broader exposition of God's glory. In their interpretations, the transfiguration looks back to a clear beginning and points forward to an expected future fulfillment. When cast in this light, certain elements of the transfiguration passage seemed to fit awkwardly and were pushed to the margins or passed over altogether (the image of the bleacher). Other textual elements contradicted this vision of clarity and fullness, as strange shadows and unexpected colorings became difficulties that did not seem consonant with what was expected (the missing face, Peter's error). And even what seemed the most apparent and self-evident images of all contained within them their own ambiguities

## Conclusion

(Jesus' transfigured robes, the disciples' fear). In scholarship, then, the transfiguration is read as a model of God's glory, and this glory, defined in terms of light and fullness, is used to clarify the glory that courses through the Gospel as a whole. This being the case, the details of this passage and the way they are read have had a significant impact on the way the broader vision of Mark's glory is understood.

In response, I proposed a rereading of the Markan transfiguration in chap. 4, one that took up these problematic elements and read them alongside a selection of Derrida's writings. This rereading sought to avoid presupposing the features and conditions of glory that were seen to underlie traditional readings of this text. Moreover, rather than focusing on what have been considered the central elements of the passage (the Sinai motif, Elijah and Moses, God's voice), this rereading brought to the fore those jarring and repressed images that have, for the most part, been pushed to the margins of the text. Although the perspective was different, certain questions were carried over from chap. 3 to chap. 4. These questions presupposed that the disciples are indeed experiencing something in this encounter—What does it mean to say Jesus was transfigured?—and looked to the appropriateness of their response. In reformulating an answer to these questions, I made connections to other places in Mark's Gospel, in particular the scene at the empty tomb. This is a site that depicts a startling absence and as such appears to be the antithesis of the transfiguration vision. Considering the conclusions drawn from chap. 2, however, I gave attention to "otherness" at both of these points and noted the impact of this on notions of subjectivity. I read the transfiguration as a scene not just about Jesus' transformation—a metamorphosis that revealed something of the fullness of God's glory—but also as a confrontation with a certain sense of "otherness," a lacking within this full vision that is also a lacking within ourselves. It is a scene that depicts the response to this otherness, a response that is fearful and irresponsible, but at the same time faithful to the "truth" of this encounter.

This notion of a transfiguration that reveals what cannot be revealed, in an encounter with the impossible, was further explored in chap. 5. Using Blanchot's development of a literary or poetic notion of transfiguration, I turned to two poems where this notion could be further elaborated. Blanchot speaks of the "sacred," of an encounter with the "opacity" of meaning and of a transfiguring sense of the poetic. Consequently, I investigated an experience of "otherness" that occurs within language, within poetry and the literary, and, moreover, charted its subsequent impact on subjectivity. In the final part of this chapter, I raised questions as to the relationship between Derridean theory and theology. I concluded here by taking Hart's suggestion that for literary theory to be a part of theological inquiry, the structures of theology need to be reformulated to some extent.

Throughout the course of this book, it has been difficult to resist the temptation to expand the field of view and attempt to account for broader elements and consequences. The themes explored in this book touch on the areas of theology and philosophy, as well as literary theory and cultural studies. Despite the larger ramifications of commenting on conceptions of God's glory, I have had to narrow my scope somewhat and keep my investigation to the image of glory presented in the Markan transfiguration scene itself, particularly the image implicit in commentators' readings of this passage. I have had to resist the temptation of moving beyond the shifting borders of biblical studies and delving too far into the theological realm. Despite the fact that the distinction between the two is uncertain, I have been interested in the image of God's glory implicit in biblical studies' approaches to this text. Throughout, I have reread the image of glory and have suggested that it can be understood differently.

Along the way, certain critical approaches have stood out as ways of integrating Derrida's approach into a way of reading biblical texts that maintains a balanced connection to the biblical studies enterprise. The most effective of these (particularly Landy) were able to balance and maintain a number of traditional scholarly aims and show that the distinctions between the literary and theological, the critical and poetic can melt away. These critical approaches have been a major reason for including Derrida's later works rather than simply proposing yet another "deconstructive reading" of a biblical text. To be sure, deconstructive criticism represents a well-known part of Derrida's overall thought, but Derridean theory extends beyond this. For instance, in attending to textual otherness, it has pertinent applications in biblical scholarship, and, in terms of this book, for the reading of the Markan transfiguration passage.

In the end, the impact of this book bears most directly on the traditional approaches that still dominate the scholarship on the Markan transfiguration. Bringing Derrida to traditional readings has revealed the need to broaden the theoretical scope of their approach. This is not to say that traditional motivations need to be relinquished altogether, but there are certainly a number of ramifications that should urge biblical scholarship toward increased interdisciplinarity, notably the incorporation of more of the literary-theoretical approach. Even the most minimal consequence of doing so will be a broader sense of what constitutes the theological. The problem with not taking up this challenge is that critics risk tacitly reaffirming longstanding interpretative boundaries around the text which will inevitably influence and determine their readings. In such a situation, they will also be limiting the potentiality for the text to be meaningful beyond traditionally prescribed boundaries.

To this end, an intriguing point of inquiry would be to consider to what extent the transfiguration imagery and the notion of God's glory have already been taken up by voices from outside the academy. Such a championing of the marginal voice is a logical extension of Blanchot's poetic encounter, in which texts are opened to infinite interpretative possibilities. Creating a space for such readings is also a clear consequence of Aichele's challenge to canonicity as is his observation of the hypotextual as a contemporary cultural context. Not only are marginal readers encouraged by such perspectives, but by attending to the structures of meaning and interpretation, alternative reading strategies also become possible. Allegoresis is but one such reading strategy.

Derridean theory implicates the reader and attends to the structures that shape readers, structures that are challenged by Derrida just as much as the structures of metaphysics. The question of otherness situates and implicates the reader/critic in the creation of meaning. In this way, the text is accessible to different readers as well as to different readings. Certainly the way is open for both marginal and mainstream voices to sketch anew the contours of glory in Mark's Gospel and beyond. In so doing, they might speak of transfiguring encounters in ways and for reasons not yet conceived.

BIBLIOGRAPHY

Adam, A. K. M. 1995. *What Is Postmodern Biblical Criticism?* Guides to Biblical Scholarship. Minneapolis: Augsburg Fortress Press.
———, ed. 2000a. *Handbook of Postmodern Biblical Interpretation*. St. Louis: Chalice Press.
———. 2000b. *Postmodern Interpretations of the Bible: A Reader*. St. Louis: Chalice Press.
Agua Perez, Agustin del. 1993. "The Narrative of the Transfiguration as a Derashic Scenification of a Faith Confession (Mark 9:2–8 par)." *NTS* 39:340–54.
Aichele, George. 1996a. *Jesus Framed*. London: Routledge.
———. 1996b. Review of *What Is Postmodern Biblical Criticism?* by A. K. M. Adam, *JBL* 115: 721–22.
———. 2001. *The Control of Biblical Meaning: Canon as Semiotic Mechanism*. Harrisburg, Pa.: Trinity Press International.
Allan, Archibald. 1923. *The Transfiguration of Jesus*. Edinburgh: Oliver & Boyd.
Allison, D. C., Jr. 1984. "Elijah Must Come First." *JBL* 103: 256–58.
Anderson, Hugh. 1976. *The Gospel of Mark*. Met Century Bible Commentary. Grand Rapids: Eerdmans; London: Marshal, Morgan & Scott.
Anderson, Janice Capel, and Stephen D. Moore, eds. 1992. *Mark and Method: New Approaches in Biblical Studies*. Minneapolis: Fortress Press.
Aristotle. 1995. *Topics*. Translated by W. A. Pickard-Cambridge. Procyon Publishing. http://libertyonline.hypermall.com/Aristotle/Logic/Topics-Bk5.html.
Audi, Robert, ed. 1999. *The Cambridge Dictionary of Philosophy*. 2nd ed. Cambridge: Cambridge University Press.
Baker, William, and Kenneth Womack, eds. 1996. *Recent Work in Critical Theory 1989–1995: An Annotated Bibliography*. Westport, Conn.: Greenwood Press.
Baltensweiler, Heinrich. 1959. *Die Verklärung Jesu: Historisches Ereignis und synoptische Berichte*. Zurich: Zwingli-Verlag.
Barclay, William. 1975. *The Daily Study Bible: The Gospel of Mark*. Revised edition. Toronto: G. R. Welch.
Barnett, Panel. 1991. *The Servant King: Reading Mark Today*. Sydney: Anglican Information Office.
Barta, Karen A. 1988. *The Gospel of Mark*. Message of Biblical Spirituality 9. Edited by Carolyn Osiek. Wilmington, Del.: Michael Glazier.

Barthes, Roland. 1974. *S/Z*. Translated by Richard Miller. New York: Hill & Wang.
———. 1977. "The Struggle with the Angel." Pages 125–41 in *Image—Music—Text*. Edited and translated by Stephen Heath. New York: Hill & Wang.
———. 1985. "Wrestling with the Angel: Textual Analysis of Genesis 32:23–33." Pages 246–60 in *The Semiotic Challenge*. Oxford: Basil Blackwell.
———. 1990. *The Pleasure of the Text*. Translated by Richard Miller. Oxford: Basil Blackwell.
Barton, John, ed. 1998. *The Cambridge Companion to Biblical Interpretation*. Cambridge: Cambridge University Press.
Beal, Timothy K. 1997. *The Book of Hiding: Gender, Ethnicity, Annihilation, and Esther*. Biblical Limits. London: Routledge.
Bennington, Geoffrey, and Jacques Derrida. 1993. *Jacques Derrida*. Translated by Geoffrey Bennington. Chicago: University of Chicago Press.
Berg, Temma F. 1989. "Reading in/to Mark." *Semeia* 48: 187–206.
Bernadin, J. B. 1933. "The Transfiguration." *JBL* 52: 181–89.
Best, Ernest. 1983. *Mark: The Gospel as Story*. Edinburgh: T & T Clark.
———. 1986. *Disciples and Discipleship: Studies in the Gospel According to Mark*. Edinburgh: T & T Clark.
The Bible and Culture Collective. 1995. *The Postmodern Bible*. New Haven/London: Yale University Press. Cited as BCC.
BibleWorks. 2001. Version 5.0 for Windows. BibleWorks, LLC.
Blanchot, Maurice. 1981. *The Gaze of Orpheus and Other Literary Essays*. Edited by P. Adams Sitney. Translated by Lydia Davis. Barrytown, N.Y.: Station Hill Press.
———. 1982. *The Space of Literature*. Translated by Ann Smock. Lincoln: University of Nebraska Press.
———. 1995. *Work of Fire*. Translated by Charlotte Mandell. Stanford, Calif.: Stanford University Press.
Blank, G. Kim. 1986. "Deconstruction: Entering the Bible through Babel." *Neot* 20: 61–67.
Blodgett, E. D. 2001. *Transfigured*. Unpublished poem.
Blodgett, E. D., and Jacques Brault. 1998. *Transfiguration*. Saint-Hippolyte, P.Q.: Éditions du Noroît; Toronto: BuschekBooks.
Boobyer, George Henry. 1942. *St. Mark and the Transfiguration Story*. Edinburgh: T & T Clark.
Boring, Eugene M. 1999. "Markan Christology: God-Language for Jesus?" *NTS* 45: 451–71.
Bratcher, Robert G., and Eugene A. Nida. 1961. *A Translator's Handbook on the Gospel of Mark*. Leiden: E. J. Brill.
Brooks, James A. 1991. *Mark*. The New American Commentary 23. Nashville, Tenn.: Broadman Press.
Brueggemann, Walter. 1993. *Texts under Negotiation: The Bible and Postmodern Imagination*. Minneapolis: Fortress Press.

Bruns, Gerald L. 1997. *Maurice Blanchot: The Refusal of Philosophy*. Baltimore: Johns Hopkins University Press.
Bryan, Christopher. 1993. *A Preface to Mark: Notes on the Gospel in its Literary and Cultural Settings*. New York: Oxford University Press.
Bubar, Wallace W. 1995. "Killing Two Birds with One Stone: The Utter De(con)struction of Matthew." *BibInt* 3: 144–57.
Budick, Sanford, and Geoffrey H. Hartman, eds. 1986. *Midrash and Literature*. New Haven: Yale University Press.
Bultmann, Rudolf. 1968. *The History of the Synoptic Tradition*. 2nd ed. Translated by J. Marsh. New York: Harper & Row.
Burgass, Catherine. 1999. *Challenging Theory: Discipline after Deconstruction*. Aldershot, U.K.: Ashgate.
Cahill, Michael, ed. and trans. 1998. *The First Commentary on Mark: An Annotated Translation*. New York: Oxford University Press.
Caputo, John D. 1987. *Radical Hermeneutics: Repetition, Deconstruction, and the Hermeneutic Project*. Bloomington: Indiana University Press.
———, ed. 1997. *Deconstruction in a Nutshell: A Conversation with Jacques Derrida*. Edited with commentary by John D. Caputo. New York: Fordham University Press.
Caputo, John D., and Michael J. Scanlon, eds. 1999. *God, the Gift and Postmodernism*. Bloomington: Indiana University Press.
Carlston, C. E. 1961. "Transfiguration and Resurrection." *JBL* 80: 233–40.
Carroll, Robert P. 1998. "Poststructuralist Approaches New Historicism and Postmodernism." In Barton 1998: Pages 50–66.
Chilton, B. D. 1979. *God in Strength*. Studien zum Neuen Testament und seiner Umwelt. Freistadt: Plöchl.
———. 1980. "The Transfiguration: Dominical Assurance and Apostolic Vision." *NTS* 27: 115–24.
———. 1992. "Transfiguration." In *The Anchor Bible Dictionary*. Edited by D. N. Freedman. Volume 6. New York: Doubleday.
Clark, Timothy. 1992. *Derrida, Heidegger, Blanchot: Sources of Derrida's Notion and Practice of Literature*. Cambridge: Cambridge University Press.
Clines, David J. A. 1990. "Deconstructing the Book of Job." Pages 65–80 in *The Bible as Rhetoric: Studies in Biblical Persuasion and Credibility*. Edited by Martin Warner. Warwick Studies in Philosophy and Literature. London: Routledge.
———. 1993. "Haggai's Temple, Constructed, Deconstructed and Reconstructed." *SJOT* 7: 51–77.
———. 1995. "Deconstructing the Book of Job." *Bible Review* 11: 30–35, 43–44.
———. 1998. *On the Way to the Postmodern: Old Testament Essays, 1967–1998*. Volume 1. Sheffield: Sheffield Academic Press.
Coleridge, Mark. 1992. "In Defence of the Other: Deconstruction and the Bible." *Pacifica* 5: 123–44.

Conzelmann, Hans. 1960. *The Theology of St. Luke.* Translated by Geoffrey Buswell. New York: Harper.
Counet, Patrick Chatelion. 2000. *John, A Postmodern Gospel: Introduction to Deconstructive Exegesis Applied to the Fourth Gospel.* Leiden: E. J. Brill.
Cranfield, C. E. B. 1966. *The Gospel of St. Mark.* 3rd ed. Cambridge: Cambridge University Press.
Critchley, Simon. 1992. *The Ethics of Deconstruction: Derrida and Levinas.* Oxford: Blackwell.
Crossan, John Dominic. 1978. "A Form for Absence: The Markan Creation of Gospel." *Semeia* 12: 41–53.
———. 1980. *Cliffs of Fall: Paradox and Polyvalence in the Parables of Jesus.* New York: Seabury Press.
———. 1988. *The Cross That Spoke: The Origins of the Passion Narrative.* San Francisco: Harper & Row.
Culler, Jonathan. 1982. *On Deconstruction: Theory and Criticism after Structuralism.* Ithaca, N.Y.: Cornell University Press.
Cutrofello, Andrew. 1998. "Derrida, Jacques (1930-)." *Routledge Encyclopedia of Philosophy.* Edited by Craig Edward. London: Routledge.
Daniel, Felix Harry. 1976. "The Transfiguration (Mark 9/2–13 and Parallels): A Redaction Critical and Traditio-Historical Study." Ph.D. diss., Vanderbilt University.
Danove, Paul L. 1993. *The End of Mark's Story: A Methodological Study.* Leiden: E. J. Brill.
———. 1996. "The Characterisation and Narrative Function of the Women at the Empty Tomb (Mk 15.40–41; 16.1–8)." *Bib* 77: 375–97.
Davis, Robert Con, and Ronald Schleifer, eds. 1985. *Rhetoric and Form: Deconstruction at Yale.* Norman: University of Oklahoma Press.
———. 1991. *Criticism and Culture: The Role of Critique in Modern Literary Theory.* London: Longman.
Dawes, Gregory W. 1996. "Derrida among the Teachers of the Law: Deconstruction and Biblical Studies." *Pacifica* 9: 301–9.
de Man, Paul. 1979. *Allegories of Reading: Figural Language in Rousseau, Nietzsche, Rilke and Proust.* New Haven: Yale University Press.
Derrett, J. Duncan M. 1990. "Peter and the Tabernacles (Mark 9:5–7) [insights from Jonah]." *DRev* 108: 37–48.
Derrida, Jacques. 1973. *Speech and Phenomena: And Other Essays on Husserl's Theory of Signs.* Translated by David B. Allison. Evanston, Ill.: Northwestern University Press.
———. 1974a. *Of Grammatology.* Translated by Gayatri Chakravorty Spivak. Baltimore: Johns Hopkins University Press.
———. 1974b. "White Mythology: Metaphor in the Text of Philosophy." *New Literary History* 6: 5–74.

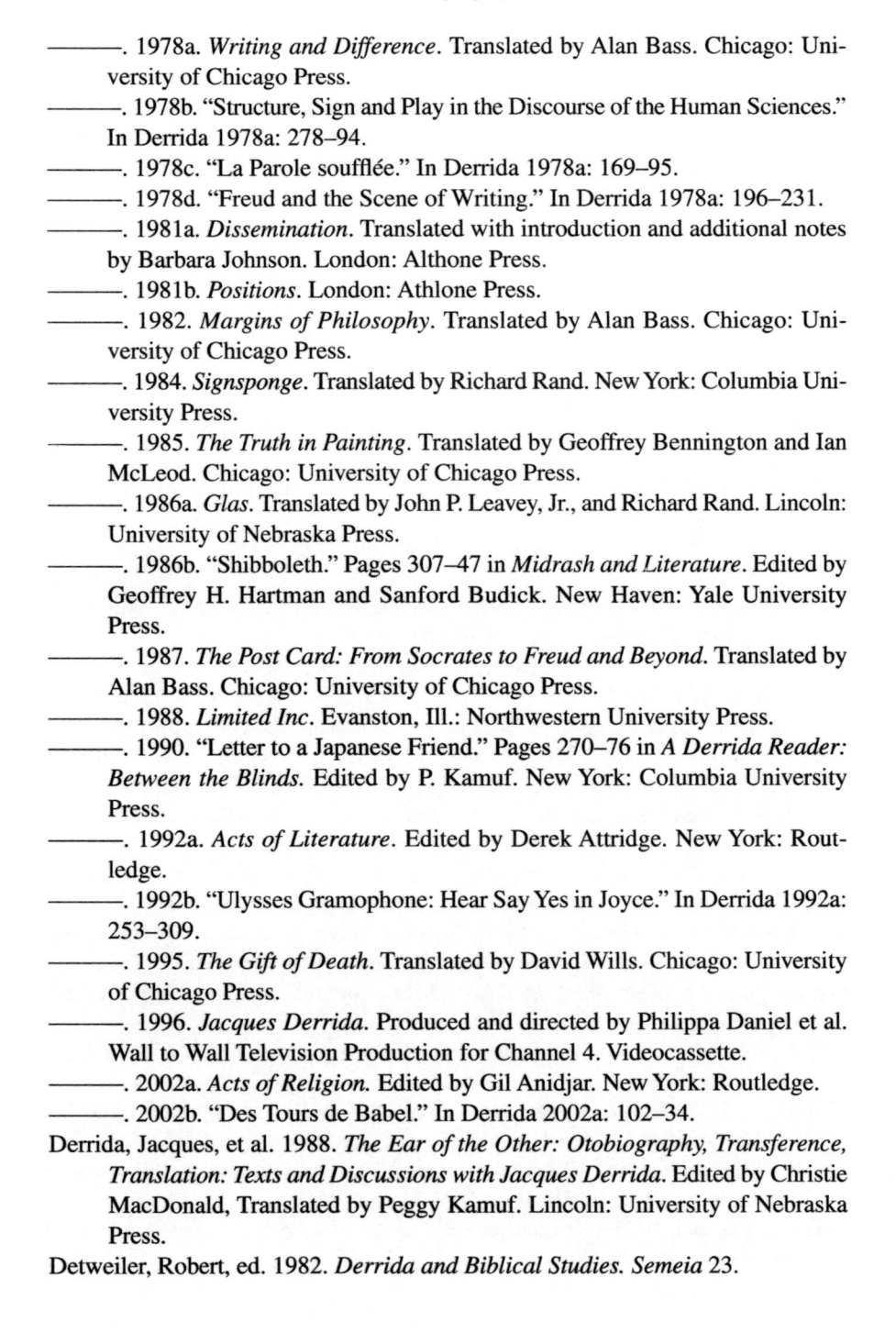

———. 1978a. *Writing and Difference*. Translated by Alan Bass. Chicago: University of Chicago Press.

———. 1978b. "Structure, Sign and Play in the Discourse of the Human Sciences." In Derrida 1978a: 278–94.

———. 1978c. "La Parole soufflée." In Derrida 1978a: 169–95.

———. 1978d. "Freud and the Scene of Writing." In Derrida 1978a: 196–231.

———. 1981a. *Dissemination*. Translated with introduction and additional notes by Barbara Johnson. London: Althone Press.

———. 1981b. *Positions*. London: Athlone Press.

———. 1982. *Margins of Philosophy*. Translated by Alan Bass. Chicago: University of Chicago Press.

———. 1984. *Signsponge*. Translated by Richard Rand. New York: Columbia University Press.

———. 1985. *The Truth in Painting*. Translated by Geoffrey Bennington and Ian McLeod. Chicago: University of Chicago Press.

———. 1986a. *Glas*. Translated by John P. Leavey, Jr., and Richard Rand. Lincoln: University of Nebraska Press.

———. 1986b. "Shibboleth." Pages 307–47 in *Midrash and Literature*. Edited by Geoffrey H. Hartman and Sanford Budick. New Haven: Yale University Press.

———. 1987. *The Post Card: From Socrates to Freud and Beyond*. Translated by Alan Bass. Chicago: University of Chicago Press.

———. 1988. *Limited Inc*. Evanston, Ill.: Northwestern University Press.

———. 1990. "Letter to a Japanese Friend." Pages 270–76 in *A Derrida Reader: Between the Blinds*. Edited by P. Kamuf. New York: Columbia University Press.

———. 1992a. *Acts of Literature*. Edited by Derek Attridge. New York: Routledge.

———. 1992b. "Ulysses Gramophone: Hear Say Yes in Joyce." In Derrida 1992a: 253–309.

———. 1995. *The Gift of Death*. Translated by David Wills. Chicago: University of Chicago Press.

———. 1996. *Jacques Derrida*. Produced and directed by Philippa Daniel et al. Wall to Wall Television Production for Channel 4. Videocassette.

———. 2002a. *Acts of Religion*. Edited by Gil Anidjar. New York: Routledge.

———. 2002b. "Des Tours de Babel." In Derrida 2002a: 102–34.

Derrida, Jacques, et al. 1988. *The Ear of the Other: Otobiography, Transference, Translation: Texts and Discussions with Jacques Derrida*. Edited by Christie MacDonald, Translated by Peggy Kamuf. Lincoln: University of Nebraska Press.

Detweiler, Robert, ed. 1982. *Derrida and Biblical Studies. Semeia* 23.

———. 1989. *Breaking the Fall: Religious Readings of Contemporary Fiction.* Louisville: Westminster/John Knox Press.

Detweiler, Robert, and Vernon K. Robbins. 1991. "From New Criticism to Poststructuralism: Twentieth Century Hermeneutics." In Prickett 1991: 225–80.

Detweiler, Robert, and William G. Doty, eds. 1990. *The Daemonic Imagination: Biblical Text and Secular Story.* Atlanta: Scholars Press.

Dewey, Joanna. 1991. "Recent Studies on Mark." *RSR* 17: 12–16.

Dillon, Richard J. 1978. *From Eye-Witnesses to Ministers of the Word: Tradition and Composition in Luke 24.* Rome: Biblical Institute Press.

Donaldson, Terence L. 1985. *Jesus on the Mountain: A Study in Matthean Theology.* Sheffield: JSOT Press.

Dorris, C. E. W. 1970. *A Commentary on the Gospel According to Mark.* Nashville: Gospel Advocate Company.

Dwyer, Timothy. 1996. *The Motif of Wonder in the Gospel of Mark.* Sheffield: Sheffield Academic Press.

Ellis, John M. 1989. *Against Deconstruction.* Princeton: Princeton University Press.

Ernst, Josef. 1981. *Das Evangelium nach Markus.* Regensburg: Verlag Friedrich Pustet.

Evans, J. Claude. 1991. *Strategies of Deconstruction: Derrida and the Myth of the Voice.* Minneapolis: University of Minnesota Press.

Fewell, Danna Nolan. 1995. "Deconstructive Criticism: Achsah and the (E)razed City of Writing." Pages 119–45 in *Judges and Method: New Approaches in Biblical Studies.* Edited by Gale A. Yee. Minneapolis: Fortress Press.

Fitzmyer, Joseph A. 1985. "More about Elijah Coming First [reply to D C Allison, Jr, 'Elijah must come first,' 103, 256–258 1984]." *JBL* 104: 295–96.

Fowler, Robert M. 1991. *Let the Reader Understand: Reader-Response Criticism and the Gospel of Mark.* Minneapolis: Fortress Press.

Franke, Chris. 2000. Review of *On the Way to the Postmodern* by David J. A. Clines. *RBL* www.bookreviews.org/Reviews/1850759014.html.

Frei, Hans W. 1974. *The Eclipse of Biblical Narrative: A Study in Eighteenth and Nineteenth Century Hermeneutics.* New Haven: Yale University Press.

Garland, David E. 1996. *Mark.* NIV Application Commentary. Grand Rapids: Zondervan Publishing House.

Garner, Helen. 1997. *The First Stone: Some Questions about Sex and Power.* New York: Free Press.

Geddert, T. J. 1989. *Watchwords: Mark 13 in Markan Eschatology.* JSNTSup 26. Sheffield: Sheffield Academic Press.

Gould, Stephen J., and Rhonda Roland Shearer. 1999/2000. "Boats and Deckchairs." *Natural History* 12/99–1/00: 32–44.

Goulder, Michael. 1979. *The Evangelists' Calendar: A Lectionary Explanation of the Development of Scripture.* London: SPCK.

Greenstein, Edward L. 1989. "Deconstruction and Biblical Narrative." *Prooftexts* 9: 43–71.

———. 1999. "In Job's Face/Facing Job." Pages 301–17 in *The Labour of Reading: Desire, Alienation, and Biblical Interpretation*. Edited by Fiona C. Black, Roland Boer, and Erin Runions. Atlanta: Society of Biblical Literature.

Gundry, Robert H. 1993. *Mark: A Commentary on His Apology for the Cross*. Grand Rapids: Eerdmans.

Guy, H. A. 1968. *The Gospel of Mark*. London: Macmillan & Co.

Hall, Stuart G. 1987. "Synoptic Transfigurations: Mark 9:2–10 and Partners." *King's Theological Review* 10: 41–44.

Harari, Josue V., ed. and trans. 1979. *Textual Strategies: The Philosophy of Structuralism and Post-Structuralism*. New York: Methuen.

Hare, Douglas R. A. 1996. *Mark*. Louisville: Westminster/John Knox Press.

Hart, Kevin. 1991. "The Poetics of the Negative." In Prickett 1991: 281–340.

———. 1997. "Jacques Derrida (b. 1930): Introduction." Pages 159–66 in *The Postmodern God: A Theological Reader*. Edited by Graham Ward. Oxford: Blackwell.

———. 2000. *Trespass of the Sign: Deconstruction, Theology and Philosophy*. 2nd ed. New York: Fordham University Press.

Hartin, P. J. 1991. "Disseminating the Word: A Deconstructive Reading of Mark 4.1–9 and Mark 4.13–20." Pages 187–200 in *Text and Interpretation: New Approaches in the Criticism of the New Testament*. Edited by P. J. Hartin and J. H. Petzer. Leiden: E. J. Brill.

Hartman, Geoffrey. 1980. *Criticism in the Wilderness*. New Haven: Yale University Press.

Heidegger, Martin. 1962. *Being and Time*. Translated by John Macquarrie and Edward Robinson. San Francisco: Harper & Row.

Heil, John Paul. 1992. "The Progressive Narrative Pattern of Mark 14.53–16.8." *Bib* 73: 331–58.

———. 2000. *The Transfiguration of Jesus: Narrative Meaning and Function of Mark 9:2–8, Matt 17:1–8 and Luke 9:28–36*. Analecta Biblica 144. Rome: Editrice Pontificio Istituto Biblico.

Hengel, Martin. 1985. *Studies in the Gospel of Mark*. Translated by John Bowden. Philadelphia: Fortress Press.

Holmes, R. 1903. "The Purpose of the Transfiguration." *JBL* 4: 233–40.

Hooker, Morna D. 1987. "'What Doest Thou Here, Elijah' A Look at St. Mark's Account of the Transfiguration." Pages 59–70 in *The Glory of Christ in the New Testament: Studies in Christology in Memory of George Bradford Caird*. Edited by L. D. Hurst and N. T. Wright. Oxford: Clarendon Press.

———. 1991. *The Gospel According to Saint Mark*. London: A & C Black.

Horsley, Richard A. 2001. *Hearing the Whole Story: The Politics of Plot in Mark's Gospel*. Louisville: Westminster/John Knox Press.

Hughes, Kent R. 1989. *Mark: Jesus, Servant and Saviour*. Volume 2. Westchester, Ill.: Crossway Books.
Hunter, J. H. 1987. "Deconstruction and Biblical Texts: An Introduction and Critique." *Neot* 21: 125–40.
Hurtado, Larry W. 1983. *Mark*. NIBC. Peabody, Mass.: Hendrickson.
Hutton, Rodney R. 1994. "Moses on the Mount of Transfiguration [bibliog]." *HAR* 14: 99–120.
Jasper, David. 1998. "Literary Readings of the Bible." In Barton 1998: 21–34.
Jasper, David, and M. Ledbetter, eds. 1994. *In Good Company: Essays in Honor of Robert Detweiler*. Atlanta: Scholars Press.
Jobling, David. 1995. "Writing the Wrongs of the World: The Deconstruction of the Biblical Text in the Context of Liberation Theologies." *Semeia* 51: 81–118.
Jobling, David, and Stephen D. Moore, eds. 1991. *Poststructuralism and Exegesis. Semeia* 54. Atlanta: Scholars Press.
Johnson, Sherman E. 1960. *A Commentary on the Gospel According to St. Mark*. London: A & C Black.
Jordan, Lynn Mishkin. 1981. "Elijah Transfigured: A Study of the Narrative of the Transfiguration in the Gospel of Mark." Ph.D. diss., Duke University.
Juel, Donald H. 1990. *Mark*. Augsburg Commentary on the New Testament. Minneapolis: Augsburg Fortress Press.
———. 1994. *A Master of Surprise: Mark Interpreted*. Minneapolis: Fortress Press.
Kamuf, Peggy, ed. 1990. *A Derrida Reader: Between the Blinds*. New York: Columbia University Press.
Kazmierski, Carl R. 1979. *Jesus, the Son of God: A Study of the Markan Tradition and Its Redaction by the Evangelist*. FB. Wurzburg: Echter Verlag.
Kearney, Richard. 2001. *The God Who May Be: A Hermeneutics of Religion*. Bloomington: Indiana University Press.
Kee, Howard Clark. 1971. "Mark as Redactor and Theologian: A Survey of Some Recent Markan Studies." *JBL* 90: 333–36.
———. 1972. "The Transfiguration in Mark: Epiphany or Apocalyptic vision?" Pages 135–52 in *Understanding the Sacred Text: Essays in Honor of Morton S. Enslin on the Hebrew and Christian Beginnings*. Edited by J. Reumann. Valley Forge, Pa.: Judson Press.
———. 1978. "Mark's Gospel in Recent Research." *Int* 32: 353–68.
Keegan, Terence. 1995. "Biblical Criticism and the Challenge of Postmodernism." *BibInt* 3: 1–14.
Keenan, John P. 1995. *The Gospel of Mark: A Mahāyāna Reading*. Maryknoll, N.Y.: Orbis Books.
Kelber, Werner. 1983. *The Oral and the Written Gospel: The Hermeneutics of Speaking and Writing in the Synoptic Tradition, Mark, Paul and Q*. Philadelphia: Fortress Press.

Kenny, A. 1957. "The Transfiguration and the Agony in the Garden." *CBQ* 19: 444–52.
Kermode, Frank. 1979. *Genesis of Secrecy*. Cambridge, Mass.: Harvard University Press.
Landy, Francis. 2001. *Beauty and the Enigma: And Other Essays on the Hebrew Bible*. Sheffield: Sheffield Academic Press.
Lane, William L. 1974. *The Gospel According to Mark*. Grand Rapids: Eerdmans.
Lechte, John. 1994. *Fifty Key Contemporary Thinkers: From Structuralism to Post Modernity*. London: Routledge.
Lectorium Rosicrucianum. 1979. *What Is Transfiguration?* 2nd ed. Haarlem: Lectorium Rosicrucianum.
Lee, Sungho. 2000. Review of *On the Way to the Postmodern*. Volumes 1 and 2, by David J. A. Clines. *RBL* www.bookreviews.org/Reviews/1850759014.html.
Lehman, David. 1995. "Deconstruction after the Fall." Pages 132–49 in *The Emperor Redressed: Critiquing Critical Theory*. Edited by Dwight Eddins. Tuscaloosa: University of Alabama Press.
Leitch, Vincent B. 1983. *Deconstructive Criticism: An Advanced Introduction*. New York: Columbia University Press.
Liddell, Henry George, and Robert Scott. 1940. *A Greek-English Lexicon*. Oxford: Clarendon Press.
Lightfoot, R. H. 1950. *The Gospel Message of St Mark*. Oxford: Oxford University Press.
Lincoln, Andrew T. 1989. "The Promise and the Failure: Mark 16:7, 8." *JBL* 108: 283–300.
Lohmeyer, Ernst. 1967. *Das Evangelium des Markus*. Göttingen: Vandenhoeck & Ruprecht.
Lodge, David. 1988. *Modern Criticism and Theory: A Reader*. London: Longman.
Louw, J. P., and E. A. Nida. 1988. *Louw-Nida Greek-English Lexicon of the New Testament Based on Semantic Domains*. 2nd ed. New York: United Bible Societies. In BibleWindows 2001. Cited as Louw-Nida.
Mack, Burton L. 1988. *A Myth of Innocence*. Philadelphia: Fortress Press.
Magness, J. Lee. 1986. *Sense and Absence: Structure and Suspension in the Ending of Mark's Gospel*. Atlanta: Scholars Press.
Malbon, Elizabeth Struthers, and Edgar V. McKnight. 1994. *The New Literary Criticism and the New Testament*. Sheffield: Sheffield Academic Press.
Mann, C. S. 1986. *Mark: A New Translation with Introduction and Commentary by C. S. Mann*. AB 27. New York: Doubleday.
Mansfield, Robert M. 1987. *"Spirit and Gospel" in Mark*. Peabody, Mass.: Hendrickson.
Marcus, Joel. 1995. "Jesus' Baptismal Vision." *NTS* 41: 512–21.
Marshall, Rob. 1994. *The Transfiguration of Jesus*. London: Darton, Longman & Todd.

Martin, Ralph. 1973. *Mark: Evangelist and Theologian*. Grand Rapids: Zondervan.
Marxsen, Willi. 1959. *Mark the Evangelist: Studies in the Redaction History of the Gospel*. Translated by James Boyce. Nashville, Tenn.: Abingdon.
——. 1968. *Introduction to the New Testament: An Approach to Its Problems*. Oxford: Blackwell.
Matera, Frank J. 1987. *What Are They Saying about Mark?* Mahwah, N.J.: Paulist Press.
McCurley, Foster R. 1974. "And After Six Days (Mark 9:2): A Semitic Literary Device." *JBL* 93: 67–81.
McGuckin, John Anthony. 1987. *The Transfiguration of Christ in Scripture and Tradition*. Studies in the Bible and Early Christianity 9. Lewiston, N.Y.: Edwin Mellen.
Moore, Stephen D. 1989. *Literary Criticism and the Gospels: The Theoretical Challenge*. London: Yale University Press.
——. 1992. *Mark and Luke in Poststructuralist Perspectives: Jesus Begins to Write*. New Haven/London: Yale University Press.
——. 1994. *Poststructuralism and the New Testament: Derrida and Foucault at the Foot of the Cross*. Minneapolis: Fortress Press.
——. 1995. Review of *Deconstructing the New Testament* by David Seeley. *JBL* 114: 729–31.
Moses, A. D. A. 1996. *Matthew's Transfiguration Story and Jewish-Christian Controversy*. Sheffield: Sheffield Academic Press.
Mouffe, Chantal, ed. 1996. *Deconstruction and Pragmatism*. London: Routledge.
Nealon, Jeffrey T. 1993. *Double Reading: Postmodernism after Deconstruction*. Ithaca/London: Cornell University Press.
Neirynck, F., et al. 1992. *The Gospel of Mark: A Cumulative Bibliography 1950–1990*. Brussels: Leuven University Press.
Nineham, D. E. 1963. *Saint Mark*. Pelican New Testament Commentaries. Harmondsworth, U.K.: Penguin Books.
Norris, Christopher. 1987. *Derrida*. Cambridge, Mass.: Harvard University Press.
——. 1983. *The Deconstructive Turn: Essays in the Rhetoric of Philosophy*. London: Methuen.
Nützel, Johannes M. 1973. *Die Verklärungserzählung im Markusevangelium: Eine redaktionsgeschichtliche Untersuchung*. Bamberg: Echter Verlag.
Öhler, Markus. 1996. "Die Verklärung (Mk 9.1–8): Die Ankunft de Herrschaft Gottes auf der Erde." *NovT* 38: 197–217.
Orr, James, ed. 1939. *International Standard Bible Encyclopedia*. Grand Rapids: Eerdmans. In BibleWindows 2001 (rev. ed. 1997). Cited as *ISBE*.
Otto, Randall E. 1997. "The Fear Motivation in Peter's Offer to Build ΤΡΕΙΣ ΣΚΕΝΑΣ." *WTJ* 59: 101–2.
Otto, Rudolph. 1926. *The Idea of the Holy: An Inquiry into the Non-Rational Factor in the Idea of the Divine and Its Relation to the Rational*. Translated by John W. Harvey. London: Oxford University Press.

Painter, John. 1997. *Mark's Gospel: Words in Conflict*. London: Routledge.
Perrin, Norman. 1969a. "Composition of Mark 9:1." *NovT* 11: 1–31.
———. 1969b. *What Is Redaction Criticism?* Philadelphia: Fortress Press.
———. 1977. *The Resurrection According to Matthew, Mark and Luke*. Philadelphia: Fortress Press.
Perry, John Michael. 1993. *Exploring the Transfiguration Story*. Kansas, Mo.: Sheed & Ward.
Peterson, Norman R. 1978. "'Point of View' in Mark's Narrative." *Semeia* 12: 97–119.
Phillips, Gary A. 1994a. "Drawing the Other: The Postmodern and Reading the Bible Imaginatively." In Jasper and Ledbetter 1994: 447–82.
———. 1994b. "The Ethics of Reading Deconstructively, or Speaking Face-to-Face: The Samaritan Woman Meets Derrida at the Well." Pages 283–325 in *The New Literary Criticism and the New Testament*. Edited by E. Struthers Malbon and Edgar McKnight. Sheffield: Sheffield Academic Press.
———. 1995. "You Are Here, Here, Here or Here: Deconstruction's Troubling Interplay." *Semeia* 71: 193–213.
———, ed. 1990. *Poststructural Criticism and the Bible: Text/History/Discourse*. Semeia 51. Atlanta: Scholars Press.
Pilch, John J. 1995. "The Transfiguration of Jesus: An Experience in Alternate Reality." Pages 47–64 in *Modelling Early Christianity: Social-Scientific Studies of the New Testament in Its Context*. Edited by Philip F. Esler. London: Routledge.
Plato. 1994. *Republic*. Translated by Robin Waterfield. Oxford/New York: Oxford University Press.
Poland, Lynn M. 1985. *Literary Criticism and Biblical Hermeneutics: A Critique of Formalist Approaches*. AAR Academy Series 48. Chico, Ca.: Scholars Press.
Porter, Stanley E. 1989. *Verbal Aspect in the Greek of the New Testament, with Reference to Tense and Mood*. Studies in Biblical Greek 1. New York: Lang.
Prickett, Stephen, ed. 1991. *Reading the Text: Biblical Criticism and Literary Theory*. Oxford: Basil Blackwell.
Radford, L. B. 1937. *The Transfiguration of Our Lord*. London/New York: Faith Press.
Rajnath, A., ed. 1989. *Deconstruction: A Critique*. Basingstoke, U.K.: Macmillan.
Ramsey, Michael. 1949. *The Glory of God and the Transfiguration of Christ*. London: Longmans.
Rawlinson, A. E. J. 1925. *St. Mark*. Westminster Commentaries. London: Methuen.
Reid, Barbara E. 1993. *The Transfiguration*. Cahiers de la *Revue biblique*. Paris: J. Gabalda.
———. 1994. "Prayer and the Face of the Transfigured Jesus." Pages 39–53 in *The Lord's Prayer and Other Prayer Texts From the Greco-Roman Era*. Edited by James H. Charlesworth, with Mark Harding and Mark Kiley. Valley Forge, Pa.: Trinity Press International.

Rhoads, David, Joanna Dewey, and Donald Michie. 1999. *Mark as Story: An Introduction to the Narrative of a Gospel*. 2nd ed. Minneapolis: Fortress Press.

Riesenfeld, Harald. 1947. *Jésus Transfiguré: L'arrière-plan du récit évangélique de la transfiguration de Notre-Seigneur*. Copenhagen: Ejnar Munksgaard.

Robbins, Vernon K. 1984. *Jesus the Teacher: A Socio-Rhetorical Interpretation of Mark*. Philadelphia: Fortress Press.

Rorty, R. 1992. "Is Derrida a Transcendental Philosopher?" Pages 235–46 in *Derrida: A Critical Reader*. Edited by David Wood. Oxford: Blackwell.

———. 1995. "Deconstruction." Pages 166–96 in *The Cambridge History of Literary Criticism*. Edited by R. Selden. Cambridge: Cambridge University Press.

Rutledge, David. 1996. *Reading Marginally: Feminism, Deconstruction, and the Bible*. Leiden: E. J. Brill.

Ryrie, Charles C. 1990. *Transformed by His Glory*. Wheaton, Ill.: Victor Books.

Salusinszky, Imre. 1987. *Criticism in Society*. New York: Methuen.

Schwartz, Regina M. 1990. "Joseph's Bones and the Resurrection of the Text: Remembering in the Bible." Pages 40–59 in *The Book and the Text: The Bible and Literary Theory*. Edited by Regina Schwartz. Oxford: Blackwell.

Schweizer, Eduard. 1970. *The Good News According to Mark*. Translated by Donald H. Madvig. Richmond, Va.: John Knox Press.

Seeley, David. 1994. *Deconstructing the New Testament*. Leiden: E. J. Brill.

Selden, Raman, ed. 1995. *The Cambridge History of Literary Criticism*. Vol. 8. Cambridge: Cambridge University Press.

Selden, Raman, and Peter Widdowson. 1993. *A Reader's Guide to Contemporary Literary Theory*. 3rd edition. London: Harvester Wheatsheaf.

Shaviro, Stephen. 1990. *Passion & Excess: Blanchot, Bataille, and Literary Theory*. Tallahassee: Florida State University Press.

Sherwood, Yvonne. 1996. *The Prostitute and the Prophet: Hosea's Marriage in Literary-Theoretical Perspective*. JSOTSup 212. GCT 2. Sheffield: Sheffield Academic Press.

———. 2000. "Derrida." Pages 69–75 in *Handbook of Postmodern Biblical Interpretation*. Edited by A. K. M. Adam. St. Louis: Chalice Press.

———, ed. 2004. *Derrida's Bible: Reading a Page of Scripture with a Little Help from Derrida*. New York: Palgrave Macmillan.

Sherwood, Yvonne, and Kevin Hart, eds. 2005. *Derrida and Religion: Other Testaments*. New York/Oxford: Routledge.

Simpson, J. A., and E. S. C. Weiner, eds. 1989. *The Oxford English Dictionary*. Second edition. Oxford: Clarendon Press.

Smith, Joseph H., and William Kerrigan, eds. 1984. *Taking Chances: Derrida, Psychoanalysis and Literature*. Baltimore: Johns Hopkins University Press.

Smith, Stephen H. 1996. *A Lion with Wings: A Narrative-Critical Approach to Mark's Gospel*. Sheffield: Sheffield Academic Press.

Smith, Stephen Harry. 1985. "Structure, Redaction and Community in the Markan Controversy." Ph.D. diss., University of Sheffield.
Stein, Robert H. 1969. "What Is Redaktionsgeschichte?" *JBL* 88: 45–56.
———. 1971. "The Proper Methodology for Ascertaining a Markan Redaction History." *NovT* 13: 181–98.
———. 1976. "Is the Transfiguration (Mark 9:2–8) a Misplaced Resurrection-Account?" *JBL* 95: 79–96.
Sturrock, John, ed. 1979. *Structuralism and Since: From Lévi-Strauss to Derrida*. New York: Oxford University Press.
Synge, F. C. 1970. "The Transfiguration Story." *ExpTim* 82: 82–83.
Tallis, Raymond. 1995. *Not Saussure: A Critique of Post-Saussurean Literary Theory*. 2nd ed. London: MacMillan Press.
Tate, W. Randolf. 1991. *Biblical Interpretation: An Integrated Approach*. Peabody, Mass.: Hendrickson.
Taylor, Justin. 1991. "The Coming of Elijah, Mt 17:10–13 and Mk 9:11–13: The Development of the Texts." *RB* 98: 107–19.
Taylor, Mark C. 1984. *Erring: A Postmodern A/theology*. Chicago: University of Chicago Press.
Taylor, Vincent. 1952. *The Gospel According to St. Mark*. London: Macmillan.
Telford, William R. 1995. *Mark*. New Testament Guides. Sheffield: Sheffield Academic Press.
———. 1999. *The Theology of the Gospel of Mark*. New Testament Theology Series. Cambridge: Cambridge University Press.
Thackeray, H. St. J. 1979. *Josephus*. Volume 3. Cambridge, Mass.: Harvard University Press.
Thrall, Margaret E. 1969–1970. "Elijah and Moses in Mark's Account of the Transfiguration." *NTS* 16: 305–17.
Throckmorton, Burton H., Jr., ed. 1979. *Gospel Parallels: A Synopsis of the First Three Gospels*. 4th edition. Nashville, Tenn.: Thomas Nelson.
Tolbert, Mary Ann. 1989. *Sowing the Gospel*. Minneapolis: Fortress Press.
Trites, A. A. 1974. "The Transfiguration of Jesus: The Gospel in Microcosm." *EvQ* 51: 70–83.
———. 1994. *The Transfiguration of Christ: A Hinge of Holy History*. Hantsport, N.S.: Lancelot Press.
Ulansey, David. 1991. "The Heavenly Veil Torn: Mark's Cosmic 'Inclusio.'" *JBL* 110: 123–25.
———. 1996. "The Transfiguration, Cosmic Symbolism and the Transfiguration of Consciousness in the Gospel of Mark" (paper presented at the annual meeting of the Society for Biblical Literature, November 1996). http://www.well.com/user/davidu/transfiguration2.html.
Ulmer, Gregory L. 1981. "The Post-Age." *Diacritics* 11: 39–56.

———. 1985. *Applied Grammatology: Post(e)-Pedagogy from Jacques Derrida to Joseph Beuys*. Baltimore: Johns Hopkins University Press.
van Iersel, Bas M. F. 1998. *Mark: A Reader-Response Commentary*. Sheffield: Sheffield Academic Press.
Veniamin, C. N. 1991. "The Transfiguration of Christ in Greek Patristic Literature from Irenaeus of Lyons to Gregory Palamus." Ph.D. diss., University of Oxford.
Via, Dan O. 1985. *The Ethics of Mark's Gospel—In the Middle of Time*. Philadelphia: Fortress Press.
Viviano, Benedict T., O.P. 1990. "Rabbouni and Mark 9.5." *RB* 97 (1990): 207–18.
Waetjen, Herman C. 1989. *A Reordering of Power: A Sociopolitical Reading of Mark's Gospel*. Minneapolis: Fortress Press.
Walker, Simon. 1997. "Challenging Deconstruction: A Look at Persons, Texts and Hermeneutics." *Churchman* 3: 239–43.
Wand, J. W. C. 1967. *Transfiguration*. London: Faith Press.
Ward, Graham, ed. 1997. *The Postmodern God: A Theological Reader*. Blackwell Readings in Modern Theology. Oxford: Blackwell.
Ward, Reginald Somerset. 1957. *The Experience of God: Meditations on the Transfiguration*. London: A. R. Mowbray.
Watson, Francis. 1985. "The Social Function of Mark's Secrecy Theme." *JSNT* 24: 49–69.
Wenham, David, and A. D. A. Moses. 1994. "'There are Some Standing Here': Did They Become the 'Reputed Pillars' of the Jerusalem Church? Some Reflections on Mark 9:1, Galatians 2:9 and the Transfiguration." *NovT* 36: 146–63.
Wentling, Judith L. 1982. "A Comparison of the Elijan Motifs in the Gospels of Matthew and Mark [Matt 11:2–19; 17:1–13; 21:12–17; 27:45–50; Mk 1:4–8; 9:2–13]." Pages 104–25 in *Proceedings, Eastern Great Lakes Biblical Society*. Edited by P. Sigal. Grand Rapids: Eastern Great Lakes Biblical Society.
Wheeler, Samuel C., III. 2000. *Deconstruction as Analytic Philosophy*. Stanford, Ca.: Stanford University Press.
Wild, Robert A. 1986. *His Face Shone Like the Sun. Encountering the Transfigured Christ in Scripture*. New York: Alba House.
Williams, James G. 1985. *Gospel against Parable: Mark's Language of Mystery*. Bible and Literature Series 12. Decatur, Ga.: Almond Press.
———. 1993. "On Job and Writing: Derrida, Girard, and the Remedy-Poison." *SJOT* 7: 32–50.
Williamson, Lamar, Jr. 1983. *Mark*. Interpretation: A Biblical Commentary for Teaching and Preaching. Atlanta: John Knox Press.
Witherington, Ben, III. 1992. "Transfigured Understanding—A Critical Note on Mark 9:2–13 as a Parousia Preview." *Ashland Theological Journal* 24: 88–91.

———. 2001. *The Gospel of Mark: A Socio-Rhetorical Commentary*. Grand Rapids: Eerdmans.

Wood, David, ed. 1992. *Derrida: A Critical Reader*. Oxford: Blackwell.

Wrede, William. 1971. *The Messianic Secret*. Translated by J. C. G. Greig. Cambridge: James Clarke.

Wright, N. T. 1987. "Reflected Glory: 2 Corinthians 3:18." Pages 139–50 in *The Glory of Christ in the New Testament: Studies in Christology in Memory of George Bradford Caird*. Edited by L. D. Hurst and N. T. Wright. Oxford: Clarendon Press.

Wright, Terry R. 1994. "Through a Glas Darkly: Derrida, Literature, and the Specter of Christianity." *Christianity and Literature* 44: 73–92.

Yee, Gale A. 1995. *Judges and Method: New Approaches in Biblical Studies*. Minneapolis: Fortress Press.

Ziesler, J. A. 1970. "The Transfiguration Story and the Markan Soteriology." *ExpTim* 81: 263–68.

# Index of Biblical Passages

## Old Testament

### Genesis
| | |
|---|---|
| 5:24 | 69 |
| 9:5–6 | 25 |
| 11:1–9 | 1 |
| 11:6 | 1 |
| 11:7 | 12 |
| 11:8 | 9 |
| 11:9 | 11 |
| 22 | 109, 110 |

### Exodus
| | |
|---|---|
| 13:21 | 80 |
| 13:21ff. | 56 |
| 16:7 | 53 |
| 16:10 | 53, 79, 105 |
| 19:9 | 79, 105 |
| 24 | 65, 66 |
| 24:15–16 | 105, 106 |
| 24:28 | 79 |
| 33:1 | 79, 105 |
| 33:7–11 | 56 |
| 33:18 | 53 |
| 34 | 65, 66 |
| 34:28 | 69 |
| 34:29–35 | 68 |
| 34:29ff. | 104 |
| 34:30 | 65 |
| 40:34–38 | 79, 105, 106 |

### Leviticus
| | |
|---|---|
| 10:1–5 | 27 |

### Numbers
| | |
|---|---|
| 9:15–16 | 106 |
| 9:15–22 | 79, 105 |

### Deuteronomy
| | |
|---|---|
| 5:24 | 53 |
| 23:15–16 | 25 |
| 34:5 | 69 |
| 34:6 | 69 |

### Judges
| | |
|---|---|
| 1:11–15 | 46 |

### 1 Kings
| | |
|---|---|
| 2:11 | 68 |
| 8 | 106 |
| 8:10–11 | 79, 105 |
| 8:11 | 106 |
| 8:12 | 106 |
| 19 | 106 |
| 19:12 | 106 |

### 2 Kings
| | |
|---|---|
| 2:11 | 68 |

### Isaiah
| | |
|---|---|
| 4:5 | 79, 105 |
| 40:5 | 53 |
| 60:1 | 53 |

### Ezekiel
| | |
|---|---|
| 1:4 | 79 |
| 1:28 | 56 |
| 11:23 | 56 |

### Daniel
| | |
|---|---|
| 7:9 | 62, 65 |
| 10:4–11:1 | 62 |
| 10:5–8 | 62, 65 |
| 10:7 | 78 |

# Index of Biblical Passages

Amos
8:9 — 106

Malachi
3:2 — 67
4:4 — 68
4:4–6 — 68
4:5–6 — 68, 70

## New Testament

Matthew
5:40 — 101
17:2 — 53, 65, 101, 103, 105
17:4 — 74
17:5 — 80
28:9 — 84
28:16–20 — 84

Mark
1:1 — 55
1:10 — 61, 62, 102, 103
1:11 — 55, 57, 62, 81
1:12 — 103
1:14 — 70
2:21 — 98
4:1ff. — 98
4:22 — 116
4:41 — 77, 78, 113
5:15 — 77, 78, 113
5:33 — 77, 78, 113
6:14a — 70
6:16 — 70
6:50 — 77, 78
8:27 — 74
8:27–33 — 77
8:28 — 70
8:29 — 57, 77
8:31 — 54, 77
8:31–32a — 58
8:31–9:1 — 82
8:32 — 73, 77
8:34–37 — 77
8:38 — 57, 58, 76, 77, 117
8.38–9.1 — 58
9:1 — 72, 73, 74, 76, 77, 78, 82
9:2 — 53, 56, 61, 66, 78, 86, 94, 124
9:2–3 — 93
9:2–4 — 77, 84
9:2–8 — xi, 60
9:3 — 53, 60, 62, 64, 65, 66, 73, 80, 86, 94, 101, 112
9:4 — 59, 67, 69, 70, 72, 73, 113
9:5 — 53, 72, 73, 74, 76, 77, 78, 79, 86, 112, 113, 117, 119
9:5–6 — 87
9:6 — 72, 73, 74, 77, 78, 79, 81, 108, 112, 117, 119
9:6b — 58
9:7 — 55, 62, 69, 79, 80, 81, 82, 105, 107, 123
9:8 — 69, 82
9:9 — 65
9:11–13 — 70
9:13a — 70
9:31 — 54
9:32 — 113
9:43 — 73
9:44 — 73
9:47 — 73
10:32 — 116
10:34 — 54
10:37 — 117
10:51 — 73
11:21 — 73
12:1–12 — 76
12:35–37 — 73
13:26 — 58, 117
14:7 — 118
14:28–30 — 73
14:40 — 78, 81
14:45 — 73
14:51–52 — 33
14.62 — 82
15:24 — 101
15:33 — 62, 106
15:35 — 102
15:36 — 102
15:37 — 103
15:38 — 61, 102, 103

## Index of Biblical Passages

| | | | |
|---|---|---|---|
| 15:39 | 55, 102, 103 | Philippians | |
| 15:42 | 78 | 2:12 | 117 |
| 16:1–8 | 116, 122 | | |
| 16:2 | 78 | 1 Thessalonians | |
| 16:5 | 62 | 4:16 | 82 |
| 16:6 | 78, 117 | | |
| 16:7 | 78, 116, 122, 123 | Hebrews | |
| 16:8 | 77, 78, 84, 87, 113, 115, 116, 117, 118, 119, 123 | 12:21 | 77 |
| | | 2 Peter | |
| | | 1:16–18 | 58 |
| Luke | | Revelation | |
| 9:29 | 53, 65, 103 | 1:9–18 | 62, 65 |
| 9:33 | 74 | 3:4 | 62 |
| 16:9 | 75, 76 | 3:5 | 65 |
| | | 3:18 | 65 |
| John | | 4:4 | 62, 65 |
| 4 | 44, 45 | 6:11 | 65 |
| 4:18 | 37 | 7:9 | 62, 65 |
| 6:54 | 42 | 7:11 | 65 |
| 6:56 | 42 | 7:13–14 | 62 |
| 8:1–11 | 152 | 11:5–6 | 70 |
| 8:3–11 | 25 | 21:3 | 75 |
| 12:23–30 | 81 | | |
| 21 | 42 | | |
| 21:24–25 | 42 | | |

### Apocrypha and Pseudepigrapha

| | | | |
|---|---|---|---|
| Acts | | Sirach | |
| 1:10 | 62 | 44:16 | 69 |
| 10:4 | 78 | | |
| | | 2 Maccabees | |
| Romans | | 2:8 | 79, 105 |
| 12:2 | 101 | | |
| | | 4 Maccabees | |
| 2 Corinthians | | 4:10 | 78 |
| 3 | 151 | | |
| 3:7–18 | 65 | 1 Enoch | |
| 3:18 | 101, 103 | 14 | 62 |
| 4:18 | 101 | | |
| 5:4 | 75 | 2 Enoch | |
| | | 22:8–10 | 63 |

## Index of Names

Abraham, Nicolas, 17
Aichele, George, xiv, 154, 155, 156, 160
Anderson, Hugh, 116, 123
Anidjar, Gil, 2
Aristotle, 19, 20, 78, 88, 89, 90, 91, 92, 93, 99, 105, 106
Austin, J. L., 17

Bachelard, Gaston, 89
Baltensweiler, Heinrich, 60, 61, 68, 78, 83, 94, 95
Barthes, Roland, 34, 35, 47
Bass, Allan, 121
BCC (Bible and Culture Collective), xii
Beal, Timothy K., 97
Benjamin, Walter, 13
Bennington, Geoffrey, xii, 15, 39
Best, Ernest, 57, 58, 59, 71, 78, 108
Blanchot, Maurice, xiv, 13, 47, 125, 126, 128, 129, 130, 131, 132, 133, 141, 142, 143, 144, 145, 146, 148, 155, 159
Blodgett, E. D., xiv, 125, 133, 134, 135, 140, 141, 146
Bloom, Harold, 16
Boobyer, George Henry, 54, 82, 96
Bratcher, Robert G., 95
Brault, Jacques, xiv, 125, 133, 134, 135, 136, 140, 141, 146
Brooks, James A., 57, 58, 60, 68, 73, 74, 75, 80, 83, 117
Bubar, Wallace W., 23, 31, 32, 50
Bultmann, Rudolf, 29, 54

Caputo John D., xii, 15, 147
Chilton, B. D., 55, 57, 64, 66, 68, 70, 73, 81, 96

Cixous, Hélène, 47
Clines, David J. A., 23, 24, 25, 26, 32, 36, 46, 49, 51
Conzelmann, Hans, 34
Counet, Patrick Chatelion, xii, 23, 41, 42, 50
Cranfield, C. E. B., 77, 78
Crossan, John Dominic, 22
Culler, Jonathan, xii, 15, 17
Cutrofello, Andrew, 16, 17

Daniel, Felix Harry, 68, 70, 74, 76, 78, 82, 99
Danove, Paul L., 116, 117
Davis, Robert Con, 16
de Man, Paul, 15, 16, 17
Derrida, Jacques, xi, xiii, xiv, 1–21, 22–25, 27–29, 31–35, 38–44, 46–50, 85–94, 96–99, 104–113, 115, 117, 119–27, 134–35, 142–50, 152, 156, 158–61, 164–70, 172–77
Descartes, René, 4, 35, 89, 92, 106
Detweiler, Robert, 148
Dewey, Joanna, 117
Dillon, Richard J., 34
Dwyer, Timothy, 78, 94, 96

Ellis, John M., 15, 17
Ernst, Josef, 77, 81, 83
Evans, J. Claude, 99

Fewell, Danna Nolan, 31, 38, 39, 46
Fontanier, Pierre, 89
Foucault, Michel, 16, 17
Franke, Chris, 24
Freud, Sigmund, 17, 97, 120, 134, 146

## Index of Names

Garland, David E., 52, 62, 64, 65, 66, 69, 73, 74, 116, 117
Garner, Helen, 154, 155
Goulder, Michael, 67, 81, 95
Graham, J. F., 2, 10
Greenstein, Edward L., 23, 27, 28, 29, 32, 49
Gundry, Robert H., 57, 58, 60, 61, 63, 66, 68, 69, 70, 72, 74, 76, 78, 79, 81, 82, 83, 96, 99, 101, 102, 104, 105, 106, 108, 112, 113, 117, 123

Haenchen, Ernst, 44
Hare, Douglas R. A., 69, 70, 116
Hart, Kevin, xiv, 6, 14, 24, 127, 143, 144, 146, 147, 148, 149, 150, 152, 153, 154, 155, 156
Hartman, Geoffrey, 16, 28, 149
Hartshorne, Charles, 2
Hegel, Georg Wilhelm Friedrich, 17, 19, 20, 35, 89, 90
Heidegger, Martin, 8, 16, 17, 19, 109, 146, 149
Heil, John Paul, 55, 69, 73, 74, 76, 77, 79, 80, 81, 83, 96, 99
Hölderlein, Friedrich, 129, 145, 149
Holland, Norman N., 43
Hooker, Morna D., 52, 55, 56, 57, 59, 60, 61, 65, 66, 67, 68, 70, 71, 72, 73, 75, 78, 79, 83, 94, 95, 96, 99, 103, 116, 117, 123
Hughes, Kent R., 52, 61, 68, 69, 73, 80
Hurtado, Larry W., 66, 71, 77, 83
Husserl, Edmund, 4, 17, 89

Iersel, Bas M. F. van, 55, 57, 58, 62, 63, 66, 69, 70, 79, 81, 84

Jabès, Edmond, 146, 149
Jobling, David, 39
Johnson, Barbara, 16
Johnson, Sherman E., 68, 95, 103
Juel, Donald H., 57, 58, 64, 68, 74, 77, 81, 83, 116

Kafka, Franz, 129
Kant, Immanuel 17

Kearney, Richard, xiv, 127, 150, 151, 152, 153
Kee, Howard Clark, 62, 65, 66, 68, 70, 75, 77, 80
Keegan, Terence, 23, 38, 39, 50
Keenan, John P., 64, 83, 117
Kelber, Werner, 56
Kitzberger, Ingrid Rosa, 35
Kristeva, Julia, 2, 47

Lacan, Jacques, 17, 43, 120, 121
Landy, Francis, xiii, 23, 47, 48, 49, 50, 158, 160
Lane, William L., 64, 65, 69, 78, 116, 117, 123
Lautréamont (Isidore Ducasse), 89
Lee, Sungho, 24
Lehman, David, 16
Leibniz, G., 93
Leitch, Vincent B., xii, 15
Levinas, Emmanuel, 17, 44, 146
Lévi-Strauss, Claude, 17, 29
Lincoln, Andrew T., 116, 117
Lohmeyer, Ernst, 73
Louw, J. P., 95, 99, 112, 114, 123
Luria, Isaac, 146

Mack, Burton L., 29
Magness, J. Lee, 117, 118
Mallarmé, Stéphane, 129, 130
Mann, C. S., 56, 57, 61, 65, 66, 68, 70, 72, 73, 76, 78, 79, 80, 81, 83, 96, 99, 116, 117
Martin, Ralph, 57, 75
Marx, Karl, 17
McGuckin, John Anthony, 56, 58, 59, 65, 66, 67, 69, 72, 73, 74, 75, 76, 79, 81, 82, 95, 96, 104, 105
Melville, Herman, 151
Michie, Donald, 117
Miller, J. Hillis, 16, 25, 26
Moore, Stephen D., xii, 23, 29, 32, 33, 34, 35, 36, 37, 38, 43, 44, 45, 46, 50, 51, 120, 143
Mouffe, Chantal, 15

Nida, Eugene A., 95, 99, 112, 114, 123

## Index of Names

Nietzsche, Friedrich, 17, 146
Nineham, D. E., 60, 68, 74, 79, 83, 94, 103
Norris, Christopher, 15, 31
Nützel, Johannes M., 64, 69, 70, 74, 78, 94

Öhler, Markus, 61, 79, 80, 83
Otto, Rudolf, 108, 109
Owens, Craig, 143

Painter, John, 102
Patocka, Jan, 109
Peirce, Charles S., 2
Perry, John Michael, 57, 65, 68
Phillips, Gary A., 23, 44, 45, 46, 50, 51
Philo, 144
Plato, 4, 7, 19, 20, 88, 89, 93, 109, 120
Poe, Edgar Allan, 120, 121
Porter, Stanley E., 94

Quilligan, Maureen, 143

Ramsey, Michael, 55, 56, 58, 60, 66, 68, 73, 82, 83
Rawlinson, A. E. J., 105
Reid, Barbara E., 56, 61, 62, 79, 82
Rhoads, David, 117
Riesenfeld, Harald, 55, 64, 74
Rilke, Rainer Maria, xiv, 128, 129, 130, 132, 133, 141, 145
Rorty, Richard, xii, 15, 16, 17, 18, 19, 20, 39
Rutledge, David, 39
Rousseau, Jean-Jacques, 4, 29

Salusinszky, Imre, 16
Saussure, Ferdinand de, 2, 3, 5, 8, 9, 11, 17, 87, 90
Scanlon, Michael J., 147

Schleifer, Ronald, 16
Schwartz, Regina M., 38
Schweizer, Eduard, 64, 66, 69, 74, 77, 79, 80, 81, 83, 96, 101, 105
Scott, Robert, 101
Seeley, D., xii, 23, 29, 30, 31, 32, 38, 50
Sherwood, Yvonne, xii, 17, 23, 24, 38, 39, 40, 41, 45, 50, 51, 108, 148, 149, 152, 154
Spivak, Gayatri, 146, 166
Stein, Robert H., 54

Tallis, Raymond, 15
Taylor, Mark C., xii, 147
Taylor, Vincent, 56, 64, 65, 66, 68, 74, 77, 78, 99, 101, 104, 105, 123
Thrall, Margaret E., 68, 75
Tolbert, Mary Ann, 55, 57, 66, 73, 80, 107
Torok, Maria, 17
Trites, A. A., 60, 66, 72, 99

Ulansey, David, 56, 61, 62, 63, 64, 96, 99, 100
Ulmer, Gregory L., 17, 120, 143, 144

Voltaire, 11

Ward, Graham, 147, 148
Watson, Francis, 54
Weiss, Paul, 2
Wheeler, Samuel C. III, 15, 18, 19, 20
Williams, James G., 122
Williamson, Lamar Jr., 116
Witherington, Ben, III, 55, 57, 58, 61, 62, 63, 64, 65, 68, 70, 73, 75, 79, 84, 96, 99, 102, 103, 106
Wood, David, 18

Ziesler, J. A., 55, 61, 71, 75, 99